When All the Men Were Gone

World War II and the Home Front, One Boy's Journey Through the War Years

Ronald G. Capalaces

To
Theresa Monica
Our Mother
Frances Ann
Our Sister
and
Richard John
My Brother

For All We Shared

When All the Men Were Gone: World War II and the Home Front, One Boy's Journey Through the War Years

Copyright © 2010 by Ronald G. Capalaces

First Edition
Published and Printed in the U.S.A.

Lazarus LLC Publishers
PO Box 189
Irvington, VA 22480
info@lazaruspublishers.com
www.lazaruspublishers.com

Library of Congress Control Number: 2010903467

ISBN Number: 978-0-615-35607-5

Cover Photo: An alley off Clinton Street. Courtesy of the Broome County Historical Society.

All photos in this book are courtesy of the Broome County Historical Society, unless marked (private).

Photo sections in book designed by Joseph D. Lops

ACKNOWLEDGMENTS

My thanks and deepest appreciation to Nick Matthews for his editorial reviews and critiques and guidance. Nick was there from the beginning and never left. Gerald R. Smith, Broome County Historian, for his review and commentary and for the support and use of historical source material from the Collection of the Broome County Historical Society. Francis Kolosna, my childhood friend, for sharing his boyhood memories and insight. To WWII veterans William and Joseph Vrabel, my uncles, for their knowledge of the times and places where stories/events took place. To Lt. Col. Ed Rhodes (retired) for his review, comment, and support. To David M. Gouldin, who provided a meticulous editorial review and who was one of the earliest supporters. To Evander Lomke for his editing and constructive comments. To Keith Korman, a unique talent and wellspring of literary knowledge. To Jack Fowler, for his steadfast belief in the book and his encouragement and assistance throughout. To my brother, Richie, who continues to share his memories and life with me. To Marie Therese, wife and mother to our Julie, Lisa, Andrea, Beth, and Mimi—our nine beautiful grandchildren Byron, Katherine, Merritt Edward, Abigail Jane, Henry John, Jill, Olivia Louise, Nicholas Gene, and Claire Marie. And to sons-in-law Chat, Eddie, Steve, Will and Tito. Your love and affection sustain me.

CONTENTS

PROLOGUE

I t came up in conversation, an item dropped during small talk. "They tore it down," the voice on the phone said. The news caught me by surprise. I reacted casually to it, but deep inside it hit like a death in the family.

This simple boxlike structure was gone—with it, all signs of the life it held vanished. Why should anyone care about its loss? Was not a vacant lot better than the slum apartment building that once stood there? Maybe so. But in its day, the Kelly block was more than stucco and wood. It was the pregnable fort where I lived during the years of World War II. It was the site of many battles among the diverse factions encamped there trying to endure and survive in a time of great uncertainty.

The Kelly block was owned by Dr. John Kelly, a practicing dentist, whose training and background all came in handy since collecting the rent money was like pulling teeth. You rarely saw him except when rents were due or overdue. He stood out from everyone else. He wore a long dark suit and a long grim face. With his stern manner and long bony hands and gray hair, he looked like death calling. When he came to collect, you tried to make yourself scarce so you wouldn't have to lie when he asked where your parent was. Mama "wasn't home" because the rent couldn't be paid. You could hide, but you couldn't run and, like death, sooner or later Dr. Kelly caught up with you.

I lived on the Kelly block at 30 Dickinson Street in the First Ward during the war years with my mother, older sister, and younger brother in the two-bedroom apartment on the second floor—the one on the left, facing the street. All the men were gone; gone for the duration of the war. Left behind were wives, mothers, children, old folks, and the military rejects all facing an uncertain future.

This all took place in Binghamton, New York, at the time a bustling blue-collar industrial city whose Main Street ran right up to the Main Street of Johnson City, a next-door neighbor, whose Main Street connected to its neighbor, Endicott. A huge stone arch spanned over the Main Streets, welcoming you from one town to the other. Endicott-Johnson Shoe Company workers built the arches and inscribed them with the words: HOME OF THE SQUARE DEAL. Together, Binghamton, Johnson City, and Endicott are called the Triple Cities of Broome County.

On a recent visit to Binghamton, I went to Dickinson Street to see, once again, where the Kelly block used to be. In its place stood a condo development, new and neat. Although the Kelly block was gone forever, I could still feel its presence. This was the site of my awakening, a place and a time of so many memories. During those years, I had no idea I would some day be a child of what was to be called the Greatest Generation. Now, despite the passing of so many years, this place and those times remain mysteriously alive and stirring.

The America of World War II stands in sharp contrast to the America of today: so much so that to appreciate the era, it is important to note some of the differences between then and now. While a World War was being waged across the Atlantic and the Pacific, we at the Binghamton home front lived in a world where television, cell phones, computers, satellites, and the internet did not exist. News came by radio, newspapers, and the newsreels at the movies, Movietone, Pathé, and the March of Times. Except for local news, world events took considerable time to report and reach home. The newspapers came twice a day—a morning paper and an evening paper owned by two competing publishers. Each paper sold for three cents.

People didn't E-mail or text message, they wrote letters. Like the newspapers, the mail was delivered twice a day, every day, except on Sundays. Mailmen (always men) walked their routes on foot in all kinds of weather carrying leather bags full of mail and packages. They were friendly and helpful, and none of them went "postal."

Talk radio did not exist nor did Oprah or Dr. Phil trying to make us feel better about ourselves. No one was terribly interested in opinions and if you offered them unsolicited, it could bring a tongue-lashing or a busted lip. All telephones were rotary dialed and when you made a phone call or dialed the operator you always reached a human being on the other end, not a computer-generated voice programmed to sound human.

Movies were in black-and-white, and the only special effects were the looks on the actors' faces. There were no Power-Ball Millions to bet on; no easy credit to float that dream vacation or buy that special car; no product spokesman telling you what to buy. The ubiquitous commercial had yet to be born.

Tabloids did not exist, no Paparazzi stalked celebrities, no *National Enquirer* to expose scandals such as cellulite among Hollywood stars, the stretch-marks of Octomom, or how much a half-ton man enjoys the Food Channel. Magazines racks carried no girlie or skin publications. They had not made their way into the culture as yet.

Political correctness had not evolved; negative attack ads were yet to be born. There was no left nor right, no blue nor red states, only United States. Campaigns and politics were seasonal activities. Bottled spring water did not exist. Spam came in a tin can and you ate it. Plastic credit cards did not choke your wallet and make your backside look like you had three cheeks. Pins and passwords did not clog your brain. Most people got around by walking or taking a bus or hitchhiking. Malls didn't exist; there were only downtown department stores and most importantly the neighborhood store.

Women wore rayon stockings (nylon was unavailable during the war) with a heavy seam running upward from the ankle to the thigh. Men whistled at women in public and called them babes, chicks, tomatoes, dolls, dishes, and broads. Women had little power. Everyone smoked—men, women, young, and old. They smoked unfiltered Camels, Chesterfields, and Lucky Strikes from packs that carried no warnings from the Surgeon General. On the street, kids even picked up cigarette butts with a puff or two left in them. Dogs roamed free of any leash laws. No one picked up dog poop. You could find droppings anywhere, most often on your shoes. You didn't need DNA to solve a crime. All you needed were Sherlock Holmes and Charlie Chan, and a dime to get into the Ritz Theatre to see them solve any caper, no matter how complex and mysterious.

Beer joints were called saloons, beer parlors, and joints. The friendly owners' sole purpose was to sell as many drinks to as many patrons as possible. Inside, patrons played juke-boxes, pinball machines, shuffle-boards, cards, and got drunk. Cars were big, boisterous hunks of heavy metal with style and character. Gasoline cost 15 cents a gallon. Seat belts and air-bags had not yet been invented. Crashes were deadly.

Consumer protection did not exist. Bologna on white bread with mustard was the favorite sandwich. Washing machines were usually women using large cakes of Octagon Soap to scrub clothes by hand on wood framed metal scrub-boards that were held upright in a tub of water. The sun dried wet clothes hung on a line in the fresh air. Baseball was the only national sport. Ballplayers bulked up on hot dogs and beer, the "steroids" of the times. A cup of coffee cost five cents and it came in only one flavor—strong. It would take over five decades to transform a simple cup of Joe into a half-calf–triple-grande–two-percent–three-pump–vanilla–no foam *latte*.

Doctors made house calls and Castor Oil was the popular over-the-counter medicine of the day. Kids got mumps, measles, chickenpox, and head lice. Smallpox vaccinations often left quarter-sized scars on the upper shoulders of kids. Outbreaks of polio came and crippled and killed children. Survivors wore braces and walked with the help of canes. Some lived for a few years inside "iron lungs" to help them breathe. Then they died.

No matter which school one attended or what subject was being taught, every classroom teacher of our era looked old. Sixty years would pass before eager young blonde teachers would find their way into classrooms. These modern teachers would bring with them a new, deep passion for teaching while giving new meaning to extracurricular activity.

The only time people thought about outer space was when they went to see Buck Rogers at the movies. Citizens revered the President, voting FDR in four terms. The big immigration problem of the times? There wasn't any. Everybody was an immigrant or the child or grandchild of immigrants. And terrorists? They were active during the war years: Lon Chaney, the Werewolf; Boris Karloff, Frankenstein's monster; and Bela Lugosi, Count Dracula. They threatened and scared the hell out people at the neighborhood theaters. The only suicide bombers were the Japanese Kamikaze pilots who sacrificed themselves against military targets during actual combat in the Pacific during the war.

Environmental issues did not exist. No one knew there was an environment. The color green had no special meaning. Streets and sidewalks and lawns and parks were the dumpsters du jour. People used them freely to throw their trash away and leave it up to the wind or a change of seasons to recycle the debris.

Winters were cold; summers were hot. Global warming did not exist. Blocks of ice, replaced regularly in an ice box, kept food edible. People kept warm by burning coal and wood in stoves. Electric fans and hand-fans kept people cool.

Mass shootings at schools and universities did not happen. Children rarely went missing, never to return—victims of child predators.

Hoboes were the homeless people of the times. They didn't have shelters to go to or social programs offering help. They slept in alleyways, on riverbanks, and in abandoned buildings and railroad cars. They moved around a lot, courtesy of hopping freight trains.

Fast Food enterprises had not been invented yet. Designer and organic food were unheard of. Eggs came from hens that never roamed free. Use by dates did not appear on perishable foods. Whatever you bought, you performed a smell test. Milk cost 12 cents a gallon; a loaf of bread 9 cents; a bottle of Coke 5 cents. Canned food, meat, cheese, butter, and cooking oil were some of the things rationed during the war.

No one talked about diets. If you happened to be fat . . . well, you were fat. Heavy women did try to appear slimmer by using girdles, a type of medieval contraption that women squeezed into. Heavy men with bulging bellies created by a steady diet of hops and barley wore large belts and suspenders at the same time. These men brought new meaning to the term "belly up to the bar."

Men did not wear earrings and women did not wear pants. Birth control for women did not exist, nor did a legal right to abortion. Men grew old without Viagra and thus avoided the worrisome dilemma of the four hour erection. Women aged naturally without cosmetic surgery and hormone replacement. The public knew little about health and medicine. Patients worshiped doctors like gods.

Formal social networks did not exist; no Facebook, no MySpace, no match-making services scoring couples compatibility. During the war years, informal social networking consisted of sharing stuff with the apartment across the hall, the house next door, the block and the street where you lived.

Teenagers went "steady." Young couples went to drive-ins to make out which usually meant kissing and maybe a little "petting." Few girls went "all the way" because they didn't want to be labeled "easy" and they were saving "it" for marriage. Most of all they feared the moral judgments, the wrath of parents and family, and being ostracized. Few guys had the guts to go to the drugstore and ask the pharmacist for a pack of "rubbers." Condoms were not sold on the aisles. Unmarried couples did not shack up, i.e., live together. This was frowned upon and viewed as immoral.

African-Americans were classified and called Negroes. With few exceptions they lived in ghettoes. There was little social mixing between races. Without a proactive political voice, most were invisible. In the South, segregation laws existed, keeping the whites and negroes separated. The military segregated units along racial lines. Neither negroes, nor whites ever thought there would one day be a black president. How absurd the thought.

During the war years, kids loved to play war whenever they could. They fought with imaginary bullets and bombs; they got wounded and some died. When their mothers called, they snapped back to life and ran home. Discipline of kids employed a number of methods. They typically got spanked by hand or whipped by leather belts. Most didn't finish school, dropping out by the eighth grade to get a job doing anything to help bring money to the family. The average yearly wage for a worker in 1942—$1,880; the cost of a new home—$3,770; a new car—$920.

Women took to the factories to replace the men called to service. Some rushed at the chance to join the military to serve in non-combat roles as WACs (Women's Army Corps), Waves (Women's Navy Service), WASP's (Women's Airforce Service Pilots), and The Army and Navy Nurse Corps.

During the World War II era, people didn't run around complaining their rights were being violated. There were no level playing fields to play on. Everybody could expect to be discriminated against, abused, exploited, and offended regardless of race, religion, ethnic origin, gender, and sexual orientation—at one time or another. It came with the times. Your real education came from people around you who "taught you a lesson."

There was no sensitivity training, and very little dialogue about hopes and dreams and feelings and fears. People knew the difference between right and wrong and took the good with the bad, and paid whatever the price doing wrong cost. The only real support system consisted of your own two feet, and you learned to stand on them one way or another—sooner or later.

There was no professional military during World War II. Our fighting forces were ordinary men freely enlisting to serve their country. Others were given a number and randomly selected by a local draft board, and then pressed into service. They were factory workers, doctors, nurses, grocery workers, teachers, construction workers, unemployed men, and high-school kids. They came from every background in the area, from eighteen to forty-five, many married with children. Most were first-generation Americans, sons of immigrants who came to America to make a better life for themselves and their families. They were men and boys who barely knew peace, let alone war. Now after a little training, they would face an enemy on strange soil and fight to kill. Death and the cry of the dying and wounded would be everywhere. Our men and boys were not taught how to die or how to watch friends or foes die. They learned this on the job.

The Americans who fought in World War II had already survived a national depression. Many stood in soup lines between looking for jobs that didn't exist. For the rare job, there was no minimum wage although every wage was minimum. Money, food, and hope were in short supply. Most persevered and did whatever was needed to survive until government programs and relief found their way to cities and neighborhoods. It was this trial that would really help prepare our men and nation to persevere in the mud at Anzio, the snow at Bastogne, the sand at Iwo Jima, and the waters of the Pacific.

Regardless of personal and communal deprivations, loss or suffering the war brought, people believed in the rightness of our national cause. Our fighting men were honored and the flag flew with respect. Citizens loved their country and were ready to fight and die for it. Though interwoven with human tragedy and suffering, the days of World War II helped define a nation and words such as *courage, valor, heroism,* and *sacrifice.*

Over the years, a lot changed.

*W*hen *All the Men Were Gone* is a salute to those of my generation, the ones who lived in the shadow of the Greatest Generation. It was our generation that also suffered many losses—our loved ones; our innocence; our nurturing. We saw the images—the toll of human conflict—the horror of the atom bomb. We saw the ravages of hatred in the gaunt faces and hollowed spirits of concentration camp survivors. We saw giant holes filled with naked and dead bodies.

As kids, most of us were on our own, without any clue where we were heading. We came of age between two powerful decades: "The Forties" and "The Sixties." Our time to serve came with the Korean Conflict and for some the Vietnam War.

This book is but a small step toward helping to define our generation and staking out a claim for a legacy. This is a remembrance of our generation . . . not the Greatest, but the one closest to it.

What follows took place between 1941 and 1946. Based on actual events, these occurrences are told as accurately and truthfully as memory permits. In many places, where recall has been compromised by the passage of time, dramatic license has been used to convey the events. In all, this is a remembrance of living through a period when men left their families and loved ones to fight a war, a war they would not return from until it was won or they were crippled or dead. This is about the struggle of life without men and its impact on those left behind. It is told through the eyes of a child as he lives through the war years.

Ronald G. Capalaces

1.

REDS CALL A-BOMB TEST BLACKMAIL

ALBANY MAN FOUND CROUCHING NEAR CANDLE STAND IN HILLCREST CHURCH JAILED FOR VAGRANCY

Bring Him Home

He had been gone a long time and had traveled far. Now, John "Jumbo" Vrabel found himself in a strange place. Someone told him if he crossed *that* bridge, he and his buddies would soon be on their way back home. He wanted very much to be home, but *that bridge* was not the Yellow Brick Road and clicking his worn and muddy boots three times wouldn't magically take him back to New York. Crossing *that bridge* meant fierce fire from Nazi arms dug in on the other side. Jumbo and his buddies knew what this choice meant. The attempt to cross *that* bridge, without any cover, would decide how they'd get home—dead or alive. This was all I ever heard about his fighting during the war. "Jumbo" Vrabel was my uncle—my mom's brother.

Uncle John was one of the first GIs to fight his way across the Remagen Bridge in Germany, the last bridge left standing over the Rhine River. The prize waiting on the other side was the road leading straight to Berlin and Hitler's headquarters. Taking the bridge at Remagen came at a high cost in U.S. forces killed and wounded.

Uncle John made it across unhurt.

Now that the war was over, it was my job to bring Uncle John safely home from the beer joints on the main drag, Clinton Street in the First Ward of Binghamton. The fighting overseas had given him a thirst that nights of drinking couldn't quench. My assignment seemed almost as tough to me as crossing the Remagen Bridge.

"Go get your Uncle John," Mama said, waking me up.

"I don't want to go, I'm tired," I answered.

"I said go get him and bring him home before I crack you!"

"Where is he?"

"Probably at Andy's Inn, but he could be anywhere up there. Just ask anyone where Jumbo is. Look for him till you find him and bring him home. Go on."

It was well past midnight on Saturday and as I walked by the bars along Clinton Street with their smell of stale beer and smoke and spittoons filled with spent chewing tobacco, I wished Uncle John were somewhere else. I wished he were still over there sending home those skinny, one-page airmail letters that told my grandmother her son was all right. He was the oldest of three sons to enlist and fight in Europe.

When he came home on furlough, he looked like a giant to me in his olive green uniform with the shiny brass buttons and the spit-polished shoes. This was how I remembered him. This is how I wanted to remember him.

At each beer joint along the way, I stopped and looked through the window for Uncle John. Inside, a few old men sat along the bar raising their drinks and taking long, slow swallows. I passed Freije's Bar and Grill, Elmo's Bar, the Marble Grill, and Metrus's, too, with no sign of Uncle John.

Only a few cars passed by late at night. Once in a while, a man and a woman left a bar and walked down the street together. Larry's Lunch was closing, and when I passed one of the alleys off Clinton Street, I saw a man in the shadows pissing against a wall.

Special overhead lights lit the large letters, ANDY'S INN, printed above its big front window. Light from inside spilled onto the sidewalk. Peering past the neon beer-and-whiskey signs hanging inside the front window, I searched for Uncle John. Through the heavy smoke inside, people moved like Zombies walking through a thick fog. I couldn't tell if Uncle John was in there. I hated stepping into the place. I had no choice.

Slowly opening the door I stepped inside for a closer look. As always, Andy's Inn was crowded and noisy. It reminded me of a John Wayne Western, with people lined up at the bar and cigarette smoke hanging in the air. Grown men walked around on wobbly legs from all the booze in their guts. Some spit old chewing tobacco into brass buckets on the floor. The place always smelled, especially the toilets splattered and stained with piss and puke. You never knew when a fight might start; it didn't take much. Most women alone in the bar were called sluts or kudvas, Slovak for whore.

I saw Andy behind the bar, grabbing a whiskey bottle from a row of shiny ones and pointing its spout to fill a shot glass. Andy, like most of the bar owners on Clinton Street, had a big belly and a big smile to match.

The Wurlitzer jukebox played Freddy Martin and His Orchestra's "Doin' What Comes Natur'lly," against the rumble of loud talk. Most of the men sitting at the bar were veterans from the war. At the tables in the back, a few older men and women drank and listened to the music coming from the Wurlitzer with its bright-colored lights. A sign nailed above the entry to the back part of the saloon read: NO DANCING. Still, a couple in the shadows held each other and moved to the music. Men played cards—Pinochle and Euchre—in a few booths opposite the bar.

On the far corner of the bar, I finally spotted Uncle John raising his hand to get Andy's attention. Andy nodded and began
drawing a beer from the tap. I crossed the barroom floor and
stood near Uncle John. On his left was an empty stool. On the bar,
in front of the empty stool, was a pack of Camels and a silver
Zippo cigarette lighter. Uncle John took a long drag on his cigarette as Andy placed a glass of light brown beer covered with
creamy white foam next to the open pack of Uncle John's
Chesterfields. He then poured a double shot into a small glass. As
Uncle John shoved the money toward him, Andy motioned
toward me and said, "Hey, Jumbo, I think you've got company."

Uncle John turned and stared at me for a moment with his
glassy eyes, then turned back. Before I could say anything he
turned toward me again, this time his eyes focused. His face
turned angry.

"Jesus, Ronnie, what in the hell you doin' here?" he asked.

"It's time to go home," I answered.

"Who shent you here? Tree?"

"Yeah. She told me to come and get you."

"What the hell's wrong with her? I ain't shupposed to be here
or what? What does she think, I'm a goddamn baby?"

I stood looking at him without trying to answer.

"Look, I know it's not your fault, but for Chris'shake I don't
need people telling me what to do. You know what I mean?"

"Sure. But I know if you don't come home with me, I'm
gonna get it."

"For Chris'shake, it's shtill early. I'll tell you what, come up
here and have a Coke and we'll have one more drink and think
about it."

"That's OK, I don't need a Coke."

"C'mon. Have a drink. C'mon, up here. Shit, you're getting
almost big enough to be in here on your own."

"I think there's someone sitting here."

"Just shove it over. There's another empty shpot."

I figured it wouldn't be bad having a drink. I was thirsty. So I climbed onto the stool next to him, shoving the pack of Camels and lighter to my left. Uncle John didn't speak; he drank his beer and smoked his cigarette. His eyes were red and I knew from experience that the way his words were coming out meant it would be a problem getting him to go home.

Andy brought a Coke over to me along with another beer for Uncle John.

"Andy, you remember Theresa's boy, Ronnie?" Uncle John asked.

"Sure. He's startin' to be a regular here on Saturday nights. How you doin' kid?" Andy asked.

"OK."

"That's good, kid."

A woman's hand reached onto the bar next to me, picked up the pack of Camels and lighter and lit up a cigarette. I could feel her look my way as she climbed onto the bar stool next to me. Andy brought her a beer and when she lifted it to her lips, I glanced at her. Cigarette smoke curled around her face. A bright shiny polish covered her fingernails and matched the same bright red color of her lips. She wore glasses and her eyes blinked as if she were about to fall asleep. I was never good at telling how old people were, but she looked old to me.

Uncle John sat drinking, almost unaware of the woman, one of the few in the bar. This wasn't the right time or place, but I had a lot of questions I wanted to ask him, questions about the war. I wanted to know if he killed any Nazis and was he ever scared. And what it felt like to get over the Remagen Bridge and if any of his friends died trying to cross it. And did he ever come close to being killed. And did he think God helped him to stay alive. Uncle John never talked about the war.

Uncle John got up slowly and said, "I'm gonna take a leak. I'll be right back."

"And then we'll go, OK?"

"Yeah, yeah. We'll go when I'm ready to go."

In the mirror, hanging behind the bar, I watched Uncle John weave across the floor to the rest room. I saw the woman next to me look over her shoulder at him and then turn toward me.

"Don't hol' your breath, kid. He's gonna pee like a racehorse. He's got a lot of beer to pish out."

I began poking the ice cubes in my Coke with the straw, hoping the woman would turn away and not talk anymore.

"Whash the matter with you, kid? Don't you look at a lady when she's talkin' to you?"

I glanced up and for a brief moment looked into her bloodshot eyes. "I'm sorry, Ma'am. I don't talk a lot."

"Then you're in the right plashe. None of these ashholes talk to ladeez. They just sit here night after night suckin' up the booze. They're sooo shtoopid and have no manners."

I shrugged my shoulders and returned to the ice cubes near the bottom of my Coke. I glanced in the mirror to check on Uncle John. He was still in the toilet.

A new song came up on the jukebox. "Shoo-fly Pie and Apple Pan Dowdy," the lady muttered when she heard the song playing. She turned toward me and said, "What the fuh's a 'Shoe-fly pie and an Apple pan dowdy'? If you can tell me what that means, I'll kish the ash of everyone sitting at thish bar, including Jumbo's . . . whenever he's through pishing his brains out."

I shrugged my shoulders again and shook my head, hoping she'd get an answer from someone else.

"You can believe me, sonny-boy, none of deez jerkoffs know what that song is about. The only thing deez guys know is how to feel sorry for demselves. Somebody needs to tell them the war's over. It's time, baby, to move on."

Her voice was getting louder and I was sure everyone in the place could hear her.

"Hey, Andy, give my little buddy here another drink. On me," the lady said. "He's the only one in dis joint who ain't feelin' sorry for hisself."

Andy placed another Coke in front of me and gave me a reassuring smile.

"Thanks," I said to Andy.

"Don't thank me, thank the lady," Andy said and then told the woman, "This is Jumbo's nephew, Theresa's kid."

She looked over at me with a blank stare and turned back and nodded.

"Thank you, Ma'am," I said, anxious for Uncle John to return.

"And the kid's got manners," the lady said in a loud voice. "Which is rare in a joint like dis."

No one paid any attention to her. It was as if she were talking to a roomful of deaf people.

"Thanks again, Ma'am," I said turning toward her.

A disgusting look came onto her face. "Yeah, kid, that's good. Now go ahead and enjoy your drink," she said quietly.

I watched her light another cigarette while Andy worked the bar, pouring drinks, wiping up spills, emptying ashtrays, and hitting the cash register. The men at the bar sat hunched over their drinks, staring at nothing. I glanced at the bar mirror again and spotted Uncle John heading back to the bar.

Turning to him I said, "You ready to go?"

"Yeah, as shoon as I finish my drink," he said climbing onto the bar-stool.

I saw the woman's lip curl when she looked at Uncle John. She took a long drag on her cigarette and crushed the lipstick-stained butt into the ashtray.

Uncle John finished his beer, set the glass down and to my surprise nodded to me. He stepped off his stool and began to walk across the floor toward the door. I slurped the last of my Coke and before I moved to follow him, the lady on my left grabbed my arm and said, "I know Jumbo and I know your mother. Make sure you don't grow up feelin' sorry for yourself, kid." I nodded and then waved to Andy as I slid off the bar-stool to join Uncle John.

Out on the street, it felt good to breathe in the fresh night air. On wobbly legs, Uncle John lit up another Chesterfield and then headed for home. Along the way, drunken men poured out of bars, coughing and hacking and spitting—not used to the fresh night air. In a silent parade they shuffled off on their perilous journeys home.

Uncle John and I walked without talking. The noise from Andy's Inn faded in the distance. On the street, my uncle's shoes shuffled against the pavement, and every now and then you could hear the snapping sound of his finger flicking ashes from his cigarette. I watched his steps so he didn't stumble on the sidewalk or slip on a mound of spit snorted and coughed up by a drunk to clear a lung. One day I planned to ask him about the war and I hoped he'd tell me about it, but the time would have to be right. I had learned from his brothers, who had also fought in Germany, that he had seen the worst of it.

I remembered how we all rushed to grab the mail when it came, hoping a light blue skinny V-Mail letter would be there from Uncle John or one of his two brothers, Joe or Bill, all fighting in Germany. You always hoped you'd learn something important from reading the letters Grandma got from her boys. But they always seemed to be the same old stuff. Nothing seemed to change except for the date on them. Things like, *I'm fine . . . got your letter and was glad to hear everyone's OK . . . the weather's pretty lousy . . . thanks, Irene, for the package. It was great getting it from home . . . Merry Christmas to everyone.* We never knew where they were or how the war was going for them. I guess the only important thing was just to get a letter. That told us all we wanted to know.

When Uncle Bill, Uncle John's youngest brother, got home after the war ended, he told Aunt Irene that he and all the other GIs were under strict orders not to write anything in their letters home about where they were or who they were fighting or how it was going. It was especially important that if they were captured, there weren't any letters on them that they had written that could give any information the Nazis could use. The Army censored the mail written by the GIs overseas.

Uncle Bill said the American soldiers listened to Axis Sally on the radio when they got to Europe. Axis Sally worked for the Nazis. In between the songs she played she would try to get the GIs homesick and to get them to stop fighting. She only played American music; all of the top hits. Songs such as: "Boogie Woogie Boy" by the Andrews Sisters, "You'll Never Know" by Dick Haymes and the Spinners, "When the Lights Go on Again (All Over the World)" by Vaughn Monroe and His Orchestra, "As Time Goes By" by Dooley Wilson, "I'll Be Seeing You," and "Long Ago and Far Away." They loved hearing the latest music from the States, even though Axis Sally only played sad songs to get the GIs down.

Uncle Bill told us how she used to read letters over the radio that the Nazis took from dead GIs or prisoners. In her friendly and sweet-sounding voice, Axis Sally would say something like, "Hey, this is for all you GIs out there. This is Sally here with a sweet letter Corporal Walter Branson from the U.S. 9th Armored Division recently got from his wife Martha in Kansas City."

Dear Walter, You're probably wondering why I've not written to you like I used to. Well, to be honest with you, I've just been so busy with this new job I got at the plant. I'm working a lot of overtime and my boss is training me for another spot. He's a real nice guy . . . a family man who goes to church every Sunday. I'll try to write more, I promise, but try to understand how things are back here without you.

Axis Sally would go on to say, "Hey, are you guys wondering about your wives and girlfriends and how they're spending their time and what they're doing on Saturday nights all alone without you? Well, Corporal Branson isn't worried about it. You see, he's dead. Yes, the poor guy got killed just outside St. Laurent-sur-Mer in France. His wife Martha doesn't even know it yet. Does fighting this war make any sense? Boys, be careful out there, please."

Axis Sally knew everything that was going on, according to Uncle Bill. He said she even knew the name of his ship and welcomed his unit, the 432nd, the code name for the 62nd Field Hospital, to Scotland when he arrived from the States. The guys didn't listen to any of her crap according to Uncle Bill, just that sweet music from America.

I realized our guys couldn't tell us much while they were over there fighting. But now they were home and they still didn't say much about the war. I guess they wanted to forget what they went through. I understood that, but I wanted to know about the war. My buddy Tootsie told me the only thing he ever heard his Uncle Ambrose say on the subject was that: "War is funny. You fight up one hill and get to the top and then you see another hill." Ambrose was wounded three times and that's about all he ever said, according to Toots.

When we finally reached the Kelly block, I got behind Uncle John for the final push up the outer stairs to Grandma's apartment where he lived. Pudgy, the family dog, barked as we pushed open the door to the apartment. Uncle John loved Pudgy, but Pudgy knew from the stink he carried home from the saloon that she wanted no part of him.

I helped my uncle onto his bed, and he lay there without moving. His jaw loosened and his mouth opened wide. His eyes were shut. He looked like the grotesque war pictures in the newsreels and newspapers of dead soldiers, frozen and twisted on the wintry fields of battle. I took off his shoes and opened his bedroom window to let in some air. He was in a deep sleep and in a place where not even his own loud, crackling snoring could wake him.

When the war ended, four years of worry seemed enough, but

now there were new worries. Battle-scarred men had brought their demons home and new fronts were opening up in a different kind of war. When would all this finally end? No one had any answers. All we had was the hope that tomorrow might be better.

"Is that you, Ronnie?" Mama shouted from her bedroom as I closed the front door of our apartment behind me.

"Yeah."

"Did you bring him home?"

"Yeah."

Crawling into bed, there was too much stuff going on in my head to fall asleep. I lay awake thinking about the war being over, how I looked up to Uncle John, all that he had been through, what he had done. As a soldier, Uncle John looked great. Now that he was home, he looked like all the other drunks up on Clinton Street. I didn't like it. But there was little I could do about it.

WE ALL WENT through the war together and it did things to all of us. By the time it ended, we all had a story or two to tell.

2.

BINGHAMTON PRESS   DECEMBER 9, 1941

FOUR FROM BINGHAMTON VICINITY AMONG AXIS ALIENS

F.B.I. Agents Pick up 12 of German, Italian Extraction in Eight New York Cities— Slated for Detention Centers

War

ar is a little word—just three letters. But for a kid it was really too big to know what it meant. No one ever took the time to talk to us about things. You were supposed to keep quiet and not ask questions. That's what grownups expected. So they never really thought about what the kids were thinking; how we felt about things or how badly we wanted to know what was happening. We just had to keep quiet.

All I knew was something serious happened and things around me started to change. Barely out of kindergarten, I learned to recognize the big letters on the front page of the newspaper: WAR. The word showed up every day in the *Binghamton Sun* and the *Binghamton Press*, the morning and evening newspapers. Although war meant little to me, I could tell it was important because everyone talked about it all the time. And whenever they did, they looked worried.

Every day corner newspaper boys shouted war news, *Extra, extra, read all about it. Draft may cover men 18 to 45. Shoes, butter, sugar, and coffee to be rationed. Red Cross sets up War Fund and asks for money and blood!* I asked my older sister, Frances, what the newspaper boys were talking about. She explained drafting meant men were being taken to go to war, even if they had families. They would be taking everyone fit to fight. Some things like shoes, butter, sugar, and coffee would be harder to get, and the Red Cross needed blood for the soldiers in case they got hurt.

The Movietone Newsreel at the Ritz Theatre changed. Before the war started, they would show the serious news and then include some happy stories about funny people or animals or sports. Now everything seemed scary. The big screen showed clouds of black smoke rising from burning boats, and men in uniforms running and carrying bloody people. The newsreel voice used words like *attacked* and *killed* and *lost*. The music behind the war pictures was sad and scary. The voice on the newsreel said a man called the President would speak. Then a man wearing glasses came on the screen and stood in front of a crowd of people sitting in a big room. When he spoke, his voice sounded strong. He said something bad happened on December 7th, and then he talked about war. When the man they called the President finished, the people in the room with him stood up and cheered and so did the people in the Ritz.

In the first grade at Daniel S. Dickinson school, we learned to put our right hands over our chests and say the Pledge of Allegiance in front of our red, white, and blue flag. Whenever all the classes came together in the big assembly room, students sang the National Anthem and "God Bless America."

I began to see older kids hauling scrap metal in wagons to Levine's Junkyard for the war. Levine weighed the metal on a scale and put it in different piles to be taken away on trucks. The boys got paid a little and then went right out again to look for more scrap.

I went to the railroad tracks behind Grandma's apartment building at 123 Clinton Street and walked along the tracks looking for pieces of coal that fell from the trains. Other kids were there looking for coal, too. Whatever I found, I'd stuff in my pockets to take back to my grandmother, and she'd put it in the kitchen stove to keep the fire going. Sometimes I'd follow other boys and climb into empty boxcars made cold from blocks of ice. These railroad cars hauled fresh fruit and sometimes, if you were lucky, you might find a few grapes that fell and you'd reach down in between the floorboards and grab them. You had to keep watch that the train didn't start moving or the railroad man didn't come by and catch you.

Sometimes I'd go to the city dump and look for pieces of wood to bring to Grandma. She taught me what kind of wood to look for, not too wet and not too hard. It didn't matter how big the pieces were as long as you could break them with your foot and they could fit in the stove.

My mother, Theresa, sister, Frances, younger brother, Richie, and I lived in an apartment building in the alley behind Elmo's Bar at 80 Clinton Street. Our mom's mother and father and their three grown sons and two grown daughters lived in an apartment building at 123 Clinton Street. Grandma watched Fran, Richie, and me while Mom worked. No matter how crowded or how many mouths to feed, Grandma always got us through the days and nights.

One Saturday morning a man showed up with a pony, a real one, right in the alleyway outside 123 Clinton. All of the kids pushed and shoved to get close to it. The man carried a big camera over his shoulder and asked if we wanted to take a picture sitting on top of the pony. It cost seventy-five cents, he said. Everyone ran to ask their moms if they could take a picture with the pony. Mama came down and asked the man when she'd have to pay. He said when he came back with the picture. Mama said OK and she watched the man put furry leggings on me and a vest and a cowboy hat. He lifted me onto the saddle and put the leather straps coming from the pony's head into my hands. I felt like a real cowboy. I could see Mama smiling as all the other boys started shouting and whistling and laughing. The man told me to look up out toward the sky and then I heard the click of the camera. He brought me down off the pony and said I did real good as he took off the cowboy clothes and put them on another kid waiting his turn. The man took Mama's name and said he'd bring the picture by. I was real excited and couldn't wait to see me sitting on that pony.

On Christmas Eve, the *Binghamton Press* ran a story about rationing tires. I asked my Uncle Bill what that meant and he told me that rubber was now needed for the war, and people who had cars wouldn't be able to buy tires for their cars any time they wanted. But he said we didn't have to worry about that because no one in our family owned a car.

Uncle Bill used to take me to the Abashians, the neighbors across the hall, where he would go to sit by the radio with them and listen to the news about the war. Christmas was coming and everyone was sad when the radio said that a soldier from Johnson City was missing in Pearl Harbor. They called him a war casualty, the first from our area. I didn't know what it meant to be missing, but it didn't sound good. When the radio news changed to music, everyone in the room talked about how they hated "the Japs" for what they did.

I got the biggest stocking I could find to hang up for Christmas. I wanted a toy soldier gun, but on Christmas morning of 1941, I got an orange and some marbles. Uncle Bill also gave me a nickel from the money he made working at Kutz's Market on Clinton Street where he swept the floor and put canned food on the shelves for a quarter an hour.

The pony-picture man came by and showed Mama and me the picture. If you didn't know it was taken on Clinton Street, you'd swear I was out West where the real cowboys live. Mama asked the man if he could come back—she had just run out of money. He told her he would try, but with the war on he said he didn't know for sure when it might be. Mama told him she would have the money for sure when he came the next time. He said he would give it to us for fifty cents. Mama said she couldn't do it right then, so he left. I watched out for that man all the time, but I never saw him or that picture of me sitting up on that pony like a real Ritz cowboy ever again.

Every day men began to sign up to go to war. Most were young, but a lot were old. Over the years, I went with my Grandma three times to watch each of her sons go to war. One by one, my uncles signed up at the Capitol Theatre Building on Exchange Street across from the Courthouse. After getting checked over by a doctor, my uncles and the others who signed up were marched down the middle of Exchange Street by a man in an Army uniform, proceeding around the corner of Court and down the middle of Chenango Streets to the Lackawanna train station on Lewis Street. All along the way, people cheered and waved flags at Grandma's sons and the other soldiers-to-be.

Large and noisy crowds waited on the platform of the station to see the men off. Everyone watched them board the train. When air from the train squealed and the big wheels started to turn, the noise from the crowd suddenly stopped. No one spoke, and except for the occasional sound of people sniffling everything was still. People stood watching the train taking their men away and waved good-bye until it disappeared around a curve. The train whistled two double toots in the distance. They sounded like *bye-bye . . . bye-bye.*

Soon, Grandma and Mama got stamps every month to take to the grocery store to buy certain foods such as sugar and butter. The ration stamps could get you just a portion of some foods because of the war. But the stamps didn't mean anything if you didn't have the money to pay for the food. A lot of families got food on a weekly tab from the storeowners, but you had to keep an eye on them so they didn't cheat you.

Once rationing started, the thing I started to miss most was the sweet taste of the penny candy and bubble gum at Simeck's and Parrish's Candy Stores on Mygatt Street. It wasn't long before you couldn't get the old candy with chocolate on top and real sugar inside, and the Fleers Bubble Gum wasn't the same; you couldn't blow good bubbles and it was so hard to chew your jaw hurt.

IT SEEMED AS IF, little by little, all the men, young and old, were leaving for the war. Only the very old, sick men, women, and kids remained. Things began to change everywhere. The streets started to look empty. People went to church to pray and light candles—for the men and boys who went away and for those of us left behind.

3.

BINGHAMTON PRESS   MARCH 19, 1942

JAPS DRIVE ON PORT OF AUSTRALIA

165 TIER MEN IN RUSH HERE TO JOIN ARMED FORCES; YOUNG AND OLD IN ALL WALKS OF LIFE BESIEGE RECRUITERS

Clinton Street

E verything happened on Clinton Street. From the time you came out of the dark shadows underneath the railroad overpass at Front Street at the east end until you covered its mile-long stretch ending at Glenwood Avenue on the west side, Clinton Street was the heart and soul of the First Ward. Its noisy, crowded sidewalks were filled with life.

If you needed anything you could find it on Clinton Street, even Gypsies.

Every spring Gypsies showed up, renting a tiny place on the corner of Clinton and Oak Streets across from the Powell Coal Company. No one knew how or why they came. One day they would just be there as though they rode in on a magic carpet. The Gypsies always caused a big commotion because they were so mysterious. The men were dark with piercing eyes. The women were short and fat. They wore skirts, with funny colors, that hung to the ground. Their children were quiet and stayed to themselves. No one knew how the Gypsies made money. Someone said they read fortunes and stole children. We were all warned to stay away from them.

Bulldog Parker patrolled Clinton Street as if he owned it. Parker, a fat Binghamton cop, kept an eye on the Gypsies and everyone else. He walked the street with his big belly and big patrol stick swinging from side to side. As with the Gypsies, it was a smart thing to stay away from Bulldog Parker.

On the street, the native languages of various First Warders filled the shops, grocery stores, and bars. From Slovak and Polish to Russian and Lithuanian, the different voices caught your ear. With a little Italian and Yiddish mixed in, it almost felt as though you lived in the Old World.

Charlie Savery owned and ran the Ritz, the local movie theater on Clinton Street. Movies changed every two days and double-feature cowboy movies ran on Saturdays. You could go to LaTorre's next to the Ritz and buy candy and comic books and baseball cards. If you wanted a really good bag of popcorn, you could go down a few doors to Lalley's where the smell of Mr. Lalley's popcorn seemed to reach out and pull you right in off the street. Whenever I asked Mr. Lalley to top off a nickel bag of popcorn, he'd always say: *Who do you-a-think I am? A John D. Rockefeller!* Then he would top off the bag of popcorn with a big smile on his face.

At night, the neon lights hanging on saloon windows lit a path along the length of Clinton Street. With so many beer joints, it seemed that was all Clinton Street was—just one long beer joint. They opened early and closed late. Inside, the buzz of loud talk was drowned out by a louder beat of polka music squeezed in and out of accordions by old men. Men and women with worried and sad faces sat in the barrooms of the Clinton Hotel, the Brass Rail, the Marble Grill, Freije's, Welcome Inn, Elmo's, Andy's Inn, Metrus's, the Lincoln Hotel, Sansevieria, and the House of Mills. Some joints didn't even have names;

they just looked like regular houses except for the neon signs in the windows advertising Piel's, Pabst Blue Ribbon, Schlitz, and Genesee Beer. The saloons were often the places where good-byes were said to the men leaving home for the war.

Across from Elmo's beer joint was an illegal gambling room. To hide its activity, gamblers were instructed to go through Harry's Lunch, a greasy spoon next to Konick's Tin Shop, and leave out the back door. Then they would walk through an alley and enter the back door of a cigarette and candy store next to Minnow's Barber Shop. Once inside, they would shoot dice and play blackjack in the back room while Joltin' Joe Banovic, a local professional boxer, ran the house and Johnny Haystack, a punch-drunk boxer with over 200 fights and cauliflower ears to prove it, walked the alley outside to keep an eye out for Bulldog Parker and the other cops.

In 1902, Joseph Paul Zukauskas was born in Binghamton to a Lithuanian couple who lived on Clinton Street. At sixteen, he left home and after joining the Navy in 1920, began boxing soon after. Four years later, fighting as a professional out of Boston, he changed his name to Jack Sharkey. You could listen, for hours, to the older guys on the street talk about how great a boxer he was. On July 21, 1927, Sharkey was beating the heck out of Jack Dempsey at Yankee Stadium in front of 84,000 fight-fans, before Dempsey hit him with a low blow. When Sharkey turned to complain to the ref, Dempsey nailed him with a left to the jaw and knocked him out. Sharkey always thought Dempsey to be the greatest heavyweight champion and Dempsey said Sharkey was the toughest he'd ever fought. Sharkey fought on to become the Heavyweight Champion of the World. That day would come on June 21, 1932, when Sharkey decisioned Max Schmeling in fifteen rounds to win the title and then lost it to Primo Carnera on June 29, 1933 by knockout in the sixth round. Clinton Street would see its share of fights and fighters, but there would never again be one like Sharkey.

Almost everyone stood out on Clinton Street, some more than others. Johnny Haystack, with his big cauliflower ears, walked the street smoking a pipe, but instead of putting tobacco in the bowl of his pipe, he put a lit cigar in it. He never looked at anyone when he strolled the streets; he just mumbled quietly to himself. When he wasn't looking out for the cops at the gambling parlor, he just walked Clinton Street shuffling on the heels of his shoes and puffing on his cigar-pipe.

Spooks and Cy lived in a cardboard box they stuffed in a narrow opening between Izzy Lipshutz's Grocery Store and Elmo's Bar. They huddled with their whiskey and kept to themselves, but if anyone called them bums, Spooks would get mad and yell, *I might be a tramp, but I ain't no bum!*

Izzy Lipshutz was one of a number of small grocery-store owners on Clinton Street who offered credit to his regular customers. He always thanked his lady customers by patting them on their rear ends when they left the store. Singer's, on the corner of Hanchett Avenue, was another grocery, but you had to keep an eye on Mr. Singer not to get cheated. He liked to sneak a little lead weight on the scales.

A character of charm and personality roamed from bar-to-bar on Clinton Street. Masti Huba, a friendly old man, was offered a free beer at every stop along the way to reward him for his pleasant manner and happy spirit. Everyone went to Mike and Pete Minnow's for haircuts. Besides cutting men's hair, the brothers specialized in butch cuts and crew cuts for kids. Women did their own hair. When they could scrape enough money together, it was a special trip for them to leave the Ward and go all the way downtown to Bennett's Beauty Shop for a perm.

Philadelphia Sales took up most of the blocks on Clinton Street between Murray and Mygatt Streets. Philly's carried everything from clothes to furniture and although most of it was cheap stuff, it was just the right price for people who didn't have much to spend. Shoppers came from all over the city looking to save a few pennies. It was always crowded and it gave you a chance to look at different faces, and have a sense of who the other people were that lived outside the First Ward.

Larry's Lunch, across from Philly Sales, served delicious hot roast-beef sandwiches with gravy and mashed potatoes for fifteen cents. You didn't even want to walk by Larry's and smell what was inside unless you had at least fifteen cents in your pocket.

Very few people went to Harry's, the greasy spoon a few doors down from Larry's Lunch. A customer once told Harry there was a dead fly in his coffee and Harry told him, "What do you want for a nickel, elephants?"

Jacob Eisenberg ran the Broome Drug Company, a drugstore on the corner of Mygatt Street. Ladies went in with prescriptions, and while they waited, sprayed on a sample of Evening in Paris perfume. You could always tell if a lady just came from the drugstore because the perfume filled the air like flowers when she passed by.

Across the street from the drugstore was French Dry Cleaners, run by a sharply dressed Negro who got a lot of business. He didn't do credit and he got awfully annoyed if you couldn't pay him right away when you went to pick up your clothes.

Kitty-cornered from French Cleaners was Olum's Store, on Mygatt and Clinton, where you could buy furniture on credit. Three doors down from Olum's was the American Store, a big grocery, whose well-dressed shoppers paid mostly in cash.

A bit farther down on the next corner was Saint Cyril's Church where people went to get married and to get their babies baptized, and to pray for those who died. A little white wooden cross, placed on a grassy spot in front of the church, had the name of the first parish soldier killed in the war. Soon other crosses would follow. Little by little I began to learn what war really meant.

On school days, you could see nuns dressed in black, their

faces squeezed into spotless stiff white collars, leading groups of silent students from Saint Cyril's Slovenska Skola to church. There was a social club behind the church where, in the evenings, some of the First Ward's best bowlers rolled the lanes and drank beer. In the summertime, on warm Saturday nights, the big hall above the club shook with Polka music and dancing at wedding receptions. And while brides and grooms smiled at flashing cameras, Saint Cyril's Hall was an easy place for uninvited guests to crash the party and enjoy the free beer and food. All you had to do was wash up and dress up for the occasion and act like you belonged.

Up the street was Greskovic's Funeral Home and just before Jarvis Street was Pecho's Funeral Home. Most everyone who died in the First Ward stopped by one of those two houses on their way to the cemetery.

Lamb's Ice Cream Parlor near the corner of West Street was a favorite place where people gathered around marble-top tables and sat on iron-backed chairs to fill up on banana splits and sodas and shakes. It was a big treat when you scraped enough money together to be able to walk in and hear the sound of the little bell ringing above the door, welcoming you.

If you didn't have the money to go to Lamb's, you could have fun by going next door to the E. J. Shoe Store where you could stick your foot in the store's new fluoroscope for free and look down into a peep-slot and see your foot bones wiggling inside your shoe. My friends and I would take turns on the X-ray-like machine until the salesman threw us out.

Down a few doors, on the corner of Jarvis Street, was the Sokolovna, a social club that gave the Slovaks a place to go to drink beer and talk to people in their native tongue. Club members bowled in leagues on the Sokolovna Lanes, while others enjoyed playing cards—Pinochle and Knock Rummy.

Farther down, on the corner of Holland Street, a place called Wesley Hall hosted a lot of wedding parties. The brass sound from Bosti Abadessa and His Band filled the air while chilled silver beer kegs rolled in to keep the fun going late into the night.

A few doors down from Wesley Hall was St. Michael's Russian Greek Orthodox Church where the Russians in the First Ward went to church. On Fridays, people came to St. Mike's from all over the First Ward to buy and savor pigs-in-a-blanket and Pirogue, Russian food made by the Russian church ladies.

The Wilson Memorial Annex, a small hospital across and down the street, made room for the sick and dying when there wasn't any room at the main hospital in Johnson City.

Holy Spirit Church on the far west side marked the end of Clinton Street. People who lived around the corner on Glenwood Avenue attended the church and weren't even considered First Warders by the First Warders on the east end of Clinton Street.

Scattered among the churches and businesses on Clinton Street were apartment buildings and small houses where people sat by windows to watch the daily parade of people go by. Kids ran through apartment hallways shouting and playing games on rainy days. The backs of the buildings overlooked alleyways that led to other apartments and other houses behind Clinton Street. Creaky and weather-worn wooden steps in the backs of the apartment buildings led down to sunless dirt yards where kids played in the constant shade of the buildings.

As men left for the war and women took their jobs in the factories, the young people ran wild throughout the Ward, but especially up on Clinton Street. Kids searched the sidewalks for cigarette butts with a little life left in them. If they were lucky, they might find a nickel or a penny to be able to go and buy a piece of candy. And on most days, kids got extra exercise by stealing a piece of fruit from baskets sitting outside grocery stores and running away from screaming owners.

When you laid your sweat-drenched head down to sleep at night, Clinton Street was still on your mind. With each new day to come you'd know you would be facing a new challenge. You didn't always know where you would find it, but somewhere among the sidewalks, the alleyways, the shops and doorways, a challenge always waited.

At night, the bright lights on Clinton Street made you feel it was the place to be. Sometimes the street went dark when the City ordered blackouts, and everyone had to turn their lights off and pull their shades down. Men who couldn't serve in the war were usually made Air Raid Wardens. They walked the neighborhood streets at night in white metal helmets carrying whistles and flashlights. When the air-raid sirens screamed into the night air across the city, the wardens' job was to make sure no lights could be seen in case enemy planes came over to bomb us.

Still, the blackouts didn't stop people from being on Clinton Street. They walked up and down the sidewalks in the pitch dark with cigarettes hanging from their lips. It looked like fireflies glowing in the night and in the cold of winter with snow covering the ground, the dancing dots of burning cigarettes made it seem like summer in winter. It was magical.

Over time, the beer joints got quieter as more and more of the men were sent to war. They still stayed open, serving a few regulars unfit to fight the war, but fit enough to have a whisky and nurse a beer or two.

YOU COULD FEEL things changing on Clinton Street. Women and girls worked real jobs, the ones men left behind. The big crowds of people were gone and you started to get a sad feeling like riding a merry-go-round when the music ends and the horses slow down. On Clinton Street, kids could remember or forget their troubles, or just waste time waiting for the day when everyone would be home again and the street would look and sound and smell the way it once did. In the meantime, you had the feeling you were on your own.

4.

BINGHAMTON PRESS   MARCH 24, 1942

TIDE TURNING AGAINST JAPS

CROWD OF 1,000 SEES 200 SELECTIVE SERVICE MEN PULL OUT OF BINGHAMTON ON WAY TO WAR

Sweethearts, Relatives, and Pals Jam Station as Largest Draft Contingent Leaves the City

No Good Deed

It started out as a game, but something went wrong.

Joe Parisi put his head down, closed his eyes, and began to count to one hundred. A hundred seemed like a lot of time to find a spot to hide in the Ruffos' apartment, but with me and two other guys running away from Joe in the kitchen, getting to a good spot before someone else did was the toughest part of the game.

Dutchie Ruffo, a friend from the apartments in the alley off Clinton Street, came up with the idea to go to his cousin Anthony's after school to play before Anthony's parents came home from work. But it was Joe Parisi's idea to play hide-and-seek. Anthony's apartment wasn't that big—a small kitchen, a living room, two bedrooms, and a couple of closets. It wasn't the

best kind of place to play a game like hide-and-seek, but Joe Parisi was older and bigger than Anthony and Dutchie and me, so
we figured if he wanted to play the game, then we'd play.

"Forty-nine, fifty, fifty-one . . . ." Joe was already into the
fifties, counting quickly toward the sixties, while Dutchie and
Anthony Ruffo and I were still checking out spots to hide while a
small radio in the kitchen played "Don't Sit Under the Apple Tree
with Anyone Else but Me."

I slid beneath the small bed in the farthest bedroom. I liked
hiding under beds, and I especially liked this bed because the bedspread fell all around the floor, making it dark underneath. I lay
still as I heard someone open a closet door and step inside. That
meant two of us had found hiding spots. Then Anthony lifted the
bedspread and began to slide underneath the bed I was under. I
put my fingers to my lips to signal to be quiet and said in a whis-
per for him to leave and find his own spot. Hearing the count in
the eighties, Anthony scooted out and I heard him shuffle behind
the stuffed chair next to the window facing Clinton Street. Then
everything got quiet.

It seemed I had heard Joe reach a hundred and yell, *Ready or
not, here I come*, quite a while ago. Laying in the quietness underneath the bed, I listened for any signs he was heading our way,
but I heard none. Then the door to the bedroom opened slowly
and I heard footsteps entering the room. I held my breath as the
closet door creaked open. Suddenly, Dutchie screamed out as Joe
yelled, *Gotcha!*

Dutchie stumbled out of the closet and left for the kitchen to
wait until the rest of us were caught. The room got quiet again.
Then I heard Joe's steps walk by the bed. *Gotcha!* Joe shouted as
Anthony muttered, *Oh, shit!* from behind the stuffed chair. He
then left to join Dutchie in the kitchen.

Joe's footsteps seemed to follow Anthony slowly out of the
bedroom. I heard the bedroom door close shut and everything
was quiet again. A smile broke across my face, but before I could

enjoy it, the bedroom door burst open and Joe dove underneath the bed and grabbed my foot as I struggled to get away. *Gotcha!* Joe yelled, pulling me out from underneath the bed.

We took turns being *it* even though it was not much of a game in the tiny apartment. By the time everyone had a turn, Anthony reminded us his parents would be getting home soon and that it was time to quit. I left and went across the large open yard to our apartment building.

I was surprised when a short time later I heard a knock on our apartment door. When I opened it, Dutchie was standing there. He looked scared and nervous when he told me, "Anthony's mother got home and said someone stole her gold watch from the glass cabinet in the kitchen and that if it isn't returned by six tonight, she's going to call the police."

"Took her watch? Who would do that?" I asked Dutchie.

"I don't know, all I know is my aunt said it was there this morning when she left for work and now it's gone. She said one of us took it."

"Christ, Dutch, I don't know anything about her watch. Did she really look all over for it?"

"I don't know. I guess. All I know is she's gonna call the cops if it's not found."

I went outside with Dutchie onto the dirt yard that was our neighborhood playground. Looking up, I saw Mrs. Ruffo standing near the back railing off her kitchen. She looked down at us and, after mumbling something in Italian, she turned and went inside.

"Boy, is she mad," Dutchie said. "Hey, I gotta go. My folks are gonna give it to me if that thing ain't found. Ain't you afraid of your mother?"

"Yeah, but I didn't do nothin'. Hey, it's gotta be somewhere. Don't worry," I said as Dutchie ran up his apartment steps.

I jumped when Joe Parisi snuck up behind me and said, "Hey, did you hear about Mrs. Ruffo going to call the cops?"

"Yeah, I heard. I didn't do it."

"Yeah, I didn't either, but if she don't find that watch, the cops are gonna come to talk to all of us."

"What will they want?"

"They're gonna grill us till someone comes up with that watch and if they don't find out what happened, they'll probably take us all in."

"All in where?"

"To jail."

"Joe, we didn't do anything."

"Yeah. I know it and you know it, but the cops will pick someone to blame it on. We just gotta find that watch."

"How are we gonna do that?"

"We just got to look," Joe said as he put his arm around my shoulder and walked me toward the alley leading up to Clinton Street.

"But, it's probably somewhere in her apartment. How are we gonna look there?" I said.

"We can't, but you never know, something like a gold watch could turn up anywhere."

"I never saw a gold watch. How will we know what to look for?"

"It's shiny, real shiny. You can't miss it. Just look for something shiny and bright. Hey! Just like that right over there!" Joe said excitedly as he pointed underneath the wooden steps going up to the apartments across the alley from Mrs. Ruffo's.

"Gee, what's that?" Joe said.

"What, Joe? What are you talking about?"

"Right there," he said, pointing as he led me toward the stairs.

"Where, Joe? I don't see nothin'."

"That shiny thing, under the stairs. What is it?"

I looked closely and then I saw it. Something shiny was sitting in the dirt underneath the back side of the steps. Excited, I ran and reached deep under the steps until my fingers felt something.

"Joe, look . . . I found this!" I said excitedly.

"What have you got?" Joe said as he looked in my hand. "That looks like a gold watch. I'll bet it's Mrs. Ruffo's. You found it."

"What should I do?"

"Take it to her and see if it's hers. If it is, she'll probably be glad and she won't call the cops."

"Yeah. And I'll tell her where I found it and she'll be sur-prised."

"Yeah. Maybe she dropped it, and it got kicked under the stairs."

"Yeah. I better go. Don't you want to come?"

"Naw, you take it to her. You found it. I'll tell the other guys we're all clear."

I ran as fast as I could up the four flights of stairs to Mrs. Ruffo's. Out of breath and excited, I knocked on the door. Mrs. Ruffo opened it; standing behind her was her husband. From the look on her face, I could see she was mad.

"Mmrs . . . Mmrs . . . I'm sorry, I'm out of breath. Mrs. Ruffo, I ff . . . found this under the stairs across the way. I dd . . . don't know if it's yours or not," I said raising my hand with the watch in it.

Mrs. Ruffo took it from me and took a close look at it. She blew on it a few times and looked at it again. I saw Anthony come out and stand beside his father. His eyes looked red and sad. I was hoping Mrs. Ruffo would say whether or not it was hers, or maybe if she smiled a little it would let me know something. Instead, Mrs. Ruffo looked at me and her eyes got madder. She turned and went inside with the watch, slamming the door behind her. I could hear yelling inside. I think I heard Anthony crying. But, anyway, the watch must be hers, I thought, and I hoped she's glad I found it.

Kids were playing outside when Mama got home from work and found a note on our door from Mrs. Ruffo. I never saw the note, but when Mama pulled me onto a chair by the window and came after me with the big leather belt she started hitting me and screaming, "Why did you take that watch?" The kids outside got quiet.

"I didn't," but Mama kept hitting me and yelling, *Why did you steal that watch?*

I didn't want anyone outside in the yard to hear me and I tried to be quiet, but each time the leather hit my bare arms and back, I cried out, *I didn't!*

But Mama didn't stop. Each time the loud crack of the leather hit, my skin felt like it was on fire. I cried out loud and soon I was gasping for air and couldn't answer when Mama asked, "Who told you to steal . . . ?" All I could say were parts of words, *Nnn . . . nnn . . . nnn . . . I . . . I . . . I . . . I . . .* and then I tried to breathe. Mama didn't stop. I screamed each time, but I couldn't answer her, even though I tried to when she asked, "Why did you steal Mrs. Ruffo's watch? She said you brought it to her."

I don't remember how many times Mama hit me. She stopped when I couldn't talk and I couldn't breathe from the crying. She put the belt down and told me to wipe my nose and stop crying, but I couldn't.

MAMA DIDN'T KNOW that I didn't take Mrs. Ruffo's watch and no matter what, I couldn't make her believe me. The silence in the yard outside was suddenly broken with sounds of kids playing, laughing, and running. They had been listening—probably thinking I was nothing but a big crybaby and a crook.

5.

ROMMEL CAPTURES MATRUH, BRITISH ARMY IN RETREAT

17-YEAR-OLD YOUTH JOINS MARINES "TO GET EVEN" FOR BROTHER KILLED IN HAWAII

Vows Vengeance on Japanese as He Enlists Here

A Death in the Family

G randpa died and everyone cried over him as he lay in the casket with his eyes closed and his hands folded together. The smell of flowers filled the air as women rolled wrinkled white handkerchiefs in their hands and a few old men sat quietly while sad music played through a little box on the wall. I never saw Grandma cry so hard or be so sad as I saw her that day.

My grandmother, Elizabeth Barish, came to America on a boat from Europe. She came by herself from Czechoslovakia when she was sixteen. Newly arrived in Binghamton, she got a job making cigars at the F. B. Richards Cigar Factory on Water

Street for five cents an hour. She met Martin Vrabel, also from Czechoslovakia, and soon they would marry.

Martin worked for the Endicott Johnson Shoe Company, at the Pioneer Factory in Johnson City, as a leather worker, making shoes. At times he also tended bar at the Sokolovna. Martin spent most of his time off drinking beer and hanging out. He broke his leg in a fight one night, rolling down the stairs with another man. When he drank too much, Grandpa could be mean.

After six children together with grandma, Martin Vrabel, the grandpa we called Pa, took sick and died in August 1942, he was fifty-eight. His funeral was held at Pecho's Funeral Home. It was there, among family and friends, that my mother lifted me up and told me to kiss Pa good-bye. Leaning over the casket, Mama lowered me over Pa's face. His eyes were shut tight; he didn't move and I was scared. Kissing him on the forehead, my lips felt his coldness. He smelled like a flower.

Pa's oldest son, Uncle Joe, was there in his Army uniform. He looked clean and polished in his olive-drab dress suit as he walked silently among the people. Drafted into service only three months earlier, the Army sent him home to say good-bye to his father before shipping him off to war. While he was home, I liked to touch the brass insignias on his coat and look at the bright patch sewn on his shoulder that showed a tank and a lightning bolt and read: 7TH ARMORED DIVISION. I didn't want Uncle Joe to go away again.

Pa was buried on a slope on the highest corner of Spring Forest Cemetery, near the tall iron fence that ran along busy Prospect Street. After the service, Mr. Shelly Park of the Shelly Park Milk Company paid a visit to Grandma at the little house they rented on Meadow Street to tell her how sorry he was. Then he reached into his pocket and took out a bunch of bills for months of milk deliveries to the Vrabel family. He ripped them up and gave them to Grandma and told her to consider them paid. The total he forgave Pa was more than the money given to

Grandma from the collection taken up by Pa's coworkers at the Pioneer Factory when he died. After Mr. Park left, Uncle Bill grabbed Pa's leather strap, nailed to a piece of broom handle hanging near the kitchen door, and buried it in the farthest corner of the yard near the little wire fence in the back. Pa used it whenever he was mad about something. Uncle Bill never wanted to see it or feel it again.

Wherever our grandma, Elizabeth, went, we always followed. Everyone called her Ma. So, when Ma and her children moved to an apartment in the Kelly block at 30 Dickinson Street, my mom moved us there too from our apartment in the alley at 80 Clinton Street.

Ma Vrabel lived in a three-bedroom apartment in the back on the second floor with her sons John, Joseph, and Bill, along with her daughters Irene and Virginia. Ma's oldest daughter Theresa, our mom, and my sister Fran and brother Richie and I lived right next door to Ma in the front two-bedroom apartment facing Dickinson Street.

When we moved to the Kelly block, the first thing you noticed inside our apartment was the smell. All the walls were faded white and they stunk like wet wallpaper. Then you noticed how small the rooms were. We had a few things, but when we put them in our apartment, it still looked empty. There was a torn dark blue sofa with two sad-looking chairs in the living room. Two beds barely fit into the bedrooms. In the kitchen, a light bulb hung in the center of the ceiling above our small metal table with two ripped chairs. Linoleum covered all the floors. A tub and a toilet and a broken sink made up the bathroom. The noise in our apartment traveled—any yelling could be heard outside in the hallways and even up the stairs.

Our apartment was not the kind of place you would invite anyone. We didn't use it so much to live in or to spend any time there. It was just a place to be when you couldn't be on the street where you wanted to be.

It turned out that most of our Christmases at the Kelly block were snow white; the winters in Binghamton were cold. In the biting wind, Mama dragged Richie, Fran, and me out into the night to buy a fresh-cut Christmas tree on a lot on the other side of the railroad underpass on Murray Street. Picking out a tree was always hard. Mama took turns fighting with us, and she even fought with the man selling the trees. It seemed we always waited till the last minute to buy a tree, and it always seemed we were out looking on the coldest night of winter.

We would end up with whatever tree Mama could get for the lowest price. Then we would drag it home and carry it into the living room. No one really wanted to, but we all helped to decorate the tree with lights, bulbs, and tinsel. We learned never to expect much from Santa. Mama did her best to make a Christmas for us, but it was hard to pretend to be happy when we opened our gifts on Christmas morning and never got anything we wanted. Mama could tell we were disappointed and she would get mad at us.

When Mama worked at the shoe factory, Grandma watched my sister and brother and me when we weren't at Daniel S. Dickinson. In school, there wasn't much talk about the war. We were there to be taught and were expected to learn words and numbers and places around the world. In gym class we learned how to run and jump and throw and catch a ball. Mostly we learned to keep quiet and to do what we were told. We walked home for lunch, which was usually soup from a can and a chocolate Tasty Cake.

Early on I learned the importance of deposit bottles. I took whatever empty deposit bottles I could find and turned them in on Clinton Street for a penny or two each. With that you could buy a piece of Mary Jane candy or some Fleers bubble gum. On Clinton Street I'd run into some of the older guys from the Kelly block who were busy going from store to store stealing whatever they could get their hands on. It didn't take long to learn this was another way to get things when you didn't have any money or empty deposit bottles.

Philadelphia Sales, a large store filled from top to bottom with all sorts of things, was a favorite place to visit. There were two floors with everything from toys to clothes to school supplies and anything else you needed. Philly's was the place to go when you didn't want to pay much. If you had no way of paying, it was the place to go and take what you needed. You took whatever you could stuff under your shirt or in your pocket and when you did, you had to watch out that one of the big people dressed in a white shirt and necktie wasn't watching you. You didn't have to worry about the First Warders who worked there. They knew who you were and what you were doing, but they looked the other way.

Vic Lorenz, a guy I had just gotten to know in my class at Dickinson, said he needed a pen for school, but he didn't have any money to buy one. I told him I would show him how to get one at LaTorre's. Vic asked me about Philly's, but I told him LaTorre's had a lot of nice pens up near the counter just sitting right out in open glass jars.

"Are you sure we can get one?" Vic asked. "I've never done this before."

"Yeah. I'll show you how, it's easy as pie," I said. "When we go in, I'm gonna go to the magazine rack and start looking at the comic books. When you come in, you look at the candy near the counter. While you're doing that, I'm gonna ask Mr. LaTorre about one of the comic books and when he comes over to me, you grab a pen and stick it in your pocket."

"What if he sees me?"

"He's not going to see you. Just keep your eye on him, and when his back is turned, grab the pen."

"What if he hears me?"

"He won't because I'll be asking him about the comics."

"But . . ."

"Are you scared?"

"No. I ain't scared. Maybe a little. Because if I get caught, my old lady will kill me."

"You're not gonna get caught if you do what I tell you. The pens are right there. Grab one and stick it in your pocket. Remember, do it fast and look at the candy again and don't act nervous. And then you just walk out and you got a pen."

"You think we can do this?"

"This is nothing. If we can't do this, we better give up."

"Well, I need a pen."

"And you'll get one."

Vic and I set off toward LaTorre's. On the way we kept going over and over the plan. I reminded Vic that I would go in first and he should come in about a minute later. We didn't want to act as if we were together or Mr. LaTorre would think something was up. And I reminded him that after we left the store, we should act as if we're going different ways in case Mr. LaTorre comes out of the store.

Vic and I split up as we approached LaTorre's. He went over to look at the coming attractions outside the Ritz while I turned and went into LaTorre's.

Inside, Mr. LaTorre was busy filling the soda case. He turned and saw me come in and greeted, "How can I help you?"

"I'm just gonna look at the comic books. You get any new ones in yet?" I said glancing at the bunch of pens sitting within easy reach on the counter.

"I don't know. You look and see what we got. And don't bend the covers."

"Yeah. I know. Don't worry."

Mr. LaTorre knew me. I came in a lot, not to buy, just to look. But he never thought I stole from him and I didn't, not too much.

The magazine stand took up the most space in the tiny store. Brightly colored magazines lined the upper rows, far beyond my reach. *Life, Look, Time, Saturday Evening Post, Colliers, Ladies Home Journal, Photoplay*, and *Screen Stars*, with their big, bold titles filled the racks. The comic books were down below. I spotted *Superman* and *Batman*, but they weren't the new ones. After looking a bit, I reached and grabbed an *Archie* and *Captain Marvel*, and began looking over the covers.

No one else was in the store when Vic made his way through the door. It couldn't have been more perfect.

"How can I help you?" Mr. LaTorre asked Vic.

"Oh, I'm . . . I'm . . . just gonna look at the candy."

I stayed looking at the comic books and I thought that Vic sounded nervous. I figured we better do this fast.

"Hey, Mr. LaTorre, can I show you this?" I asked.

"What is it?"

"It's something in this comic book."

Mr. LaTorre came over and I pointed to an ad in the back of the book.

"Do you think this guy is for real?"

"Who?"

"Charles Atlas. Do you think those muscles are really for real?"

"What are you talking about?"

As Mr. LaTorre looked at the book, I glanced over to see if Vic had made his move. Vic was looking at us. I opened my eyes wide to signal him to grab the pen. He still didn't move.

"Of course he's real," Mr. LaTorre said.

"Well, look at the skinny kid on the beach getting sand kicked in his face by that big guy."

"Yeah."

"And then after he takes the Atlas Course he's strong and chases the big guy away."

"Yeah."

"Well, do you think if I sent away for this I could look like that?"

"Sure. If you work hard like Atlas. But, you're a little boy yet and you got plenty of time to look like him."

I sneaked a quick peek at Vic and just as he finally went to grab the pen, Mr. LaTorre turned around and caught Vic with the pen in his hand about to put it into his pocket.

"Hey, boy! What are you doing?" Mr. LaTorre yelled.

Vic froze. His face turned red, then white. A strange look swept over his face as though he were sick. He was caught. Vic let the pen drop out of his hand and he rushed out the door before Mr. LaTorre could take a step. The pen hit the counter and fell to the floor.

"Son-of-a-bitch! If ever I catch you, I'm gonna. . . ."

Vic rushed by the window like a blur. I turned and put the comic book back on the stand.

"Did you see that?" Mr. LaTorre said, as he picked up the pen and wiped it on his pants.

"What happened?"

"This crazy son-of-a-bitch tried to steal from me. I see him again, I'm a gonna kill him."

"Why does he have to steal from you?"

"Everybody steals. Everybody. Even probably you."

"Me? I didn't steal nothin'."

"You better not."

"I won't."

"You can't trust nobody."

"Well, I'll see you later. Thanks for letting me look at the comics."

"If you see that boy, tell him never to come here again or I'm gonna call the cops."

"I don't even know who he is. But, if I see him, I'll tell him."

Once outside LaTorre's, I looked for Vic. The busy and crowded street was filled with mothers wearing Babushkas wrapped around their heads. They carried their packages while little kids chased each other, dodging through and around their mothers. There was no sign of Vic. He was gone. It should have been so easy. Why did he say he could do it and then just stand there with the pen in his hand?

LATER ON MY buddies and I tried from time to time to get Vic to learn to steal like we all did, but he didn't seem to have the heart for it. Besides, he always looked guilty even when he wasn't doing anything wrong. This was not good for stealing.

6.

GERMANS BATTERED BY RED BLOWS, RETREAT ALONG STALINGRAD FRONT

TRANSMISSION OF BLACKOUT MESSAGES CALLED HOPELESS FAILURE

Performance Is Disgraceful, Says Colonel

Daniel S. Dickinson

From the Kelly block it looked like a fortress sitting on a hill. A one-way street circled the dark brick building like a moat. This was our school, it stood at the end of Dickinson Street, just a few blocks from number 30 where we lived, and this is the place where each morning my sister Fran, my brother Richie, and I along with the rest of the kids in the Kelly block trudged off to in a sleepy parade. Along the way, kids streamed from houses and apartments and side streets to join classmates on the walk to Daniel S. Dickinson Junior High School. We'd do this from kindergarten to the ninth grade; then on to high school.

I often waited for Bernie Shapiro to come along. He was a few years older than me, and lived on Front Street, just around the corner at the far end of Dickinson Street. He was a funny guy with a big laugh. I liked walking to school with him.

I was lucky. The teachers liked Fran and by the time I reached their classes I was welcomed as Frances's younger brother. If I wore out my welcome, my brother Richie would pay the price when he came through.

Up to the sixth grade, you sat in the same classroom with the same teacher for half the year and then changed to another room and another teacher for the second half. The same teacher taught you reading, writing, arithmetic, geography, spelling, and social studies. In the seventh, eighth, and ninth grades there were teachers for each subject and you went to them in their different classrooms.

If a teacher liked you, at the end of the class, you'd be asked to take the chalk-dust filled erasers from the blackboards to the basement where you'd pound them together till all the chalk dust flew out. When you were through, the erasers looked clean, but you'd be covered in white chalk dust. I never understood the honor of being selected to do chalk eraser duty.

Having my own desk felt special. Though ink-stained and scratched, it was my desk, something that belonged to me if only for a while. Behind this desk I learned to read and write and do arithmetic. Oftentimes I'd run my finger over the initials carved into the top of my desk and try to guess who they belonged to.

Our teachers taught us by going over and over the subjects until they got stuck in your head. We ran through multiplication tables, spelling, and reading over and over. Even handwriting meant filling up a piece of lined paper with one alphabet letter making sure we kept it inside the lines and as close to perfect as we could make it. Using black ink and straight pens meant no erasing. Every mistake stood out. Smelly black ink spotted our hands and stained our clothes delivering lessons of another kind when we got home.

There wasn't much talk about the war in school. Air-raid

drills were added to the fire drills. When a loud alarm bell rang, everyone lined up and exited the school, walking single file to the playground. Once there, we stood without talking until the loud bell rang again to signal the end of the air-raid drill.

Students were encouraged to save dimes in Victory Cards to buy War Bonds, but only the few kids whose parents had some dough could do that. Recess was fun time; the playground buzzed with kids running and jumping and kicking balls and skipping rope and screaming while all the time knowing that soon the sound of the big whistle would bring recess to an end.

On the playground, girls played with girls and the boys stayed with boys. Girls passed notes around to each other and laughed and giggled when they snuck off and read them. In third grade, Mary Milo, one of the students in my class, slipped a piece of paper into my hand on the playground and walked away. When I unfolded it, she had written that she loved me. She was a nice girl with a voice like a bird, but her note scared me more than the recess whistle, so I stayed away from Mary on the playground and everywhere else.

One girl stood out from all the others and most of the guys tried hard to get close to her. Angelina Liciandrello was in our class and she lived in a clean brick house right next to the schoolyard. Her milky smooth skin and dark eyes and long wavy hair made her look like her name, an angel. Every day she dressed in freshly ironed clothes with ribbons in her hair. Angelina's mother, a classy lady, always dressed and proper, guarded her "angel" from all the boys who came anywhere near her. She'd chase the boys away as if the devil had sent them. So, nobody ever got too close to Angelina. All they could do is look and wonder from afar how anyone could be so clean and heavenly and live in the First Ward.

At noontime, we walked home from school to eat lunch. Alvin Kyle, a Negro classmate of mine who stuttered, came up to me and tried to tell me that my brother, Richie, was calling him *nigger* and could I get him to stop. I wanted to help, but catching

Richie was not easy. He was fast and could run from sun up to sun down without being out of breath. I spent many a lunch hour chasing Richie and keeping him away from the Hightowers on Meadow Street, the Browns on Saint Cyril Avenue, the Backuses on Clinton Street, and especially the Kyles on Dickinson Street. It turned out Richie went through a period when he called anyone who was Negro names. It finally let up when a Chinese family moved into the ward.

The teachers at Dickinson didn't fool with student misbehavior. Yonkie Warner, a classmate, snapped a towel at me after taking a shower after gym class. When I yelled, *Stop that shit!* Mr. Lewis, the gym teacher, overheard me and ordered me back into his office. His eyes looked like they were on fire as he warned me about cursing. He vowed to keep an eye on me. When New York State ordered square dancing in gym class, where boys and girls joined together, I was thrown out of class and restricted for one year from any sports for being accused of trying to touch Shirley Franks's boobs on a "grab-your-partner-and-dosey-do."

Mr. Frenchko taught Social Studies and when I said *Geez* out loud in class one day, he thought I said "Jesus." I tried to explain to him the difference between Geez and Jesus, but Frenchko wasn't interested. He sent me to the principal, Mr. Smith, where I was yelled at and ordered to stay after school for punishment.

Mr. Joseph, our biology teacher, said "toe-*mah*-toe" in class one day and when I snickered, he asked me in front of the class what was so funny. "It's toe-*may*-toe," I responded. He yelled at me for questioning his pronunciation and ordered me to stand in the corner.

You had to be careful you didn't become too big a problem. You could get sent to live at St. Mary's Home for bad kids. It was run by nuns, the Sisters of St. Joseph of Carondelet and it was scary. The Home was on top of a big hill on the west side of town with a big fence around it. It was like prison—you were sent there for a time until they thought you had learned a lesson or two. No one wanted to go there. Some kids sent to St. Mary's ran away until they were caught and faced worse punishment. Just the mention of the place straightened you up a bit.

One day at Dickinson, I was asked to take some papers to a classroom down the hall and give them to Mrs. Petro, the teacher of a class of older kids. I was a little nervous because in that class there was a girl named Sally Carmen. I didn't really know her, but I liked her. So when I walked in, I stared straight ahead at the teacher. Mrs. Petro's face was round and puffy. She never wore lipstick and when she spoke her mouth was dry and she made smacking sounds with her lips. She took the papers from me and as I started to leave she said, "Students, Ronald here lives in the Kelly block where all the poor kids live. I walk by there every day because I live farther down on Dickinson Street." I felt my face turn a burning red. I had no idea why she had to say what she did. Maybe it had to do with something she was teaching, but it was too late to take it back. I didn't like being used to teach a lesson and I didn't like being called poor. I was also mad that Sally Carmen heard this. She wouldn't want anything to do with someone from the Kelly block.

All the older guys talked about Mrs. Kane, the English teacher, about how pretty she was and how they couldn't wait to be in her class. She wasn't that pretty, but compared to how the other female teachers looked, she was the top pick. There was something about the way she wore her sweaters and the way her skirt pinched her waist and hung off her and the way she crossed her legs. Guys smiled at her when she passed in the hallway and when she smiled back, the guys got excited and at recess they'd talk about what they wanted to do to Mrs. Kane. They wondered out loud about going to her house after school to see if she wanted to fool around. But nobody had the guts.

Of all the teachers at Dickinson, Margaret McNulty, the math teacher, was my favorite. A small woman, she limped around the classroom with a big shoe on her crippled left foot. No one knew why one of her legs was shorter than the other, but it didn't matter with Mrs. McNulty—there was something about the way she talked to you and looked at you that made you feel special. She smiled and laughed a lot when she taught and that made her different from all the other teachers. She never asked for anything; but if she did, you'd give her everything. You couldn't let her down. Inside that little person was one of us.

AFTER SCHOOL, BOYS met on the playground. This was the time and the place where you felt free and alive. It was on the playground where you learned bad words and bad ideas; where plans got made and real friends were won and lost. Dares were made and acted on to see if you were good enough to join a gang or who was chicken. On the playground, challenges were made, to see who was the fastest, the strongest, the most fearless, the most daring. The playground at Dickinson brought adventure—with fun and laughs and fights and tears. For most of us, this was home.

7.

BINGHAMTON PRESS   AUGUST 20, 1942

EYEWITNESS TELLS OF DIEPPE RAID

CITY STARTS COLLECTION OF TIN TOMORROW

Housewives Urged to Have Cans in Proper Shape

A Club for the Boys

There was always something going on there, somebody said. It was a good place to go to help you through long rainy and cold days with nothing to do. It wasn't much to look at on the outside, just a dull looking two-story brick building on the corner of East Clinton and Washington Streets. A large gray eagle made of stone spread its wings above the front door. Below it a sign read: BOYS' CLUB in big letters. But once you stepped inside, you entered a special place.

Someone in a hurry bumped me out of the way when I couldn't pull open the heavy glass and metal doors right away. When he yanked it open, a bunch of guys rushed in off the street behind him and I followed. This was my first time there and when the roar of noise from inside hit me, I didn't know what to expect.

"I want to join," I said again louder to the young guy straining to hear me from behind the counter.

"You want to join, did you say?"

"Yeah."

"This your first time here?"

I nodded my head.

"How old are you?"

"Almost eight."

"How old?"

"Seven."

"OK," he said. "Just sign here in this book. Print your name and I'll give you a card."

It only took a minute. When he handed me my official membership card, I stared at my hand-printed name. I now belonged . . . to the Boys' Club.

"Go ahead and look around. My name's Dick Maples. If you need anything, come and see me," the young man said. "And welcome to the Boys' Club."

I stayed near the front counter for a while and just looked around. Boys of all ages yelled and screamed as they ran through the club in a hurry to get to some place. Boys were everywhere. I never saw so many, ever. Scattered among them were older boys whose jobs were to make sure everyone got along.

The main floor was a big open space with high ceilings. There was no furniture, just a few benches, and every sound seemed to echo off the bare walls. I walked around and watched kids shooting pool and playing ping-pong while others argued over who had the next game. Next to them boys played checkers at tables while other boys watched, waiting to play the winner. Some games stopped suddenly while the players argued about whether something was fair or not. Sometimes they stood face-to-face until staff supervisors moved in to break them up. When I went through a set of large open doors leading to another bigger room, I saw a kid come out holding a bloody handkerchief to his nose. It looked like the supervisors got there a little late.

And no matter what game was being played, the loud shouts and waving arms told you who won. I couldn't count all the guys running around and yelling down the hallways to get to the rooms where different activities took place, like meeting-rooms and crafts-rooms and reading-rooms.

I noticed kids running up a set of wide metal steps opposite the check-in counter near the entrance. An urge sent me rushing up the stairs with the others while sidestepping those running down. Everyone moved fast, and as the stairs turned sharply up to the second floor you stayed on your toes so as not to get run over.

Once I made it to the top, I saw kids covering the second floor like ants on a bread-crumb. Most were shooting basketballs at metal nets attached to rims hanging on the walls at each end of the gym. Sweaty kids screeched across the scuffed tiled floor in worn high-top E. J. sneakers while the pounding sound of rubber balls echoed above their shouting. Shirts and jackets lay in piles around the floor, and the strong smell of dirty socks seemed everywhere. Chain-metal fencing protected rows of steamed-over windows that circled the stuffy gym.

In another area, some kids practiced tumbling on padded mats while others wrestled. Behind this area, kids bounced up and down on a trampoline trying unsuccessfully to touch the high ceiling. In a small room opposite the gym was an exercise room where older boys huffed and puffed, lifting heavy bars above their heads; their faces turning red with every lift.

I felt something hit my leg, and I turned to see one of the rubber basketballs at my feet. Looking up, a sweaty kid came running and yelling, *Hey, throw me the ball!*

I reached down and picked it up with both hands and threw it back. He grabbed it and turned and heaved it through the air. I watched it as it came down and fell through the net with a clanking sound. The kid raced to get the ball again, fighting through a crowd of kids waiting underneath the hoop for a turn to shoot at the basket.

I wandered around the gym to watch some boys taking turns climbing a thick rope attached to the ceiling. One by one they tried to pull themselves up the rope to the very top. No one could do it. Then an older negro guy with big muscles tried it and everyone backed away. He pulled his body up, first one hand and then the other, while his bare feet squeezed and pushed against the rope. The muscles and veins in his arms got bigger as he lifted farther and farther off the ground toward the ceiling. When he reached the top, he touched the ceiling and looked down at us. There were a lot of "oohs" and "aahs" from the guys watching as he slid down. I wondered how hard it was to climb that rope. And how that kid got those muscles.

"You gonna try that?" the Negro boy asked.

"Me?" I said surprised.

"Yeah, you."

"Naw. I don't think so."

"Why not? It ain't so tough."

"I don't know how."

"What's to know? You just keep pullin' till you're up there."

"I gotta go, now."

"Just throw your coat over there and take off those galoshes."

"Naw, I gotta go."

"Let's see your hand."

"What?"

"Gimme your hand."

I held my hand out and he grabbed it and put it palm to palm against his. He looked at it and said, "Yeah, your hands are OK. You can grab that rope."

I took my hand down and stared at it. It looked small next to his.

"You gonna be here tomorrow?" he asked.

"I don't know."

"Well, I'm here every day. So, I'll see you tomorrow and I'll try the rope with you, OK?"

"Yeah, if I come."

"Well, come for Chris' sake. There ain't nothin' else to do."

"I don't know," I said turning to leave.

"Say, what's your name?"

"Ronnie."

"My name's Walter, but everyone calls me Bucky. Come back tomorrow and we'll do this."

All the way home, the sounds I had heard were still in my head, like a song playing over and over. The names I heard at the Club kept running through my head, different sounding ones . . . Chubby, Zink, Lenny, Frannie, Alberto, Bucky. . . .

Lying in bed that night, I thought about all that I had seen, all those faces from all over Binghamton, faces I had never seen before. Kids with black hair and blonde hair . . . kids who looked friendly, kids who looked mean . . . kids who played hard, kids who played rough . . . kids who talked tough, kids who talked not-so-tough . . . fat kids and skinny kids . . . tall kids and short kids . . . kids with big laughs, kids who cried . . . kids who won, kids who lost.

MOST OF ALL I thought about tomorrow and about Bucky and that rope.

8.

JAPS STALLED ON ALL FRONTS

IBM TO DEDICATE MUNITIONS FACTORY IN CEREMONY

Plant Is Now Turning out War Material

Chickens Ain't Easy

This was my very first experience with a chicken, a real live chicken. It happened on a sunny Sunday morning, the day Mama sent me to an address on Oak Street. I was given a dollar and told to go to this lady's house and pay her ninety cents for one of her chickens—and to make sure I got a dime back. Mama told me we were going to have a nice dinner.

When I arrived at my destination and gave the lady the money, I was surprised to see her having such a difficult job catching one of the many chickens in her fenced yard. I was also surprised at how fast the chickens were and how they dodged all around like leaves in a windstorm. Clucking in their high voices, the chickens seemed to know what being caught meant and they definitely didn't seem to like it.

When the lady finally got hold of a chicken, I didn't exactly understand why the chicken was upside down when she handed it to me. The only thing I knew was the chicken she caught had a mean look in its eyes and the spongy red skin hanging around the chicken's face made it look spooky and ugly.

"You ever carry a live chicken before?" the lady asked, breathing hard.

"No, M'am," I answered, wondering why she asked.

The lady grabbed my hand and wrapped it tightly around the skinny legs of the chicken's razor-sharp feet. Breathing heavily, she said to me, "No matter what happens, don't let go. Cause if you do, you'll never catch it again."

"M'am, what about the change?"

She reached into her apron and poked through some change and started to stick a dime in the pocket with a hole in it. "M'am, please put it in the other one, it's better for me."

I felt funny carrying the chicken by the feet down the street, with its head hanging and bobbing and its big white feathers spread against my side. From time to time it twisted and jerked its crazy-looking head to peck me so it could get away. When that happened I squeezed tighter because I knew I had to get this chicken home.

Every step I took, the chicken got heavier. My arm hurt and it started to drop slowly bringing the chicken closer to my side. Frightened by the chicken and what the lady said and what Mama would do if the chicken got away, I jerked my arm out straight and held on out of fear. I could feel my shirt start to stick to me from the sweat coming out. Nothing mattered right now except the chicken and me.

It was a relief when I reached home and showed Mama the prize chicken. Mama took one look at the chicken and the look on her face changed in a bad way. When she reached out and took the chicken from me, I felt I had done my job and was finished. But before I could go she told me to shut all the doors and windows around the kitchen.

"What for?"

"Don't ask me stupid questions right now. I don't want the chicken to get outside when I go to kill it."

"You have to do it?"

"Who do you think's going to do it? You want to do it?"

"Not me," I said as I started to close the windows.

Suddenly, I found myself closed up in the kitchen with Mama and the chicken. I had no idea she had to kill this chicken. When I saw her grab it by the neck and begin to squeeze and twist it with both of her hands, I couldn't move. The chicken fought for its life. Its wings flapped against Mama, its sharp feet scraped and slid against the linoleum floor. It was hard to tell who was winning, but when Mama, her face straining and sweating, began to call the chicken a *son-of-a-bitch* and a *bastard*, I was worried that the chicken might be winning.

The fight went on and I felt somewhat relieved when Mama twisted the chicken's neck and head completely around and held it with all her might. It looked like it was all over for the chicken.

Out of breath, Mama let her grip go and the chicken hit the floor, but instead of dropping lifeless, it jumped up and began to run all around the kitchen with its wings flapping and its head flopping down and from side to side from a broken neck. It still clucked, even louder than before. I didn't know for sure, but I thought this chicken would never die.

I jumped up onto one of the kitchen chairs to escape the wild and crazy animal. Mama took a deep breath and set out to get *the son-of-a-bitch*, *the bastard*, as she pursued the skidding chicken. The chase took her all around the kitchen and with the chicken's head flopping between its feet, Mama couldn't grab it. Every now and then the chicken's head bounced up and its fearsome eyes looked like Count Dracula's stare when he was ready to suck the blood out of someone's neck.

Finally, out of breath, Mama stopped running after the chicken. She grabbed the broom from up against the wall and began to chase the chicken once again, this time beating it with hard blows as it dodged around the linoleum floor. Finally, *the son-of-a-bitch, the bastard*, lay on the floor without moving. Mama gasped for breath. I could see the fear and anger in her bulging eyes begin to ease. The fight was over.

Mama picked up the chicken and put it into a pot of hot water in the sink and began to pull out its feathers. In what seemed like no time, the chicken was bald. Mama then stretched the chicken out on the counter and reached for a knife.

Unlocking the door, I figured I had seen enough and it was time to leave, but before I got through the door, Mama yelled, "Make sure you're home in time for dinner. This chicken will be ready about six."

I closed the door behind me and ran down the stairs thinking about that chicken. The idea of eating that bird made me feel queasy. It put up a heck-of-a-good fight and at times I even felt myself pulling for it, but in the end Mama got it.

I HAD LEARNED two things that day. Chickens ain't easy and neither is Mama.

9.

PRODUCTION MIRACLE MEANS SMASHING NAZIS, JAPS IN OWN LANDS, SAYS F.D.R.

SELL TEEN-AGERS RIGHT IDEAS, DELINQUENCY CONFERENCE TOLD

Confused Because of War Conditions, Says, Cortland County Welfare Commissioner— Role of Parents Discussed

Victory Volunteers

T hings were happening there all the time. You always had the feeling that if you didn't hurry and get there, you might miss out on something. Every day after school, I ran out the Kelly block door, up Oak Street, onto Clinton Street, under the Lackawanna and Erie Railroad overpass and over the Clinton Street Bridge, all the way to the Boys' Club. Sure enough, in big handwritten letters in white chalk on the blackboard behind the check-in counter, a new activity was being started. Club members were being asked to join up as Victory Volunteers because of the war.

It surprised me to see so many kids already in the meeting room for the first get-together of the Victory Volunteers. I stood and listened to a man explaining what it was all about.

"For those of you just coming in, I'm Mr. DuBock, George DuBock. I'm in charge of getting this program started at the Boys' Club. I'm glad to see so many guys here. In case you're wondering what I'm doing here and why I'm not in the Army fighting the Japs and the Nazis, I have a medical problem that keeps me out. But just because a person can't serve doesn't mean he can't do something, and this is what the Victory Volunteers is all about. It's a chance to do something, something important to help our men fighting the war. I know if you guys were old enough you'd be over there too. But you can't. By the way, if at any time I'm not making myself clear or if you have a question, don't hesitate to speak up."

Mr. DuBock looked about the room and as he did, a lot of the guys sitting up front turned around to see if anyone had a question.

"OK. Well, I'm sure the questions will come. So, if you get one, don't be afraid to raise your hand and ask it. Now, you're probably wondering, *What do I have to do to be a Victory Volunteer?* The answer is, all you have to do is sign up and come to our regular meetings. They're probably going to be in this room, twice a week. There's no restriction on age. You are all OK to join and you don't have to bring anything, just yourself. And it doesn't cost anything; it's free. And the best part of it is we're going to try to get you guys uniforms."

When he said *uniforms* a kid next to me poked me and nodded with his eyes wide open with excitement. You could hear kids mumbling things to each other. A big smile came over Mr. DuBock's face. His eye caught a kid's hand raised to ask a question and pointing to him said, "OK! Hold it down. We've got a question up front."

What kind of uniforms? the kid asked.

"Khaki-colored. Just like real Army ones."

The idea of uniforms set off a buzz in the room. Everyone started looking around, smiling at one another. Somebody yelled out, *When are we gonna get the uniforms?*

"We have to work that out," Mr. DuBock said. "But, they're not just going to be given to you. You're going to have to earn them and we won't have uniforms right away. We have to raise the money. But to those who join, I promise you'll have a uniform some day."

Another kid raised his hand and Mr. DuBock pointed to him. *When you say uniforms, just like the Army, what do you mean? How will they look?*

"You've probably seen guys in an Army uniform or at least you've seen pictures. Well, the Boys' Club Victory Volunteers are going to look a lot like real soldiers. There'll be pants with a canvas belt and a shiny brass buckle, and a shirt and necktie and cap. You'll have to keep your shoes shined."

One of the kids jumped up and pointed to a hole in his shirt and a rip in his pants and said, *You mean I gotta give up deez fine duds for a uniform?*

The room exploded with laughter.

We'll wear the uniforms every day to school, too? another kid asked.

Mr. Dubock smiled and said, "No, you'll wear the uniforms only when you're at meetings here or doing special duties assigned to you."

What about da stuff on the uniforms? a kid shouted. *You know like what the real soldiers have.*

"Oh, yeah, that's good you reminded me," Mr. DuBock said. "You'll get patches and stripes or bars depending on what rank you earn."

What's dis rank mean? another kid asked back.

"Rank means how hard you work to be a leader. The harder you work, the higher the rank you'll be and people will know your rank by the stripes or bars you wear. Everyone starts out the same and you get promoted to a higher rank depending how hard you work."

You know, rank is like private or sergeant or lieutenant or captain, one of the older kids said out loud.

"That's good. That's right. What's your name?" Mr. DuBock asked the kid.

Williams, Lowie Williams. I know that from goin' to Harris's Army and Navy Store down the street. They got all that stuff.

"That's right, Lowie," Mr. DuBock said.

What we gotta do for dis uniform and stuff? a kid shouted out.

"OK," Mr. DuBock said. "If you join the Victory Volunteers, you're going to have to work hard, doing things around the community and the Club to help the war effort. There'll be a lot of different things to do. And whatever you do, you always have to do your duty with honor not only for your country, but for all the other boys at the Club you'll be representing. People all over Binghamton are soon going to hear about the Victory Volunteers. They're also going to be seeing you when we march in the parades downtown."

We don't know how to march, a kid spoke out.

"That's one of the things we're going to teach you. Don't worry, it's not so bad."

When do we start? a kid asked.

"You already have. Just take this paper home and have your mom or whoever watches you fill it out. Bring it back at our next meeting this Thursday night at seven. We'll meet right here."

Kids grabbed a paper from Mr. DuBock on the way out. "Thanks for coming. See you guys on Thursday," Mr. DuBock said to each boy.

I looked at the paper I had to take to Mama and I knew that no matter what she said, I had to get her to sign it. I wanted the uniform Mr. DuBock promised, and I wanted to help our guys fighting the war.

In the hallway outside the meeting room, I passed one of the older kids and I heard him ask whether we were gonna get guns or if we were going to have to fight anybody. I just shrugged my shoulders without stopping.

ON THE WAY HOME, there was a lot to think about. There was that stuff Mr. DuBock said about duty and honor and about having to keep your shoes polished. Those sounded OK. But I didn't have any shoes, just a pair of old sneakers. Swiping a pair of shoes wasn't gonna be easy.

10.

BINGHAMTON PRESS   MARCH 6, 1943

YANKS SEIZE KEY TOWN, ENTER PASS

GAETA IS HELD PRISONER

Air Hero Had Been Listed as "Missing in Action"

Tootsie

N o one called him *Francis*, except the Nuns at Saint Cyril School. To everyone else he was Tootsie. Whenever little Francis Kolosna walked the two short blocks from his house to Shipko's neighborhood store on the corner of Elm Street, the only thing he ever bought with the penny in his pocket were Tootsie Rolls.

On his way home, Francis passed by an older guy who always hung out on the corner with a cigarette hanging off his lip. He watched Francis pull the Tootsie Roll out of the little brown paper bag from Shipko's. One day the guy decided to call Francis "Tootsie," and the name stuck. The guy on the corner liked to rename the kids in the neighborhood after the things they bought. That's how John Jones's love for the Archie comics got him the name "Jug-bug."

Father Matthew at Saint Cyril School named Billy Machovec "Peewee" because he was small for his age. When we first met on the playground at Daniel Dickinson trying to choose sides for a baseball game, I knew them as Tootsie, Jugbug, and Peewee.

Tootsie lived with his grandmother, Anna Komacek, upstairs in her married son's two-story wooden house at 21 Mygatt Street. Ambrose, the son, lived downstairs with his wife, Ann, and five-year-old daughter, Patty. Tootsie's mother died when he was two, and his grandmother took him and his younger sister Muzzy in when Tootsie's father couldn't bring up his five children any longer. Besides Tootsie and Muzzy, there were two older sisters and an older brother. A sister, Anne, was called *Undo*, a brother, Robert, was called *Kiki*. For no known reason, Helen, the oldest child, was just *Helen*. "Muzzy"—her real name was Mary Jane. Slovak immigrants liked to add a little Slovak to their American names for flavoring.

Uncle Ambrose's wife, Ann, tried to get Tootsie and Muzzy sent away to St. Mary's Home because they were always running loose while their Grandma drank beer on Clinton Street. Tootsie and Muzzy never went to the Home, but they sure were scared. When they found out what their uncle's wife was up to, they kept a sharp eye on her.

The nuns at Saint Cyril, where Tootsie went to school, had another name for him. They called him *the Orphan*. Tootsie didn't like this because he had a father even though he wasn't around. Tootsie didn't say anything since the nuns liked him and treated him well, except for Sister Anatolia, the principal, who whacked his palms with a thick yardstick whenever he messed up. With encouragement from the nuns, Tootsie became an altar boy when he was seven, and was given the honor of carrying the Mass candle down the aisle in his starched white cassock.

Tootsie loved baseball and the New York Yankees. He was always eager to get a game going on the pebble-strewn dirt play-

ground of Daniel Dickinson School, which sat on the hilltop directly above Saint Cyril's Church and school. Saint Cyril's didn't have
any sports for the kids who went there, so the guys and girls hung
out on the playground at Dickinson. On after-school hours and
weekends, the air was filled with the sounds of kids yelling and
screaming until the sun went down and darkness sent sweat-soaked
kids on their way home.

Nothing stood still on the playground at Dickinson. Rubber
hand-balls rocketed off the school's brick walls as players
slapped them with their bare hands. Girls skipped rope while
singing rhymes until the speed of the rope turned their legs to
Jell-O and left them struggling for air. Older guys played Gorilla,
in which guys ran and jumped on top of other guys who formed
a bridge by bending over at the waist and wrapping their arms
around each other in a straight line. More guys leaped and
crashed down on the others. The test was to see how many guys
and how much weight it would take to collapse the human bridge
beneath. The heaviest guys went last. Everyone braced when big
"Poop" Hidock got ready to take his turn.

Team captains took turns wrapping their fists around the handle of a baseball bat, racing to see which hand would cover the
bat stub and who'd get to choose first among the crowd of players waiting to be picked. Clouds of dust rose when someone trying to stretch a double into a triple slid into third base. Kids yelled
all the time, arguing over rules; whether a player was safe or out
or the ball was hit fair or foul. Everyone yelled on the playground, there were no umpires or adults, just kids trying to argue
their way to an extra base or a chance to win.

Tootsie was a lefty and a good hitter. He could hit the ball
anywhere he wanted, but he was best at lining it over first base
and down the right-field line. Tootsie used to like to pretend he
was Mel Allen, the Yankee announcer, calling the game when we
played. *Kolosna's up. The bases are loaded. Kolosna swings and
there it goes, folks, a line drive down the right-field line into the*

corner! Kolosna is in at second with a stand-up double, clearing the bases and putting the First Ward Bombers ahead!

Tootsie and I never talked about the scarcity of money in our families. We never kept track of who had what. Whatever we had, we shared. We always found a way to make a little money, one way or another. We set pins at the local bowling alleys, dodging rock-hard wooden pins flying at us, and returning the balls by hoisting them into the channel that carried them back to the bowlers. This went on late into the night. After three hours in the pit, our sweat-soaked bodies limped home with the three quarters we earned jingling in the one pocket that didn't have a hole in it.

In the wintertime, Tootsie and I watched for the snow to come and when heavy snow covered the streets and roads a foot high, Tootsie and I got jobs with the city, shoveling snow off the side-walks downtown. The cold air and wind tore through our clothes while regular city workers, with steam shooting out of their mouths and noses like dragons, yelled at us to shovel harder and threatened us that we wouldn't get paid.

I helped Tootsie on his paper route. The *Binghamton Sun* was the morning paper and delivering it meant you would be up to see the day start.

Trucks screeched in front of darkened coffee shops on Main Street, leaving boxes of warm glazed doughnuts for pickup by the manager when he came to open. Our growling empty stomachs shortened the count in one of the boxes by one whole row. The doughnuts melted in our mouths and tasted like sweet gifts from heaven.

On the route, Tootsie folded his papers into tightly wrapped packages and shot them at the houses, hitting their targets flaw-lessly. I carried my papers to the houses so I could go around and check the back doors for any milk money left inside the neck of an empty milk bottle for the deliveryman to pick up.

We always made it a rule never to take the money if the front window had a Mother's Gold Star on it. That sign meant some-one at this house had been killed in the war.

From the newspapers we delivered, we'd come to learn the funny-looking names where our guys were fighting: El Agheila, Tobruk, Kasserine, Stalingrad, Anzio, Normandy, Malmedy, Bastogne, Midway, Leyte Gulf, Bataan, Manila, Corregidor, Iwo Jima, Okinawa.

At Christmastime, Tootsie and I sang carols at the nice homes on the west side, the part of town where the money was. Tootsie sang well. He knew all the words and he hit all the notes, cour-tesy of Professor Harendza, the music director at Saint Cyril's. The professor used his hands a lot when he taught, Tootsie told me. A "missed note" or "singing in your throat" brought swift and painful reminders about the sacredness and beauty of music. I sang along with Tootsie as best I could. We never knew what to expect when we knocked on the door of a house, even the ones with bright lights twinkling inside on the Christmas trees. When someone opened the door, we'd start singing; if the door stayed open and we sang several songs, we knew we would get a little money. Sometimes the door shut before we cleared our throats.

Tootsie stole but wasn't particularly good at it. He served Mass on Sundays and he hated going to confession all the time. He tried to change his voice in the confessional, but he was sure the priest knew who he was. That meant I usually went to Philadelphia Sales or Kresge's or The American Store and swiped the special things Tootsie and I needed, like school supplies or fishing line, or candy and cigarettes.

We tried shining shoes on Clinton Street to make a few bucks; I got our supplies by stuffing them inside my shirt during a visit to Woolworth's Five and Dime. With our shoeshine kit inside an old cigar box, Tootsie and I worked every beer joint up and down Clinton Street shouting, *Shine Mister? Can you use a shine, Mister? Only a dime. What do you say, Mister? How about a shine?* Every now and then, you'd get to shine a pair of scruffy, old shoes. It didn't take long to see that shining shoes on Clinton Street wasn't a good business. There just weren't any guys around with shoes worth shining.

Not having a dime for a movie never kept us away from getting into a show we wanted to see. Tootsie loved *The Purple Monster* at the Star Theatre. This serial always left the stars, John Archer and Mary Mcleod, trapped without any way out and facing certain death. Tootsie and I always checked the outside exits to see if a door could be opened to sneak inside. If that didn't work, one of us would ask the ticket taker if we could go in to see if our brother was in the movie theater. *Our mother sent us.* Once inside, one of us would go straight for an exit door and open it to let the others in. Then the ticket taker would be told the brother couldn't be found and the person would leave and go around to the exit door and be let in by the others. Sneaking in during daytime, we always tried to beat the shaft of light that rushed into the dark theater when the exit door opened. It helped if the inside guy timed it so that the ushers weren't around. We never left a show without vowing to see the next episode, because we were both convinced the two stars had died for sure this time. We ended up saying the same thing for all twenty-eight episodes.

You had to have real money to go to Larry's Lunch on Clinton Street where for fifteen cents you could get his hot roast-beef sandwich with gravy and mashed potatoes. Tootsie and I dreamed about the taste of it in our mouths and how good it felt going into our stomachs. If we happened to get the money somehow, sometimes we'd argue whether to go to Larry's or to Eddie's, where they sold "City Chicken" made of mariinated veal and pork, breaded and fried and served on a stick. Eddie's was Tootsie's second-favorite place to eat.

It was never hard to talk Tootsie into going for a piece of pie at the G&H Diner on Front Street or for a vanilla milkshake next to the Cameo Theatre. No matter where we went, there was nothing like the feeling you had when your stomach was stuffed.

One day, Tootsie asked me to come with him to visit his father at Binghamton City Hospital. He didn't see his father much, but he was told his dad just had surgery and he should get there to see him. Tootsie and I came into his father's room. The sickening smell of medicine filled the air. I remembered Mr. Kolosna was a small man. Now as he lay in his white gown and white-sheeted bed, there was very little left of him.

I stood against the wall and listened while Tootsie quietly talked to his father who was lying in pain from an operation that cut him from his neck to his stomach. Mr. Kolosna's face twisted with pain whenever he tried to speak. As if with all the strength he had, he reached up and put his trembling hand around the back of Tootsie's head and pulled him down close to him and whispered something into Tootsie's ear. When his hand slid off, Tootsie turned toward me, his eyes red with tears. I left the room and waited in the hallway. Two days later his dad died.

Tootsie's grandma died not too long after. He and I sat together at Greskovic's Funeral Home and watched the people passing by as she lay in her casket. After everyone was gone, we watched Mr. Greskovic lift her stiff body and remove a pillow from underneath her head and set her back down before closing the casket.

Every year the Boys' Club had an Annual Dinner to give out awards to supporters and members who achieved something special during the year in community service or sports or volunteering. Tootsie and I always liked to go because they served everyone a nice hot meal. Usually it was fried chicken, mashed potatoes and gravy with corn-on-the-cob, and ice cream and cake for dessert.

The Dinners were held in the gym on the second floor of the club. It was always packed. Club members were seated next to old men, too old to go to war, who were all dressed up in fancy suits and ties. The dinners always started out with everyone standing and saying the Pledge of Allegiance followed by the singing of the National Anthem. Then they would play a recording of "God Bless America" sung by Kate Smith and we were all asked to sing along.

One of the conditions of getting a meal was sitting through a lot of speeches. Then there was more singing. We all had to stand up and sing along from the song sheet they passed out: "Take Me out to the Ball Game," "Casey Would Waltz with the Strawberry Blonde and the Band Played On," "Old MacDonald Had a Farm," and "My Darlin' Clementine." The old men around us encouraged us to sing out with a lot of spirit as they were doing. Along with their spirit, they also had a lot of gas. When they sang "Dinah" and got to the words, "Dinah won't you blow, Dinah won't you blow . . . " they'd let off gas like they were farting to the music. Tootsie and I used to look at each other and laugh each time it happened. The old men always thought we were having a great time.

When ex-Heavyweight Champion of the World Jack Sharkey came back to Binghamton when his mom died, Tootsie served the funeral Mass and afterward he got to shake the champ's hand. Tootsie thought his looked like a baby's inside Sharkey's huge mitt.

I never asked him to do it and I never asked him how he did it, but it turned out that Tootsie voted for me over thirty times when I ran for Boy Mayor of Binghamton and was elected. This annual event at the Boys' Club let the winner "run" the City of Binghamton for a day. I met with Mayor Walter B. Lounsbery who turned over his office to me for the day. I got my friends "jobs" at City Hall and we all got to skip school legally.

Tootsie was given the City Comptroller's job; Jug-bug, Welfare Commissioner; Mike Ganisin, City Treasurer; Vic Lorenz, Superintendent of the Water Bureau. Yonkie Warner and Peewee Machovec were left out of my administration on purpose so that I could order the Public Safety Commissioner, my brother Richie, to send a police squad car to Dickinson School to pick up Yonkie and Peewee, and take them to city jail. Mr. Smith, the principal at Dickinson, wrecked my plans when he substituted two other boys, behind my back. He said he picked them because they were better students. I barely knew the two guys the principal picked, who left Dickinson in handcuffs in full view of the students and teachers and were driven off in a police car with flashing lights.

I wanted real bad guys. I wanted Yonkie and Peewee to come out of school like two gangsters in a Cagney movie. I wanted Yonkie and Peewee locked up in a jail cell and questioned under the hot lights. And just when they were covered in sweat and ready to break, I wanted to declare that Yonkie and Peewee were innocent and order them to be set free. When my plan was changed by Principal Smith, it turned out to be the worst time for me "in office."

I FELT I had let down my friend Yonkie and my buddy Peewee. I had only been in politics for a day, and already I was sick of it.

11.

BINGHAMTON PRESS   MAY 7, 1943

AMERICANS PUSH INTO BIZERTE, 1ST ARMY DRIVES INSIDE TUNIS

TWO BINGHAMTON SOLDIERS DRIVE GENERAL PATTON'S SCOUT CAR IN AFRICA

Captain Harry Borst Writes Mother that He and Corp. John Parsons Can Be Located through the News from Front—Likes His Job

We Regret to Inform You

My second-grade teacher said I could go home early from school this day even though all my other class-mates were still at their desks and school wasn't over. I wondered why. I left Daniel Dickinson and walked away from the school and within a few minutes I was heading down the alley off Clinton Street. Coming up was Loretta McDonald, a young

70

woman who watched Richie and me after school when Mama was at work. For some reason she put her arm around me and we walked down the alley together.

Someone told me that day that my father had been killed in North Africa fighting the Nazis. I don't remember who said it. The news in the paper said Pvt. Frank J. Capalaces, killed in action on May 3, 1943. With the story was a picture of him in a suit and tie, not an Army uniform. He was thirty-three-years old. I didn't know the man they said was my father. I could not ever remember seeing him or hearing his voice or feeling him touch me. No one ever spoke of him. My mother didn't say anything about him that day or any other day. It was a subject that never came up in our family; Fran, Richie, and I never talked about it.

A package came in the mail to the Kelly block for Mama. Inside was a certificate signed by President Roosevelt. The words printed on it looked important. Some words were too big for me to understand, but I got the idea that the President was sorry for what happened. Fran read it out loud to us: *He stands in the unbroken line of patriots who have dared to die that freedom might live, and grow, and increase its blessings. Freedom lives, and through it, he lives—in a way that humbles the undertakings of most men.*

A velvet box also came in the package. Inside the box was a medal on a ribbon. It was in the shape of a heart. Fran, Richie, and I took turns touching the medal. Our fingers traced the gold silhouette of the head of George Washington mounted on a purple stone. Someone said the medal was called The Purple Heart.

THE LAST THING in the package was a small, stained leather wallet. It was empty.

12.

BINGHAMTON PRESS   JUNE 3, 1943

QUIT LEWIS, AID U.S., F.D.R. TO ASK; PRESIDENT BELIEVED READY FOR ACTION TO END COAL STRIKE

REFUSAL TO HIRE ALIENS IS ILLEGAL, AREA WAR PLANTS TOLD

Ruling Includes Procedure to Obtain Consent

Fat

*L*eft foot on the beat! Shoulders back! Head high and chin tucked in! Eyes straight ahead! Forward, march! Left-right-left-right. Hut-hut, hut-hut-hut. Horns blared, drums banged, our chests stuck out as we marched down the middle of Main Street in front of cheering crowds lining the curbs all the way to the Courthouse.

We were a small part of a big Memorial Day parade, and though a light mist had fallen earlier, it seemed like all the townspeople were there to applaud and wave little flags. As we marched under a dark and gloomy sky, two of our guys held a banner that read: VICTORY VOLUNTEERS, BINGHAMTON BOYS' CLUB.

As Volunteers, we were told our job was to help our guys over there win the war. With twenty of us now signed up, we were organized like a real Army unit, but we didn't have any uniforms yet. Mr. DuBock was still working on it. He said we could make up for not having uniforms by marching as if we had them on.

Commander DuBock seemed to like the fact that if there were a job to do, he could count on me, whether the floors needed sweeping after our meetings or the windows needed cleaning. No matter what the job, I'd be volunteering to do it. Over time, my rank kept rising and when Commander DuBock made me a Captain, he said he liked the way I led the men. Now here I was, in formation, leading our guys in the big parade as we marched down Main Street.

As we passed the stand in front of the Courthouse I could see Bucky marching next to me looking like a real soldier. Walter (Bucky) Bonsell was one of a small number of Negroes who came to the Club. He was older than most of us—no one knew exactly how old he was—in fact, no one really knew much about him. He lived somewhere near Levene's Junkyard. Everyone liked Bucky; he had a lot of friends. No one messed with him; he was tough. I begged Bucky to become a Volunteer for a long time. I never gave up, and sure enough, it was the khaki Army belt and brass buckle I gave him that did the trick. He never asked me where I got it and I never told him that I had slipped one for him and one for me under my shirt during a visit to Harris's Army and Navy Surplus Store next to the Riviera Theatre on Chenango Street.

A week after the parade, Commander DuBock surprised us by giving us our first real job to do besides learning how to march and take orders. You could hear a pin drop in our meeting room at the Club after he explained what we were to do and how we were to do it. "Any questions, men?" Mr. DuBock asked as he glanced at his watch.

One of the guys in front raised his hand. Mr. Dubock pointed and said, "What is it, Corporal?"

Well, Sir, what do we tell the people when they ask us?

"Fat. You're collecting fat," Commander DuBock answered. "You tell them it's used to make gunpowder for bullets for our soldiers."

"Sir, I know you told us, but if you don't mind telling us again, what kind of fat do we collect?" another volunteer asked.

"Any kind of fat at all. Most of the people save it in cans after they cook. From things like bacon and meat. How many of you eat bacon or meat?"

Two guys raised their hands. Commander DuBock looked at them and said, "You know when your mom fries the meat on the stove, you hear it spittin' and poppin'? Well, that's the fat coming off the meat. In the pan it's oily and runny, but then after the meat's cooked, your mom takes the meat out and what's left in the pan, the oily and runny stuff, she probably pours it into a can. When it cools down it turns hard. That's fat and that's what you ask for, that's what you want."

You could tell from how quiet the guys were that we were all scared, but Commander DuBock told us, "It's going to take courage and guts, but I and Mr. De Sotis, the head of Club Programs, know you can do it. Troops, you have your assignments. Remember your mission and don't let anything stop you. Time now for action. You've all received your areas. Good luck and do us proud."

Commander DuBock pulled me off to the side to talk to me about my assignment. "Captain Capalaces, tomorrow you're going into action. You've been given Riverside Drive because it's a tough assignment. The Boys' Club has never gone knocking on doors in that neighborhood before asking for anything. The people there aren't used to strangers knocking on their doors. Do you understand, Captain?"

"Yes, Sir. I guess, Sir."

"Remember, we want, we need, we must have the fat."

"Yes, Sir."

My collection area started at the odd-numbered houses on Riverside Drive. At my side was Sergeant Tootsie Kolosna. He was given the even side of the street. I was hoping to add Corporal Bonsell to our team, but Commander DuBock assigned him to work in another area of town where he thought Bucky would do better.

All the rich people lived on Riverside Drive. They were doctors, lawyers, and bankers. We had heard about Riverside Drive, but we had never been there. When we finished the walk to the end of Front Street, pulling our borrowed wagons packed with empty cans, Tootsie and I stopped and looked down the long, straight, and wide street called Riverside Drive.

"Geez, Cap."

"Holy shit."

Tootsie and I couldn't believe the houses. They were so big, with tall trees and fences around a lot of them. They looked like the castles in the movies where kings and queens lived.

"Geez, Cap, I don't know," Tootsie said.

"Yeah, I know what you mean. But we gotta do it. We can't turn back. C'mon."

I watched Tootsie cross the street. He wasn't doing what Commander DuBock taught us . . . head high, shoulders back, but I couldn't worry about him now; I had to worry about myself.

It was an early Saturday morning and it was so quiet, the only sounds on the street were the birds chirping and the clatter of the empty cans bouncing inside my wagon every time the wheels hit the cracks in the sidewalk. The noise helped cover up the flapping of the sole coming off the bottom of my right sneaker.

The first house I came to had a long path from the street that curved to the front steps of a huge stone house surrounded by large trees and big bushes. It looked dark inside and pulling my wagon toward the front door, I was hoping that no one was home.

As I stared at the mean-looking lion's head hanging at the top of the heavy wooden door, I remembered Commander DuBock's warning: *It's going to take courage and guts.* I knocked just below the lion and waited, listening for any sound inside. Hearing none, I knocked again, this time a little louder. My heart pounded as I heard the lock opening inside and watched the door begin to swing open. A woman's face appeared above a chain stretched tightly inside the door. Her face was smooth and clean. Her dark hair was streaked gray and combed tight against her head.

"Ma'am. I'm, ah . . . I'm, ah . . . a Victory Volunteer with the Boys' Club and we're . . . ah . . . we're . . . ah . . . collecting fat for the war."

"Collecting what?" the lady said closing the door slightly. Her ritzy voice sounded like the fat lady in the fancy dress in the Marx Brothers' movies.

"Fat, Ma'am."

"Fat?"

"Yes, Ma'am. You know like bacon or meat drippings. The fat."

"Why on earth would they send you here for fat?"

"It's used to make gunpowder for bullets. It's to help our guys win the war."

"I had no idea."

"Yes, Ma'am. I didn't know either."

"Do you have any idea what day and time it is?"

"I know it's Saturday, but I don't know the time."

"This is not a good day or time to be knocking on people's doors. Don't the people who sent you here know that?"

"All I know Ma'am is that they said to get the fat."

"Who did you say you were with, young man?"

"The Victory Volunteers at the Boys' Club."

"What are you going to do with the fat if I give you some?"

"We take it back to the Boys' Club and and they weigh it in the basement. Then we put it in these big metal drums and when they get full, a truck comes and picks it up and takes it to the Army to make bullets for our soldiers."

"Why do they weigh the fat you bring in?"

"Because they write our name in a book and count how much each volunteer brings in."

"Well, how much do you have so far?"

"Me, Ma'am?"

"Yes, you."

"Well, this is my first day and this is my first house."

"Mmmm."

The lady looked at my sneakers and then her eyes went up to my head.

"If I have some . . . fat, what will you put it in? I'm not going to give up the tin I keep it in."

"I can scoop it into one of my cans," I said as I moved to show her the wagon.

She opened the door a bit wider and looked closer.

"Take that thing around back and I'll give you what I have."

I followed the path around to the back. The birds sang and flew among the beautiful green trees that shaded the big back-yard. When I finally got to the back door, she was waiting, holding a can in her gloved hands. A radio in her kitchen was playing, "Comin' in on a Wing and a Prayer."

"Scoop this inside your wagon. I don't want a drop of that grease, you call it fat, on my patio or grass. Do you understand?"

"Yes, Ma'am."

The can seemed heavier than the writing on it that read, A&P COFFEE—2 POUNDS. Setting it inside the wagon, I got my first real look at fat. My spoon sank deep inside the white stuff and it wasn't as hard as I thought it would be. As I slammed a spoon-ful of fat against one of cans in the wagon, a strong and sickening smell hit my nose. I turned a little, but kept scooping. I could feel the lady watching me and I was worried that some of the slippery fat at the bottom of the can would splash out and some did, but luckily for me it fell inside the wagon.

"Are you through yet? What's taking so long, for God's sake?"

"I'm almost finished Ma'am."

Handing the lady back her coffee can, she wiped it off with a cloth and checked inside it.

"Well, it's pretty clean," the lady said.

"Yes, Ma'am. It's a little tough getting it all out."

"Before you go, son, let me give you some advice. Tell your superiors at the Boys' Club that bothering people early on Saturday mornings is not a good idea. Do you get that?"

"Yes, Ma'am."

"Also, tell them that they shouldn't be sending out boys with ripped and dirty clothes and sneakers that are flapping around. Do you understand?"

"We're supposed to get uniforms soon, Ma'am,"

"Uniforms? Tell them you need haircuts."

"Yes. Ma'am."

"That's all I have to say."

"Thanks for the fat, Ma'am," I said, wanting to get far away.

"And go slowly so that wagon of yours doesn't spill anything on the way out."

"Yes, Ma'am."

I never turned back, but I knew she was watching.

We worked the whole day but Tootsie and I only covered a small part of Riverside Drive. Together we didn't do too badly for our first time out. Some of the people were nice, some told us to get off their property. Some we didn't bother because of the big dogs on chains sitting out front. But the cans in our wagons were pretty full.

TOOTSIE AND I knew two things from our first day of collecting: the people on Riverside Drive had a lot of fat, and we'd be back to get it.

13.

INVASION FLEET MOVING, SAYS ITALY

POLICE SMASH DRAFT CARD RACKET OF SCHOOLBOYS WHO FOOL BARTENDERS

River Rats

The summer sun danced on the river through the early morning mist and rode the currents downstream. The long days spent staring out the window of Mr. Frenchko's social studies class, waiting for the snow to melt, had finally paid off. A blanket of green, spotted with bright wildflowers, covered the big hills overlooking Daniel Dickinson School, and the day-dreams of summer had blossomed into wishes come true. As if under a magic spell, the river called us and we answered, knowing adventure waited.

As rivers go, the Chenango isn't big. Flowing down from the north, the river twists and turns its way through the city, running parallel to Front Street until it joins the Susquehanna River at Riverside Drive. From there the river journeys south under the name Susquehanna, through Pennsylvania and eventually giving up its waters to the Chesapeake Bay.

My friends and I swam at the dam behind the Cutler Ice

Company on upper Front Street. Cutler's made and sold blocks of ice for home and business ice boxes, keeping milk and meat fresh for a few days, depending on how warm it was outside. Cutler didn't own the dam, the city did. But everyone called the structure behind Cutler's, *Cutler's Dam*.

Unlike the Deforest Street and First Ward bathhouses with their changing rooms, showers, and lifeguards, Cutler's Dam was just a swimming hole and you swam at your own risk. The dam was a solid concrete structure spanning the entire width of the river. Ranging about five feet above the normal height of the river, the dam was designed to work with nature when the heavy rains came and the waters rose. No one knew exactly how or when, but a large sixty-foot section of the concrete span broke away and disappeared beneath the water about two-thirds of the way across the river. Between the jagged edges of the concrete still standing on each side, the river waters raged through the sixty-foot hole, leaving dangerous whirlpools on the far side. The whirpools created big circles that twisted the roaring water into a deadly funnel. The funnels, once formed, waited patiently, ready to drag any unsuspecting fool under, to what everyone believed was a bottomless pit. The whirlpools could swallow you whole as if it were having its lunch. Every summer someone drowned at Cutler's Dam. Sometimes you never knew anyone was missing or in trouble until a pile of clothes lay unclaimed on the dam for a day or two.

Even though it wasn't much to look at, my friends and I liked Cutler's Dam. We had the run of the place and no one told us what to do. Almost everyone who went there was a First Warder. Girls didn't come to the dam because it was a guy's place.

My friend Bucky never got to go to the dam. We went to where he lived and begged him to come. He said he couldn't; he had to help his father who worked for Levene's. Bucky told us that during the summer and on his days off from school they worked together to keep the scrap in the yard in order. We knew we'd see each other at the Club, but not when it was hot and sunny.

Everyone knew the rules. Every day of summer you showed up at the dam to wait until your friends came. There were no excuses for not being there. When everyone was present and accounted for, the games began. We stripped to the bathing suits we wore under our pants and left our clothes in piles on the concrete dam.

"Eenie Meenie, Mienie, Mo . . . ." Each one of us was tapped on the chest to the rhyme until the last "Mo." Who would be "it?" Tootsie? Jug-bug? Mike? Vic? Yonkie? Peewee? Me? This time, "it" was Yonkie.

"One, two, three." Yonkie began counting with his eyes closed. We ran to the edge of the dam knowing we had till a hundred to make our decision. I looked at Peewee as he dove into the fast-flowing water rushing between the broken concrete. Peewee was a strong swimmer and he stroked nonstop upstream, fighting the current pulling him downstream toward the whirlpools. He made it to the other side, grabbing onto a piece of jagged concrete just above the swirling waters below.

"Fifty, fifty-one, fifty-two!" Yonkie yelled as the others dove in, scattering in different directions. If Yonkie tagged you, you had to help him catch the others until all were caught. I liked to tease Yonkie because although he was a stronger swimmer, he wasn't as fast as I was out of the water and part of the chase would be on land.

"Ninety-eight, ninety-nine, one-hundred!" Yonkie said taking his hand away from his eyes. He spotted me at the end of the dam, just standing there looking back at him. Yonkie rose and ran after me. I waited until he got about twenty yards from me, and I dove into the calmer water on our side of the span.

The water felt fresh and clean as I rose from underneath and heard Yonkie diving in behind me. I stroked as fast as I could toward a small island in the river. Once at the island, I could either dive into the shallow rapids running beside it and be swept downstream by the currents, or I could just walk across the river to the other side at a spot where the river was shallow for most of the way. In the shallows, feet could playfully skip over the slippery stones below, splashing all the way. When the water came up to your waist, the river started to show its power. All the lower muscles in your body seemed to move in slow motion.

I chose to cross in the shallow part on foot. Soon I was up to my waist in water, straining against the currents. The sharp stones and rocks stabbed and poked at my feet. Over a summer on the river, the soles of my feet would get as hard as the rocks in the water.

Yonkie chased close behind, thrashing water in every direction. Reaching the far bank, I turned to see Yonkie in the waist-deep water moving in slow motion against the currents. Once on the dry bank, I opened up the distance between us, distance I needed for my next move.

I ran the rocks as if in a trance, peering down so as not to step on a rotting fish washed up from the shore. My eyes scanned the terrain in front of me and my feet burned as I skipped over stones baking in the hot sun.

I looked back at Yonkie and once he made it ashore, I was surprised to see him closing in on me. Up ahead, I glanced at the whirlpools to my left, passing close enough to hear the eerie sounds deep inside them. I could see the powerful twisting funnel sucking everything down within its reach. It seemed alive, like an octopus without a head. The sickening smell of dead fish seemed to be everywhere.

I spotted Mike and Tootsie up ahead waiting at the edge of the concrete break. I jumped on the concrete and as I neared, Mike and Tootsie dove upstream into the strong currents above the break. I stopped to catch my breath as I glanced at Yonkie coming fast and then at Mike and Tootsie stroking furiously upstream to escape the pull of the current.

I dove into the water and came up stroking with all my strength. I reached and pulled the water as I felt the current dragging the strength from me. I swam harder, knowing whirlpools waited downstream if I didn't break through the grip of the river. My arms got heavier, my lungs sucked for air, and my heart pounded. My shoulders burned and tightened. Fear shot through my body as I pulled harder against the current.

I felt the river let go and began drifting downstream, to the safer side of the break in the dam. My weak arms paddled the calmer waters far from the whirlpools. I reached the concrete and joined Mike and Tootsie. Together, we watched Yonkie thrashing across the break. On the island across the water, Vic, Peewee, and Jug-bug yelled for us to join them. As Yonkie drifted in, sucking for air like a beached fish, we dove into the water from where we had started just a few feet from Yonkie. Once on the island, we caught our breath from our effort crossing the break, and waited for Yonkie to come after us.

As Yonkie closed in, he swam with a look determined to catch one of us. We yelled out at him, teasing him by not making a move as he got closer. Toying with Yonkie made him mad and mean. We all liked it that way because it made the chase more interesting, more of a test.

Suddenly Yonkie was on his feet, coming ashore. I dove into the current stretching myself out to let the fast-moving water running alongside the island carry me quickly downstream. As the water deepened at the end of the island, I reached out and grabbed a branch hanging over the water and swung myself out of the rapids and climbed ashore. I glanced back to see Yonkie right on my tail. Running through the island brush I reached the north end from where we started. I turned sharply and ran along the edge of the island toward the viaduct where I could take another route back to the dam.

"I've got your ass now!" Yonkie yelled from behind.

"You don't have shit," I answered as I ran through mud and rocks in patches of dirty water near the viaduct.

I heard Yonkie breathing hard on my back as I tore through

the puddles of water to reach the base of the smooth, concrete viaduct. I knew that once I made it to the viaduct, I could put some distance between Yonkie and myself.

My feet splashed through the puddles, kicking up a spray of water. Jumping into a patch of mud, I felt a stabbing pain on the little toe of my right foot. I limped to the viaduct as Yonkie grabbed me from behind.

"I got you! I got you!" Yonkie screamed.

"Yeah, yeah, you got me! You idiot! I cut my foot!"

Glancing down at the blood, Yonkie's eyes opened wide.

"Go get the hankie out of my pants, quick."

"Hold on, I'll be right back," Yonkie said as he ran off toward the dam where our clothes were.

I squeezed my toes together with my hand to slow the bleeding. Looking down at the river's edge, I saw the jagged piece of a broken beer bottle sticking up in the mud I had just run through. The deep cut burned and throbbed with pain. Warm blood oozed out between my fingers and onto the concrete and flowed slowly into the river. The bright colored blood stood out against the dull, murky river water.

THE RIVER WAS our playground, a dangerous one; it could hurt you in many ways. On this day, the river cost me a little blood. On some other day, if I made a mistake, it could cost me my life. Though we knew about the many lifeless bodies pulled from the river each summer, my buddies and I still pushed hard to make each day there exciting. Though none of us ever said it out loud, we all feared the river and entered it as if we were swimming for our lives.

14.

"IMPREGNABLE" ROME LINE WRECKED; UNCHALLENGED NAVY HITS JAP NAURU

SGT. J. H. HOWARD IS CITED BY GENERAL EISENHOWER FOR GALLANTRY IN ACTION AT SALERNO

Louis Mizera Is Awarded Oak Leaf Cluster for Courage

Body Shot

L ine up, we're loading up! a voice said in the darkness. That call filled the cold night air with a rumble of excitement and confusion. Climbing aboard the Greyhound Bus idling outside the Boys' Club I thought about our trip to Utica. This was the first time any of us twenty-five boys had ever been on a bus, let alone facing off against guys in another city; and doing it in front of wounded soldiers at a hospital.

The rumble of voices turned silent as the line moved forward and the silhouetted figures of my frosty-breath teammates climbed, one-by-one, onto the bus steps and disappeared inside. Coach Steve

Buchta checked off each name on his list. When my turn came, I climbed the steps, catching a glance of the heavy bus driver inside writing on a small clipboard. The buttons on his shirt were straining to burst as he pushed back his sweaty cap. As I walked farther back, I watched some of the guys struggling to open windows to escape the smell of exhaust fumes. I managed to sit next to my pal Jug-bug. He had opened a window. I couldn't tell whether the open window was good or bad; whether the freezing cold air coming in was better or worse than the smell of what was inside.

Tumbling coach Buchta and boxing coach Charley Ketchuk were the last ones to climb onboard and, after a brief talk with the driver, they took a seat up front. The bus door hissed shut. The lights inside the bus went out and sitting in the dark we jumped in our seats when the air brakes squealed and the gears crunched. Then, with the hum of the motor, we felt ourselves moving.

It remained quiet on the bus as we passed through the city, down one street, up another until we were on Front Street, heading north. Soon, the street lights were gone and the bus roared its way deeper into the darkness. Most of us just sat, staring out the windows and watching gusts of snow stream by while others napped. The silence was strange because the guys on the bus were usually the loudest and toughest guys at the Boys' Club. You could tell those of us who were tumblers and those who were boxers. The tumblers were all skinny and did all the listening when the boxers talked.

As a member of the tumbling team, you had to have the guts to complete your routine, which included back and front flips, hand springs, cartwheels, and monkey rolls. You had to have a rhythm and a sense of timing to do these smoothly. If you panicked you could break your neck. Tumblers always pulled for each other.

The guys on our boxing team were tough kids who loved to fight. Some of them had broken noses; some even had scars on their faces. Outside the ring our guys were OK, but when the bell rang they seemed to turn into monsters. It was a good idea to stay out of their way and make yourself scarce if they came around, or else you could end up with a busted nose or a fat lip or get the shit pounded out of you for little or no reason. Cocky and loud, they were always looking for a good fight. I had managed to stay clear of them because I was a skinny kid with little fighting experience, except for a few neighborhood scraps.

Most of the boxers on the Boys' Club team were Italians and Russians with names like Della Rocco and Ciancio, Mikolasko and Fedish. My buddy, Bucky Bonsell, was the only boxer on the team I really knew. On the bus, Bucky wanted to be with his boxing teammates. None of the boxers used their full name, only nicknames. If you didn't know a guy's nickname, you knew him by his physical traits, like "the guy with the eye" or "the guy with the nose" or "the guy with no teeth."

One of the boxers was fifteen, most were around thirteen. These guys were from the ward and east side of town and they were always at the Club. I had a rough idea where they lived, but I never went over their way because if you didn't belong, chances are you'd get beaten up. I never saw their fathers or uncles or older brothers with them, so I figured, like most of the other men, they were far away in the war.

It sure looked funny seeing the boxers sitting there on the bus. I never saw them so quiet and looking almost harmless. I guess maybe we were all thinking the same thing. No one said, but I'm sure everyone was scared wondering about how tough the guys from Utica were and how tough it would be to compete in front of a crowd.

As a member of the Boys' Club Tumbling Team, I would be performing in front of a big audience for the first time. Although we weren't told much, we knew we were going to do our show at a hospital as a warm-up to the boxing matches against the Utica Boys' Club Boxers. I heard a boxer in the seat in front of us say to another boxer across the aisle, "Coach Ketchuk said the Utica guys are tough." No one said anything. It stayed quiet.

By the time we reached Utica, the guys were talking and laughing and having a good time. You could feel the excitement when the bus made a long, slow turn into the parking lot, past the sign that read: RHOADS MEMORIAL VETERANS' HOSPITAL.

The bus stopped and the driver let off one last blast of air from the brakes. The lights came on and Coach Buchta yelled, *Don't forget your stuff!* The driver swooshed the door open and we all piled out of the bus. Coach Ketchuk raised his hand to get our attention and said, with his voice lowered, "Stay together and follow me and keep quiet. This is a hospital."

Walking through the parking lot, you could see the hospital behind the large trees that went around it. It looked very big and different from any hospital I had ever seen. It was a cold winter night and while lamp-lights lined the walkway, bare trees swayed in the wind casting their dancing shadows on the cold ground. A few scattered lights were on inside. It looked dark and spooky.

By the time we reached the front door to the hospital, I was freezing to the bone. The light jacket, with all its buttons missing, and the old sneakers I was wearing were no match for the cold wind hitting me. My bare head and hands hurt, especially my ears. You could see the steam from our breath in the night air. Most of the guys wiped their noses on their sleeves as we waited while a man inside opened the door and let the coaches in. They seemed to talk forever, until the door opened again and the guys began to move inside.

Once inside, the man led us through another door and down a long hall. The feeling was coming back to my body as we walked through the warm air of the hospital. The only sound we made was our shuffling feet echoing off the white walls as we walked the hallway on polished and spotless floors. A funny medicine smell had everyone's head turning, with some guys holding their noses and others trying to hold back their laughter. The few snickers that came through were enough to get the coaches' attention and, with one stern look the snickering stopped.

The door to the locker room opened and in no time the clanging sounds of the metal lockers stopped and we were all dressed and seated, waiting for Coach Buchta. It didn't take long to dress. All we had were white T-shirts and old swimming trunks and the sneakers we wore.

We all liked Coach Buchta because he was a nice guy. He was in his late forties, and lucky for us he was still willing and able enough to show us some stuff. Most of the men left behind during the war were old and some men from the old country still hadn't even learned to speak English. No one knew why Coach wasn't in the war and no one asked.

"First up are you guys," Coach Buchta said to the tumblers. "You know the routine. Take your time and concentrate." He paused. "Any questions?" No one moved. Coach Ketchuk looked at his watch and said, "Boxers will go up and watch the tumblers and then when we get close to the end of the tumbling I'll signal the boxers and when I do, you come back down here and wait for me. Any questions?" None of the boxers said anything.

"OK, it's time to go up. Make sure you tuck in your shirts. Good luck and do good. Remember you're representing the Binghamton Boys' Club." Coach Buchta nodded to the man from the hospital as he stood and motioned us to follow him.

As we walked up a long set of wide stairs, the sound of voices grew louder. We entered a doorway and stepped inside an empty space with a lone light overhead. On the other side of a high, thick red curtain you could hear people talking and laughing and moving chairs. One of our boxers peeked through the curtain and turned around and nodded at us as if to say, *Wow, that's some crowd out there.*

Coach snapped his finger and motioned for us to line up for the start of our routine. The boxers moved to the side as we formed a single line for our entrance. You could feel the excitement and feel your heart pounding like crazy.

A voice on a loudspeaker came from the other side of the curtain: "Is this on? OK? OK? Testing one-two, testing one-two. All set. Ladies and gentlemen, it's a great pleasure tonight to present to you an evening of exceptional entertainment." The speaker paused briefly and you could hear the sound of metal chairs moving about. "Now," he continued, "as we all get settled in, tonight's program starts with an exhibition by the Binghamton Boys' Club Tumbling Team and after that we will have ten bouts of boxing between the Utica and Binghamton Boys' Clubs. Let us welcome the Binghamton Boys' Club Tumbling Team with a rousing round of applause."

The curtain opened and my heart leapt against my chest. Coach nodded to give the lead tumbler the go-ahead to start. The applause from the audience grew louder as we entered the brightly lit stage on the other side of the curtain. There was a large ring set up on the stage and as we approached it you could see the audience applauding down below. I snuck a look at the crowd and it seemed as if everyone were wearing white. I didn't look long because Coach's words kept reminding me to concentrate.

We followed our lead into the ring and began a series of front summersaults and cartwheels around the ring. From this warm-up routine, we moved from hand springs to front flips. Coach snapped his fingers to keep us on pace. This had a good look to it with fifteen guys moving one right after another across the mat. And the faster we moved, the more difficult it was to spot how dirty or ripped our worn white T-shirts were. The crowd clapped when our last guy snapped a tight back handspring to signal that tougher stuff was coming.

I looked at my best friend on the team, Jug-bug Jones, who was a really terrific tumbler. He looked happy and strong. Like Plastic Man in the comic books, he could bend and stretch in ways you could not believe. Jug-bug wasn't a freak, not double-jointed or anything, but he might as well have been. As I looked at the other guys, they seemed to be relaxed and having a good time. Even our boxers seemed to be enjoying it. Coach was smiling too, so we must have been doing pretty well.

As I waited my turn in the routine, my eyes drifted to the audience. The people watching us were all seated or standing around big round tables. At first I couldn't believe what I saw. There was a guy in a wheelchair who looked like he didn't have any legs. I stared hard to find them, but I couldn't. I saw a nurse in a little white cap and starched white uniform talking to a guy next to her. He was missing an arm. A guy next to him was sitting up in a hospital bed with his head and eyes all bandaged and tubes hanging all over him. The nurse bent down and spoke through the bandages where his ear would be. Coach snapped his finger at me. I hesitated for a second because I had never seen anyone with all the parts not there and it made me sick and scared. No one warned us about what we might see. Maybe they didn't think it was important for us to know.

I ran across the mat toward Coach squatting with his hands cupped together. Reaching him, I placed my hands on his shoulders and planted my right foot into his cupped hands and stiffening my leg and sprang with Coach's strong boost, high into the air and tucked into a tight back flip. Feeling myself floating, I remembered seeing Lloyd Nolan in *Guadalcanal Diary* and one of his men flying through the air when he was hit by a Jap hand-grenade. It seemed like I was just floating like that. Clapping began as soon as my feet slammed onto the canvas ring floor.

We went through our tumbling with front and back flips, monkey rolls, and walking on our hands. We were in what Coach said was a good rhythm, a good flow. Every now and then some guy in the audience would let out a whoop and a holler. They seemed to like it. Coach Ketchuk knew it was time and signaled the boxers and they got up and headed down to the locker room.

I didn't want to look anymore, but I couldn't help myself. The guys out there watching us were the real guys I had seen played by actors in the war movies at the Ritz on Clinton Street. These were the guys with their guts sticking out and their faces covered in blood. In one movie scene, one of our guys runs through the jungle to throw a grenade to blow up a Jap machine gun. After lobbing it, he gets cut down. The actor in the movie probably played the real-life soldier who saved some of the guys cheering our tumbling routine.

I felt bad because I could run and jump and see and hear; most of these guys watching us left to fight in the real war and would be coming back to their families, friends, wives, and kids with parts missing. A lot of them looked like kids themselves, maybe just a little older than some of the guys on our boxing team.

Seeing them dressed in their white hospital gowns and pajamas, I realized these wounded soldiers looked a lot different from the heroes we saw in the movies. The war movies always made our guys the bravest, ready to fight and die to defeat the bad guys. Seeing these real soldiers right there in front of us with no movie music playing you wondered what real heroes looked like. They didn't look like John Wayne or Robert Taylor. They looked more like kids.

We formed a human pyramid for our final tumbling routine. Because I was skinny, I was up near the top, helping to support the lightest guy on the very top. While the audience clapped and the guy with the microphone thanked Coach Buchta and the tumbling team, we all froze and gazed out with our heads up high. Then, on cue, we collapsed into a pile and ran off behind the curtain.

We sat in the locker room after Coach Ketchuk took the boxers up. A lot of the guys were talking about how good we were and were laughing and taking bows. Others were quiet. They had seen what I saw and they felt the way I felt—sick. No one said anything; they just got dressed slowly, and one by one left to go up to see the fights. A few of us stayed, not wanting to see anymore.

I was looking at an old comic book when the locker-room door opened and Coach Buchta came in. He said Coach Ketchuk needed one extra boxer because Utica had an extra fighter. He looked at us quickly, one by one, then his eyes stopped searching. "C'mon Cappy, we can use you."

"But, I've never boxed before," I said hoping he'd pick someone else—anyone else.

"You can do it. There's no time, the crowd's waiting. We need a man. The soldiers out there are counting on it."

Coach held the ropes up for me to climb into the ring. My legs were shaking. They felt so heavy, I almost tripped stepping over the rope.

The noise was so loud I could barely hear as Coach Ketchuk shoved the thick boxing gloves onto my hands. Lacing them, Coach gave me a quick lesson in boxing. "Keep your gloves up high to protect your face and move a lot so you're not an easy target. And when you punch, punch hard. Just listen to me when you're in there." The guys said boxing coach Charley Ketchuk was a heavyweight boxer himself and was supposed to be very good. That made me feel a little better.

Across the ring was the boxer from Utica. He was taller than me and he looked older. I watched him as he did this funny stuff, dancing around and throwing punches rapidly into the air where there was nothing to hit. He was wearing a bathrobe and when they took it off, he didn't look skinny; he looked like all muscle. His arms were long and his stomach was tight and he kept staring at me.

I looked at Coach Ketchuk with a look that said this was a mistake. Sensing my desperation, Coach said, "Remember to listen to me and don't worry, you can do this." I wasn't as sure as Coach, but there was no way to go back now. I turned and looked out at the crowd and remembered Coach Buchta saying, *It was for them—the soldiers out there.*

The bell rang and I heard Coach Ketchuk yell a final word of encouragement over the cheers. Then, out of the crowd, I heard Bucky and Jug-bug cheering for me. I was on my feet and as I met the Utica fighter in the middle of the ring, he started to go in a circle. He didn't throw a punch, he just kept dancing around nervously. I held my hands up high, like Coach said. I thought for a moment that this might not be so bad. I even smiled a tiny bit when I heard some of our boxers yelling, "Kill 'em, Cappy, kill 'em!"

And that's when it hit. It happened so fast, I never saw it. The blow struck my belly and it seemed to go all the way to my backbone. I tried to breathe, but there was no air. My lungs heaved in and out, but I was suffocating. The room was spinning. My mind flashed to Richard Jaekel in *Corregidor* diving on a *live* grenade to save his buddies. That's how I felt, my stomach ripped open and burning and gasping for air. Like the sergeant played by Richard Jaekel, I too knew I was dying.

The room stopped spinning and everyone was quiet. It probably looked like something the audience had seen before—a guy down. Coach helped me to my feet and I started crying because I couldn't breathe. There was snot running out of my nose and I looked back and saw the Utica fighter putting on his robe and dancing and throwing punches into the air again. Slowly, I started to walk back to my corner when the sound of applause started. With tears filling my eyes, I looked out to see one of the patients clapping. He had two metal hooks for hands.

One of our boxers, whose face was puffy and red from an earlier fight, looked at me in disgust. I hadn't thought about it before, but I was sure our boxers would probably kick the hell out of me for putting up such a lousy fight.

In the locker room, Coach Ketchuk and Coach Buchta tried to console me, but I was too busy trying to force air into my lungs. I didn't want to cry, but I couldn't control the huge sobs pouring out of me.

THIS ISN'T THE way it ended in the war movies. When you took the hit, you did it to save someone and you were a hero. All I had to show for it was a pain in my gut and snot running out of my nose.

15.

REDS INSIDE POLAND ON 50-MILE FRONT

TWO TRIPLE CITIES SOLDIERS "GUINEA PIGS" IN FORT MEADE MEDICAL RESEARCH PROJECT

Van Bell, Kithcart Cited for Services "Above the Call of Duty"

Snow Job

The Appalachian Mountains ranged high above the Susquehanna Valley; so high the mountains could have even told the sun where to shine most of the time. In the valley, our town and the neighboring towns seemed to go on forever, faithfully following the natural path made in the shadow of the mountains. Wherever the mountains stretched, the valley and the people in it followed.

In spring and summer dense green trees covered the mountains. In the fall the leaves turned to burning color. When the winds began to stir, then whip, the trees were stripped of their autumn coats. Now barren, they soon began to feel winter's snow. What snowflakes the evergreens could not gather in their branches on the mountainside, the valley below welcomed.

When the snow fell long and heavy, we could get jobs shoveling the streets for the city. You got paid by the hour, twenty-five cents and in cash, but you had to bring your own shovel. Tootsie had an extra shovel for me and I knew he'd be showing up soon.

The snow had fallen throughout the day and continued into nightfall. The streets were empty and covered white. Nothing moved except windswept snow. It flurried against the Kelly block and whistled a chilling sound as it raced by. In the night air, the streetlight outside my bedroom window highlighted the thickness of the falling snow. I thought of snuggling back into bed against Richie and sleeping through the night. But I soon put that out of my mind. On a night like tonight they would definitely need all the help they could get and Tootsie would be showing up soon.

I watched the snow fall and for some reason I started thinking, *I wish I had a cigarette.* I thought about the time this past summer when I went to meet Tootsie at his house. I was surprised to see him sitting on his back steps with a lit cigarette dangling from his lips.

Toots, what're you doin'?

Nuttin'.

Nothing? What about that cigarette and what about your Grandmother?

She ain't here. I got these off Kiki.

Kiki knows you smoke?

He knows someone's taking his smokes and I think he knows it's me. Have you tried it?

No, I ain't never smoked.

Here, try one.

Tootsie reached out his hand toward me. In his palm was a pack of Lucky Strikes. He flipped the pack and out came one for me. I reached over and took it. Looking it over, I saw the tobacco tightly packed inside the white paper. I put it to my nose and took a deep sniff. The tobacco inside smelled strong and it made my stomach make a funny noise.

Here's a light, Tootsie said as he struck a match and pointed it toward me.

Bending forward I put the tip of the cigarette into the flame and sucked on the other end. It began to burn and smoke curled upward. I took the Lucky from my mouth and smacking my lips, tasted the strong, bitter flavor of the tobacco.

Now I'll teach you how to really smoke, Tootsie said. *Just do what I do. Puff and then suck in the smoke and breathe it in. Go ahead.*

I puffed and sucked in the smoke. As soon as it entered the back of my throat I began choking and coughing, sending Tootsie into wild laughter. The harder I choked, the harder he laughed. My stomach felt sick from the taste of the smoke and my eyes began to water.

Jesus, Cap, you look like you're gonna pass out, Tootsie said through his laughter.

I . . . I . . . didn't know smoking was this hard, I said.

Hey, don't worry about it. Everyone goes through the same thing when you try to inhale. Kiks told me that once you smoke, you're on your way to being a real man.

How'd you learn to smoke?

I been doin' it on the sly, so no one sees me, Tootsie said as I watched him take a deep drag on his Lucky and swallow the smoke and then blow it out his mouth and nose like a dragon. *Just keep doin' it and it'll get easier each time, until you're doin' it like a pro.*

I didn't want to look like a sissy, so I finished my first cigarette choking and spitting and coughing all the way. All the guys I knew smoked, so I guessed this is what I'd have to do to be a real man.

What made me think of this? Maybe because of that feeling I wanted a smoke.

I reached under the bed for the bottle to pee in, but it hadn't been emptied since the night before. It was too full to use without the risk of it overflowing. That meant I had to go to the toilet and piss. I thought about trying to hold it until I could pee outside and carve my yellow initials into the snow, but I had to go and go now. I had no other choice but to use the toilet.

In my bare feet, I passed from my bedroom through our small living room to the kitchen. Straight ahead and to the left was a small bedroom where Mama and Fran slept. In the pitch blackness I felt for the bathroom door and pushed it open and entered the dark space closing the door behind me.

The toilet was only a few steps away, but I didn't budge. Holding onto the door handle, I reached forward in the darkness, as far as my balance would let me, to find the chain connected to the only light in the bathroom. My arm stretched and swung at the air until I felt the chain hitting my hand. Grabbing it, I yanked the chain and the bare lightbulb overhead lit up in a flash. I looked down, knowing what I'd find. The linoleum under my feet was alive with thousands of cockroaches running in full panic as if each were Count Dracula running from sunlight.

There was nothing I could do. They were like an invasion of Jap soldiers taking cover, squeezing through tiny cracks, and disappearing. Like a Flamenco dancer, I tiptoed to any spot bringing me closer to the toilet. Pulling the toilet seat up, I uncovered more roaches on the run. I took aim and let go a stream of piss in hopes of blasting one or two into the toilet bowl.

At the same time, I continued to dance in place hoping to discourage any stray cockroaches from using my bare feet as a hiding place. I was thankful I didn't have to sit on the toilet and do number two. Then I'd have to become a Cossack dancer kicking my legs high while at the same time spinning my head to check for any roaches roaming behind. Mama complained to Dr. Kelly about the cockroaches and he even attempted to clean them out once with a roach bomb, but nothing happened. The roaches liked the Kelly block and from the looks of their numbers it was obvious they had no intention of moving out. And besides, for them, rent was free.

It was almost eleven o'clock at night when I decided to wait for Tootsie underneath the enclosure of the Kelly block's front door. Looking out now and then through the snow storm I hoped Tootsie would show up soon. Rocking back and forth, I moved my toes inside my sneakers to keep them from getting cold. My Levis were tucked inside the rubber galoshes covering my sneakers, their metal buckles locked in place. The second button on my coat was missing and the top one felt a little loose. I pulled the flaps on my hat over my ears and rubbed my wool gloves together to stay warm. Every winter I had a stuffed nose. My sister Fran used to make fun calling me *Snots*, as I was always spitting up mucous. This winter was no different.

Peering out, I could see the outline of someone on the street. Through a wall of swirling flakes Tootsie appeared. He struggled lifting his legs in the deep thick snow covering the sidewalk.

"Jesus, it's freezing," Tootsie said handing me one of the shovels.

"Yeah, It's cold as hell. Hey, Toots, you got any smokes?"

"Christ, Cappy, where are yours?"

"I'll pay you back later. Don't worry about it."

Smoking made you think you were warm. Tootsie and I walked with our heads down against the wind and snow whipping against us. It seemed we walked forever, stopping often to try to figure out where we were heading. Going under the train overpass at the bottom of Clinton Street, we stopped to catch our breath outside the reach of the snow and wind, and to light up again.

"Toots, you sure they're going to put us on tonight?"

"They're gonna need anyone crazy enough to come out."

"And they'll pay us tonight, right?"

"Yeah, right after we finish."

"And how long do we work?"

"As long as we can."

"How do you know all this?"

"I did it last year with my brother, Kiki."

"And they didn't screw you?"

"Nope."

"What if they ask us how old we are?"

"Just tell 'em you're twelve. Don't worry, Cappy, we're gonna be out here soon enough shoveling our asses off."

We walked on through the blinding snow over the bridge and down State Street. Up ahead we could see figures leaving the Snow Maintenance Office. No one spoke and everyone looked like a shadow against the white snow. Tootsie and I walked into the office just as some guy was leaving.

"Leave those shovels outside," the boss man inside shouted out to us. "And close that door."

Inside a coal stove crackled and Tootsie and I joined a couple of guys standing near it to warm up. I glanced over and watched the man in charge writing in a book. He didn't look any older than a high-schooler, except he was big and his nose was crooked. When he spoke, his lips moved, but the sound seemed to come out of his nose. We had never seen him before, so we knew he wasn't from the Ward.

"OK, sign in here," he told us. "Put your name down and a start time of 11:30."

Taking the ice-caked glove off my stiff and cold hand, I scratched out my name and starting time on the sign-up pad.

"Where you guys from?" the man in charge asked.

"The First Ward," Tootsie said.

"The First Ward, huh? Well, I hope you work better than you write," he said looking at our names on the sign-up sheet. "Capa— what? What kind of name is that? Who's Capa— whatever?"

"Capalaces. It's just a name."

"It sounds like a Wop name to me. You a Wop?"

I stood there not knowing what he meant.

"There's mostly dumb Polacks and Slovaks in the Ward," the man in charge said. "A Wop must have snuck in. Hey, is your milkman a Dago? Or maybe he's a Greek and you're a Pousti."

I stood there without answering because I didn't know what he was talking about. He then turned to Tootsie.

"Kolosna? What are you, a Polack?"

"It's a Slovak name."

"Whatever. Don't they feed you guys in the First Ward? You look pretty skinny. You sure you can lift a shovel?"

"Yeah, we can shovel. I did it last year with my big brother," Tootsie said.

"What'd you say his name was?"

"Kiki. Kiki Kolosna."

"Kiki Kolosna. Yeah, I know Kiki from Central. He's a Vocky. He's all right . . . a tough guy. Hey, you better not be a sissy."

"I ain't no sissy."

"How old are you?" the man in charge asked me.

"Me?"

"Yeah, you."

"I'm twelve," I said.

"Twelve, huh?"

"Yeah, he's twelve," Tootsie said, lying to get me on.

"Hmmm. Wait over there till we get a couple more guys and then we'll send you out."

Tootsie and I stood with the others by the potbelly stove to warm our hands and feet. They were already hurting. It was toasty next to the stove and the smoky smell burned our noses a little, but nobody complained.

The door swung open and a blast of cold brought in three more workers. They were guys from somewhere outside the Ward. After signing them in, the man in charge said to us, "OK. You seven are gonna shovel the Clinton Street Bridge. I'm putting this guy . . . what's your name?"

"Leonard."

"I'm putting Leonard in charge. You do what he says. Now go out there and move some snow."

Leonard was the biggest guy in the group. He looked old enough to be a war vet. No matter, you never asked anybody their business or you might end up on your ass.

Once outside, it didn't take long before you felt the cold again. At the bridge, Leonard split us up to work on opposite sides to clear the sidewalks so people could walk across it. Tootsie and I and another guy worked together, while Leonard and the other three worked directly across the road from us.

Our shovels struck deep into the snow and with every lift, we heaved our heavy scoops over the concrete bridge rail where it dropped fifty feet into the ice-filled Chenango River below.

Progress was slow. No sooner had we cleared some of the snow off the sidewalk than more snow fell covering it up again. We kept on. We worked in silence and listened to our heavy breathing, with each icy breath hurting our lungs.

"Cap. How're you doin?" Tootsie finally spoke.

"Cold, Toots, fucking cold."

"Me too. I'm freezing my balls off."

"Toots. Let's have a smoke."

Tootsie put down his shovel and reached into his pocket and handed me a Lucky Strike from a wrinkled pack. He cupped his hand and struck a match, but it didn't light.

"Here, let me try it," I said taking the matches from Tootsie's shaking hand. "Bullshit," I yelled, unable to light the cigarette. "It's too wet and cold to get a light."

"Don't worry," the guy next to us said. "We'll get a break after two hours."

"How long we been here now?" I asked.

"I don't know. Maybe an hour, I guess," the guy said.

"An hour? Holy shit. We've only been out here an hour?" I said.

"Just think Cap, that means we already got a quarter in our pockets," Tootsie added.

Leonard suddenly appeared out of the falling snow.

"What's going on here? Why aren't you shoveling?" Leonard yelled over a howling wind.

"We just took a smoke break," I said.

"There're no breaks out here. You guys better start shoveling; you're not keeping up with the guys on the other side."

Over the next hour we shoveled as hard as we could and yet we were only a short distant from where we started. Snow plows had roared by clearing the roadway and dumping more snow onto our path. Over and over, we did the same thing, stick the shovel, slide it forward and scoop, lift, rotate and slam the shovel's shaft against the four-foot-high barrier wall, to send the snow splashing into the river below. The scoops were getting heavier with each lift.

"OK!" Leonard shouted coming across the road, "Let's take a break."

We followed Leonard back to the office and once inside, we crowded around the heat of the stove and cursed the cold. Leonard and the man in charge talked in the corner. We couldn't hear what they were saying, but we figured Leonard was reporting on our progress.

The heat from the stove brought life back to our frozen parts. Tootsie and I lit up a cigarette while we dried our gloves on top of the stove.

Soon we were shoveling again. Through the night, the snow slowly let up. I lost track of time, thinking only of break-times and that it was Saturday now and there would be no school, and how it would feel to be back in bed and out of the cold.

The morning light rose and I watched my last shovel of snow fall all the way to the river below. It fell between two sheets of ice and splashed in the cold, dark water. The Clinton Street Bridge was finally cleared and we would soon be heading home.

The man in charge sat behind his desk with an open notebook and a metal box. We lined up to get our money and to be on our way. When our turn came he looked up and asked, "What's your name?"

"Capalaces."

"Did you work tonight?"

"Gee. Yeah, I worked."

"It looked like you spent most of the time wipin' snot on your sleeve."

I looked down and saw my sleeve covered with frozen mucous.

Checking his book and marking it with a pencil, he reached into the metal box and counted out the money. "That's six hours. Here's a buck fifty."

I turned and looked at Tootsie behind me. We had figured we worked seven hours, not six. Tootsie shrugged his shoulders and shook his head.

"OK. Let's move it. I don't have all day for this," the man in charge said.

I stood by the stove, even though the coals had burned out, and looked at my money and waited for Tootsie. I could tell from the look on his face he wasn't happy either. We lingered for awhile deciding whether to say something to the man in charge. He closed the metal box with the money in it and wrote something in his notebook. Tootsie and I came close, but we left without ever saying anything to him about that extra hour we worked—the one we worked our asses off and didn't get paid for.

Tootsie and I were pissed, cursing the cheating boss man and moaning about the quarter he owed us as we dragged our shovels home.

"That cheating son-of-a-bitch," I said.

"The son-of-a-bitch! The friggin' bastard," Tootsie added.

"I hope that ass-hole chokes on it."

We were hungry and tired. Everything was closed, so we decided to just go home. I watched Tootsie pulling the two shovels after we parted company at the Kelly block. He looked pitiful, like Charlie Chaplin in *The Gold Rush*.

I took off all the wet clothes in the hallway outside our apartment door, happy finally to be out of the cold. Clutching the money in my hand, I went quietly inside the apartment, and closed the door carefully behind me. I stood listening momentarily for any signs of life. I was glad everyone was still sleeping. I had run out of places to hide things and with all the money in my pocket, I'd have to find a special place.

A while back I had gotten a cigar box from LaTorre's just to keep any money I had in it, but the problem was where to hide it? Looking and thinking, I talked myself out of every spot I thought of because I knew if anyone saw it, my money would be gone. Then I looked up and saw a round black tin sitting high on the wall near the living-room ceiling. This is where a stove pipe would be if we had a stove in our living room.

Without making a sound, I pulled a chair up to the wall and climbed onto it. I reached up and slid my fingernails under the thin tin plate sitting snug against the wall. Little by little I pried the tin plate until it came away from the wall. Lowering the plate, I could see what looked like a large hole with a shelf on it. I carefully raised the cigar box holding my money and placed it on the shelf. Then I stepped down to see whether it could be seen from the floor. A part of the box still showed. Concerned that it could be spotted if anyone took the cover off, I climbed back up and reached into the hole, and pushed the cigar box deeper. Stepping down, I looked up once again at the hole. Now, only a tiny edge of the box could still be seen. Just a little more I thought and my money would be safe from everyone and this would be the best place I ever had to hide things—no question about it.

Climbing up, I reached in and nudged the box back into the opening a little farther. Suddenly, I lost contact with the box. I heard the sound of the coins rattling inside and then the sound stopped abruptly. The box disappeared. Quickly, I balanced myself on the back of the chair to get as high and as close to the opening as I could. Reaching my arm deep into the dark hole, I ran my hand inside and my fingers felt a metal edge of what felt like a big stove pipe facing downward. My money box had slid over the edge and down into the hole somewhere beyond my grasp. I stretched with all my might, but I could not reach it. All I could feel was nothing.

I sat on the floor below the opening, looking at the black soot covering my arm. Only moments before the money was in my hand. Now, in a flash, it was gone. I stared at the opening high on the wall and wondered what had happened and why. It was then a cockroach crawled out of the hole to the edge and remained there, without moving, probably waiting for me to put the pie-tin back and close his door.

I COULD NEVER tell anyone what happened. Worse than being broke was being stupid.

16.

BINGHAMTON PRESS   JUNE 7, 1944

EXTRA!
INVASION STARTS

AMERICANS AND BRITISH STORM INTO FRANCE; CHUTISTS, GLIDER TROOPS GRAB AIRPORTS; NAZIS SAY WE'RE 10 MILES INSIDE COAST

HOW D-DAY IS GREETED IN TRIPLE CITIES

Prayer First Impulse of Many as Invasion Breaks Tension; Churches Open throughout Day

Fever

All night long the fire went through me. My pillow and sheets were soaked with sweat and underneath the wetness had brought up the stale smell of pee on the old mattress. Richie was mad at me for keeping him up all night, but there was nothing I could do.

Mama worried all the time. She never liked to hear bad news, especially about her kids. For Mama, just hearing bad news was worse than the bad news itself. I learned it was better to hide things from her than to see her get all nervous. But there was no way to hide this. I heard Mama say she was going to Grandma's next door to call the doctor and this meant we would have to wait for Dr. Goundry. He worked for the E. J. Shoe Company and took care of the factory workers and their families. He would have to make a house call, because I was too sick to move.

My sister and brother went to school that morning, and Mama stayed home from work and brought me water and a wet towel to put on my forehead. No sooner was the towel on my head than it turned hot from my fever. I pulled the sheets over me because I was suddenly cold and underneath them I huddled to stop shaking, but the more I shook, the more my bones ached. Then the fire returned and I needed more water and a freshly rinsed towel. When would the doctor get here? My head ached. My throat felt almost closed shut; it hurt to swallow.

The wait seemed forever. Mama brought in an empty milk bottle and put it under the bed and told me to use it to go if I needed to. When she left the room, I crawled out of bed and slid to the floor where I reached underneath and grabbed the bottle and placed it in front of me. The pee burned as it left me and the bottle turned warm from the dark yellow liquid. I began to shake from a sudden rush of cold and after placing the almost-full bottle down, I crawled back into bed.

Mama came into the room and placed another wet towel on my forehead. I asked her to take it away because I was freezing and it was making me even colder. Where was Dr. Goundry?

I don't remember when I fell asleep or for how long, but I was awakened again by the burning fever. I heard Mama in the other room asking out loud, *Where the hell is he?*

I stopped wondering about Dr. Goundry. I think Mama was surprised when I asked her if I was going to die. She looked at me and I could see she was afraid. She said, No, I wasn't and not to worry . . . I'd be fine. I wanted to believe her. I prayed to live and I prayed for the fire to leave.

It was quiet and I listened for any car going up or down Dickinson Street. Eventually one came to a stop and I heard the car door open and slam shut. Then I heard the front door open downstairs and the heavy sound of footsteps. They got louder and stopped at our front door.

I heard the voice of Dr. Goundry. I always felt better when Dr. Goundry took care of me. Of all the E. J. doctors, he seemed the nicest and I was glad that the war hadn't taken him away like a lot of the other doctors. He came into my room and I felt too sick to worry about the smell of pee and the dirt. He put his black bag on the bed and snapped it open. Saying little, he went about his work. He asked and I told him how I felt. With steady hands, he placed a thermometer under my tongue. He reached in and pulled out his blood-pressure equipment and after wrapping the band around my arm, it began to tighten with each hissing squeeze of the little ball in his hand. He placed the stethoscope on my arm and listened while the pressure released around the cuff on my arm. Listening to the air escaping, I thought about the newspapers reporting that polio in Binghamton was infecting kids and some were even dying from it. I hoped I didn't have polio.

Dr. Goundry's fingers squeezed my wrist. I watched him look at his watch for a time and then he wrote into a little black book. He took the thermometer from my mouth and looked at it. Placing a wooden stick on my tongue, he looked inside my throat with a tiny flashlight. His fingers poked under my chin and around my neck. Turning my head, he looked into my ears with a light. He pulled up my sweat-soaked undershirt and I felt the cold head of the stethoscope walk around my chest as Dr. Goundry listened to my heart. He stared at my stomach and asked me to sit up so that he could put his stethoscope on my back. He asked me to breathe in and out while he listened to different places on my back. My face turned even redder when he reached under the bed and held the milk bottle up to look at the pee. I was too afraid of the answer so I decided not to ask Dr. Goundry if I were going to die.

Dr. Goundry packed his things into his black bag and left the room. I could hear him talking quietly to Mama and after a few minutes I heard the door open and the heavy footsteps of Dr. Goundry walk down the stairs. Mama came into the room. She told me I had to go to the hospital. I had a 104-degree fever. Before I could ask her, she said they were sending an ambulance to take me. I asked her what was wrong? She told me Dr. Goundry said: *Scarlet Fever.*

It felt funny seeing so many people from the Kelly block and the neighbors across the street come out to watch me being carried down the stairs on a stretcher and then onto the street where a big ambulance was waiting. Most of the people just waved, some tried to smile at me, but they couldn't hide the worried look on their faces. A voice yelled out, *You'll be all right, Ronnie! Hurry back!*, another said, just as the rear doors shut and the ambulance moved slowly down Dickinson Street.

The place they took me was not the main Wilson Memorial Hospital in Johnson City, but a plain old house a few doors down. This is where they planned to keep me, in isolation, for twenty-one days until the rash above and across my stomach was gone. Isolation meant no visitors. It also meant that anything sent in to you had to be thrown away and burned when you left so that the Scarlet Fever didn't spread to others.

There were two beds in my windowless room. The second bed sat empty, its stiff white sheets starched and tucked tightly around its mattress. The white walls and white ceilings were spotless, and with a bedpan next to me there was nothing else to do except look at the whiteness of everything. I was told not to leave the bed or touch the floor. I waited for the nurses to come in and talk to me and clean me and bring me food and change the sheets.

The hours passed slowly and, without a telephone, I was shut off from the world. Once in a while I could hear music playing somewhere outside the room. I strained to listen to the words of "As Time Goes By" while wondering why time took so long. I thought about my friends and wondered if they even knew where I was. I was hoping I'd hear something, but they were probably having too much fun listening to the Yankees games just starting the new season or seeing a good movie at the Ritz or starting to think about the summer on the river.

My heart jumped when the nurse brought in a letter for me after a few days had gone by. It was from Mama. She wrote and told me that she let Tootsie know where I was and what happened. She told me that the teachers at school sent their best wishes and to tell me not to worry. She said Fran and Richie said Hi and Mama wrote she'd be sending me a package soon.

The next day a small package came for me, but it wasn't from Mama; it was from Tootsie. I opened it up and inside was a note sitting on top of three new comic books. After looking at the covers of *Superman* and *Batman* and *Archie*, I opened the note and read:

Dear Cappy,

What the heck happened? We didn't even know where you were or even that you were sick. I heard at the schoolyard that they sent you away, but I didn't believe any of that, so I finally went to your house and your mom told me what happened. Gee, we never heard of Scarlet Fever. All the guys in the gang hope you're OK. They all ask about you. It's no fun without you around and we got some games coming up and need you behind the plate. Dick Maples at the Boys' Club said he might send us to Camp Arrowhead this summer for two weeks. The camp is owned by the YMCA, but he said Mr. De Sotis worked a deal so some of us could get a chance to go. He said there's a lot to do there like swimming, canoeing, and shooting with bow and arrows and stuff, but I ain't going unless you go. When you get out, Triplet baseball should be starting. We ought to plan to sneak into as many games as we can this year.

We hope you like the comic books. They're a present from all the guys. Hey, if you can give us an idea where you are, the guys will come up and sneak in to see you. Let us know if you can. So long for now.

Your Buddy,
Toots

Yeah, I wish I could see you guys, too, but I didn't even know how to tell them where I really was. It didn't seem there was any way of breaking into this place and, if you did, you didn't want to end up with Scarlet Fever and then get locked up in here. I couldn't even let Tootsie know that I got the comic books, because I couldn't send any letters. The nurses said I just had to stay away from everyone for twenty-one days and after they checked me, I'd be able to leave. But twenty-one days was a long, long time to be sick and alone, and although I wouldn't wish this on anyone, I had to admit I was happy when, after a week had gone by, they rolled another kid into the room and put him in the bed next to me.

I didn't know the kid. He was a little younger and from Johnson City, so it was hard to talk to him about different things or about guys and places in the First Ward and things we did. So we shared comic books that he and I got, and he never knew how really glad I was to have him there with me.

We each started to get letters and packages with candy and cookies and comic books and we had fun passing stuff back and forth. We laughed and told jokes and used bad words and it all made the time pass a little faster.

One morning the nurse brought in an envelope for me. It was a note from Peewee. I opened it and inside was an article cut out of the *Binghamton Press*. The headline read: SGT. LOUIS

MACHOVEC, ONCE REPORTED MISSING, IS NOW KNOWN DEAD. *Peewee's oldest brother.*

The article had a picture of Sergeant Machovec in his uniform with a big smile on his face. The article read:

> S/Sgt. Louis Machovec, 22, who was reported missing in action a year ago this month, now is reported to have been killed at that time.
>
> In its message to the sergeant's parents, Mr. and Mrs. Isadore Machovec of 44 Elm Street, the War Department expressed regret "that unavoidable circumstances made necessary the unusual lapse of time in reporting your son's death to you."
>
> An aerial gunner on a Flying Fortress, Sergeant Machovec had been listed as missing in action over Germany on March 23, 1944.

Besides the article, there was a note from Peewee. It read:

Cap,

> An Air Force officer came to the house to tell us about Louie. We also heard from another guy that was in a plane behind my brother's. He said Louie's plane went down in the English Channel coming back from a run in Germany. At least we all now know for sure.

Peewee

All the time Peewee's brother Louie was reported missing, Peewee and his family never talked about it. I think they never gave up hope that one day he would be back. Mrs. Machovec prayed a Novena every week for her son to get home safely. Now there would be a little white cross with Louie's name on it next to the others in front of Saint Cyril's Church.

I felt bad for Peewee and I was worried about him. With a

beer in his hand, tobacco in his cheek and a leather belt nearby, Peewee's father could be rough on Peewee and his eight brothers and sisters. Now with his son Louie lost, would Mr. Machovec get meaner?

The days in that hospital bed moved like years. I stared at the same things from morning till night. Finally, the day came when I was to leave. A last bath, combed hair, and clean pajamas would send me on my way.

I SAID SO long to the kid in the bed next to me. Then the nurses lifted me onto a stretcher and carried me down a long flight of stairs. The door opened. Daylight struck my eyes blinding me. I shut my eyes tight, but felt the sun on my skin and heard the sound of cars going by. I could hear kids yelling and smell the fresh air mixed with the scent of cowhides being turned into shoes in the factories nearby. I was almost home.

17.

BINGHAMTON PRESS   JUNE 7, 1944

NAZIS ARE HURLED OFF BEACHHEADS, ALLIES RACE INLAND, REPULSE ATTACKS

STORK STAGES OWN D-DAY IN TRIPLE CITIES

Two of Four D-day Babies Born to Wives of Men in Service

Beachhead Assault

Talk about D-day was everywhere. Our guys landed in Normandy and were on the move. The excitement ran throughout the First Ward. Newspaper boys hawked Extras on street corners, church bells rang out, radios reported nonstop the assault on the French beaches, barbershops chattered about what our guys would do to the Nazis, and grocery stores were filled with smiling moms and wives who knew an end might be in sight.

Newsreels at the Ritz soon showed the D-day invasion. Landing barges carried our men onto the beaches. Some soldiers jumped from the crafts and waded through the rough waters. The

Nazis fired nonstop and our dead dotted the beaches. In the waves offshore, more dead bodies bobbed up and down. They rolled in and out with the waves. Those who made it never quit fighting.

Little did I know that I would soon witness another invasion, of a different kind, right here at home.

In Binghamton, some summer days were made for doing nothing. It was on this kind of day you could find simmering bodies covered in cocoa butter littered across the concrete abutment spanning the river at Cutler's dam.

There was no excuse, on this kind of day, for Tootsie, Peewee, Jug-bug, Mike, Vic, Yonkie, and I not to be together on the river. Once there, we'd join in with the others to see what the day would bring.

We lay patiently in the hot summer sun on the searing concrete waiting to turn our white skin golden brown and to start arguing about who had the best tan. A good tan depended on a good sun. There were summers when the sun didn't shine, where one gray day turned into another until the summer was gone. You didn't want to waste a sunny summer day, not in Binghamton.

Above, the sky was blue, without a hint of a cloud. Below, the sun-drenched Chenango River wrapped around the long concrete slab, the man-made dike meant to tame the river at flood stage. When the river ran low in the summertime, the dry concrete dam became our sandy beach.

Cutler's Dam was crowded on this day, but you hardly knew it. The sun made everything still. There was little talking going on, maybe an occasional mention of yesterday's Yankees win over the Tigers. There was little movement. Now and then a sunbather turned over to offer his other side to the sun. Once in a while, a loud splashing sound told you one of the guys was in the river cooling down. From time to time, you could hear the striking of matches lighting cigarettes. Even the river was silent, barely moving under the hazy summer sun.

The scent of the cocoa butter cooking on flesh along with the smoke from burning cigarettes was a welcome relief from the foul stink of the river with its banks baked dry, smelling like rotting fish.

Only certain people came to the river. No one really knew why they came. The river could be sneaky and dangerous. What was there about it? Was it the unknown? The fear? The challenge? The company? No one ever said; no one ever asked.

A strange yet familiar smell drifted through the air. It was the smell of fish frying and this smell made me hungry.

One by one we got up to see one of the older guys, Jake Linko, holding a small sunfish, wedged on a stick, over a pile of burning sticks gathered from the nearby river bank. Next to him laid a makeshift fishing pole and a can of worms used for bait.

"Can you believe that shit? Look at how puny that fish is!" Mike said, under his breath.

"It's about three inches long!" Tootsie added. "There won't be anything left by the time he cooks it!"

We watched as Jake pulled the fish out of the fire and picked a piece of meat off it and ate it. I could feel my stomach rumble. It wasn't much of a fish, but the man eating it didn't care so why should I.

"How's my tan?" Mike asked, as he stood up with the sun to his back.

We all turned and squinted at Mike.

"Yeah, it's good," Tootsie said.

"The back looks OK?" Mike asked as he spun around.

We all raised up for another look.

"It looks good," Yonkie said.

"Real good," Peewee added.

Mike always needed to ask a couple of times.

"Who's got a cigarette I can borrow?" Yonkie asked.

I reached over to my shirt and pulled out my pack of Lucky Strikes and gave one to Yonkie.

"You got a match?" Yonkie asked.

"Yeah, your face and my ass!" Mike answered.

"Funny, funny. You got a match, Cap?" Yonkie asked.

"Matches are scarce. Light yours on mine, and for Chris' sake stop bumming!" I said.

"So, I'm out of cigarettes. Big fucking deal!" Yonkie shot back.

"You never have shit!" Tootsie joined in on Yonkie.

"That's not true. I, I just . . . ."

"Bullshit!" Vic interrupted. "You bum everything!"

"Why don't you just go to the A&P and get some, like we do?" Peewee added.

"I can't go there. They've got their eye on me," Yonkie said.

"They've got their eye on everyone, for Chris' sake! That can't stop you!" Jug-bug added.

"If I get caught, my old man will kill me!" Yonkie said.

No one said a word. Yonkie's father was a coal miner from West Virginia. He worked for the Powell Fuel Company delivering coal to heat homes and stoves all around Binghamton. He seemed like a mean son-of-a-bitch.

"Who do you think has the biggest tits at Dickinson?" Mike asked turning to one of our favorite subjects.

"In our class or the whole school?" Vic asked.

"I don't know. Both, I guess," Mike said.

"In our class there aren't too many girls with tits," I said.

"What about Frances Minnow?" Jug-bug said.

"I mean tits you'd like to touch," Mike added.

"Yeah, no one would touch her tits," Vic chimed in.

"OK, so if Frances stuck her tits out at you, you wouldn't touch 'em?" Yonkie asked.

"I wouldn't touch 'em," Vic said. "But, you'd touch anything you could get your hands on!"

"You wouldn't? You asshole!" Yonkie shot back at Vic.

"Don't sweat it. Frances ain't gonna let anyone touch her titties! If you tried she'd probably kill you!" I said.

"Anyone else at Dickinson?" Mike asked.

"What about Bertha Frayer?" I threw out.

"From the Kelly block?" Mike said. "You gotta be kidding. She's in your brother Richie's class, ain't she?"

"Yeah, but you should see the tits she's got . . . even at her age." I answered.

"She doesn't count," Tootsie said. "She's too young."

"Hey, I can't help it. You want tits . . . Bertha's got 'em bigger than most of the older girls at Dickinson. Check her out the next time you see her; you'll see what I mean," I said.

"Hey, you know who's got nice tits?" Vic said. "Mrs. Kane."

"The English teacher? How do you know that?" I asked.

"I heard some of the guys in ninth grade talking about her on the schoolyard one day," Jug-bug jumped in.

"What did they say?" Mike asked.

"They were talking about her tits and how nice they were and how she wears tight sweaters and how sometimes they think her nipples show," Jug-bug said.

"Anything else?" Mike asked.

"Yeah. One of 'em said he'd like to screw her," Jug-bug said.

"I've seen her in the hallway a couple of times. Yeah, she'd be a good screw," Yonkie said.

"Oh, like you're the expert on screwing," Vic said. "You probably ain't even kissed a girl yet, except playing Spin the Bottle where the girl didn't have a choice."

"Oh, so you're the big kisser, you asshole!" Yonkie responded.

Mike waited for Vic to answer and when none came he asked: "What about at Saint Cyril's? Who's hot?"

Tootsie and Peewee looked at each other and Tootsie said, "I think Betty Bederka's hot."

"Yeah, she is. But she doesn't have big tits. She just has something else that's nice," Peewee added.

"Yeah, I've seen her. She's got a nice ass," Mike added.

"You know who we forgot," Vic said. "Angelina Liciandrello."

"Hey, yeah. I forgot Angelina. She is really sweet looking," Mike said.

"Bad choice," I added. "Her mother is a nice lady, but she's always on the watch. Hey, you know, who can blame her with all the jerks hanging around the schoolyard."

"Yeah, especially you dirty boys," Yonkie said.

Holy shit! Look at what's over there! a voice suddenly shouted from farther down the dam.

Everyone sat up and turned to look. On the far bank, across the river, two girls were walking slowly through the edge of a thick stretch of woods that hugged the river bank. We watched as they weaved in and out of the trees, appearing briefly then disappearing into the dense cover. I turned and saw one of the high-school guys holding binoculars up to his eyes. *It's Annie and Jane!* the guy with the binoculars yelled out. All along the length of the dam, the sunbathers rose to their feet; their eyes fixed across the river, on the woods.

The two girls came out from the trees and moved toward the bank of the river. Now in full view, both were wearing skirts and blouses. One went to the water's edge, lifted her skirt and stuck a bare foot into the water. This brought yells from the guys on the dam.

The girl looked up at the guys and raised her skirt a bit more and then wiggled her toe in the water. The two girls smiled at each other. The guys on the dam began to stir. You could feel an energy building. Up and down the dam word began to spread. The two girls across the river were well known in Binghamton. They lived somewhere outside the First Ward. Once, downtown, I remembered seeing them. Neither one was much to look at. The one named Annie seemed to be the older one. She was short and big around the middle. The other one, Jane, was taller, thinner and more shy.

No one ever walked out on the other side of the river where the girls were; it was not an easy place to reach. There was only one reason the girls were there and the older guys thought they knew why.

One by one, the guys left their spots on Cutler's Dam. Climbing into the river, they pushed against the water, slipping and sliding on the mossy rocks under their feet. The water rose swiftly as their progress brought them closer to the edge of the main current—where hidden forces could test even good swimmers. Most of the guys, who moments before were content to lie lazily in the late morning sun, were now stroking hard against the strong currents of the Chenango River. For a moment I thought I was at the Ritz looking at a Movietone newsreel of our guys landing at Normandy. One big difference in this homeland invasion was the only weapons these guys carried were between their legs. Another was Annie and Jane looked like they weren't going to put up much of a fight. And surrender would be quick.

Watching from Cutler's Dam, our eyes focused first on the guys, then on the girls. On the far shore, the girls played in the shallow water as if unaware of the force moving toward them.

"Let's go, you guys!" Yonkie yelled.

No one in our group moved.

"What's wrong with you? This is it! We can get some!" Yonkie said.

"They're just a couple of pussies!" Vic said.

"And? Yeah, and so what! How would you know?" Yonkie asked.

"Kiki told me about them," Tootsie broke in.

"What's wrong with a couple of pussies?" Yonkie asked.

"You want to get crabs?" Tootsie answered.

"Crabs?" Yonkie said.

"Yeah, crabs. They got 'em, you get 'em! They jump on you and you'll scratch so much, your dick will fall off!" Tootsie answered.

Yonkie thought for a moment, then added, "You're full of shit!"

"Also, the odds ain't so good. There're two of them and only about fifty guys!" Peewee added.

"You guys are so screwed up!" Yonkie said.

In the strongest part of the current, the swimmers heads bobbed up and down, their mouths turned downstream sucking in air as they struggled against the power of the river. Their arms thrust and pulled, their legs pumping beneath the water. On the shore the girls looked on with amusement as the guys struggled against the tow of the river.

From the dam, we watched the guys finally overcoming the grip of the current, their strokes slowing, their watery struggle almost over. With their legs touching bottom again, the guys began to rise in the shallow rapids on the far side of the river, gasping for breath as the water trickled down their sun-drenched skin. Nearby, the girls moved about with more energy.

"How many times are a couple of girls going to fall in your lap like this?" Yonkie reminded us.

Still none of us budged. We stood watching as the girls went into the woods. The guys following close behind.

"You bunch of sissies!" Yonkie said.

"Why don't you go?" Tootsie said.

"I will. You're gonna be sorry you didn't get in on it!"

Those were Yonkie's last words before he dove into the water toward the other side. We watched until he made it across and vanished, like the others, deep into the woods. Among the guys in our gang, none of us really knew Yonkie. None of us knew his real age. He looked older even though he was in our class. He always seemed to be hiding something.

Yonkie was a good swimmer. He was an even better liar and we knew no matter what really happened in the woods on the far shore with Annie and Jane, he'd come back with a story or two, telling us what we missed or maybe just complaining about the long line.

"Hey, you guys, make sure we don't run out of cocoa butter, I'm really started to tan up nicely," Mike said.

"Don't worry, we got plenty. If we start to run short someone can make a quick run and steal some more at the drugstore," Jugbug said.

WE LAY BACK down on our spots on the dam. No one spoke as we put more cocoa butter on our bodies. We lay motionless and listened. It was quiet and windless and the hot summer sun beat down.

18.

BINGHAMTON PRESS　　　　　AUGUST 1, 1944

U.S. TANKS STRIKING TOWARD PARIS; WARSAW FIRED AS NAZIS LOSE HOPE

THREE AREA SOLDIERS GIVE THEIR LIVES, FOUR WOUNDED IN BATTLE FOR SAIPAN

Harry C. Peterson, Bernard B. Kiznis, L. L. Hromaik Killed in Combat; Others Are Recovering from Injuries in Pacific

Zero at Two O'clock

I knew something was up when I spotted the crowd in front of Levine's Junkyard. Climbing the crest of the Clinton Street bridge on my way home from the Boys' Club late one afternoon, I saw people running and pushing and jumping to get a look at something. I couldn't tell exactly what they were trying to see, but from the size of the crowd milling about from underneath the railroad overpass heading west toward Clinton Street and stretching south around Front Street past the A & L Diner, I knew something big was happening.

At first I thought it was an accident, so I ran to see what was going on. Pushing my way through the thick crowd, I saw what was causing the fuss. Sitting no more than twenty feet from me was a Jap Zero. The whole plane rested on blocks of Levine's jagged scrap metal, densely packaged for pickup. This made it difficult to get too close. The plane was painted dark green from front to back with bold red circles on top of the Zero's wings and on the side of the tail section.

How Levine got it no one knew, but there it was as big and as real as if a Jap pilot had landed it himself—a Jap Zero perched nose forward on Levine's junkyard lot at the corner of Front and Clinton Streets. This was a big deal for Binghamton and people were coming from everywhere to catch a glimpse of the Japs' best fighter plane.

I checked the enemy plane carefully to see where bullets from a U.S. fighter probably ripped through it to bring it down. The front section looked clean; no visible damage to the propeller. I looked carefully at the open cockpit where a Jap pilot would have sat at the controls with his fingers on the gun-trigger while he swooped out of the clouds toward one of our carriers in the Pacific. Again, I saw no damage around the cockpit. I checked what I could of the wings. I could only see their tops; the bottoms rested on the bed of scrap metal. From what I could see there were no gaping holes. I moved toward the tail section, expecting to see it shredded from the fifty-caliber machine-gun bullets from our men on the carrier. Again, nothing. Overall, the plane looked in almost perfect condition. But what brought it down? And where did it come down? Over the Pacific? Over Pearl Harbor? Over Binghamton?

The daily newspapers reminded us that the war with the Japs was being fought in places like Corregidor, Bataan, and the Philippines. The newsreels at the Ritz showed the Jap Zeros attacking our ships and men. Jap pilots dove at our ships with guns blazing across the Pacific sky filled with giant clouds. Our men below responded with a stream of machine-gun fire from the decks of their ships. The air was streaked with anti-aircraft fire. When a Zero got hit, a trail of black smoke poured out of its wings, sending it into a steep dive to sink into the rolling black ocean water below. Some Jap pilots fought to keep their burning planes up until they could crash into our ships. These were the fight-to-the-death Kamikaze pilots. But what happened to the pilot of Levine's Zero? Did he parachute out? Was he captured? Did he desert to our side? Fly his plane to America? Sell it to Levine's? How much did Levine give him for it? What was this Zero doing in Binghamton? No one standing in front of Levine's that day seemed to know anything about it. They just looked on, shaking their heads, amazed at the sight.

Pushing through the crowd to reach the sidewalk curb, I jumped into the street and ran alongside a line of slow-moving cars crawling by Levine's. Dipping underneath the railroad overpass, I took off running up Clinton Street. I had to see Tootsie to find out if he had seen the Zero.

Nearing Tootsie's house, I slowed to a crawl since Tootsie had warned me about Busa, the Russian butcher across the street who chased kids with a cleaver if they ran near his store. Busa used to wait in the dark on Halloween night for the kids to come by who would pound on his big glass store window and run. He'd jump out of the dark and chase the kids, waving a cleaver over his head. Busa was one crazy Russian.

I ran up the back steps and knocked on the door where Tootsie lived. The smell of cabbage cooking meant it was getting close to suppertime, so I figured the odds were pretty good that Toots would be home. Tootsie's sister, Muzzy, came to the door and when she saw me she yelled for Tootsie. I waited on the porch outside with the door slightly open. Tootsie stuck his head out and I motioned for him to come.

"Did you see what's at Levine's?" I asked Tootsie.

"No, what's there?"

"You're not going to believe this! A Japanese war plane!"

"Bullshit!"

"I'm not kidding you. It's a Jap Zero!"

"What do you mean? A piece of the plane?"

"No, the whole thing!"

"Why would a Jap plane be at Levine's Junkyard?"

"That's what everyone is asking! No one knows!"

"Is it all shot up?"

"No, it looks brand fucking new!"

"Holy shit!"

"Yeah, right!"

"No damage?"

"None that I could tell. But you couldn't really see the whole thing because it was sitting flat on a pile of scrap metal and you couldn't climb around it."

"No shit . . ."

"You want to go see it?"

"Shit yes, but I can't go right now."

"What about later on?"

"Yeah, I'll come over to your place in about two hours, OK?"

"I'll be waiting. You'll never see anything like this, I swear!"

Waiting the two hours for Tootsie seemed like forever. I couldn't wait to show him the plane. But where was he?

I didn't think he was going to show, but then I heard the echoing sound of the front door opening in the hallway and footsteps climbing the noisy stairs of the Kelly block. I opened our apartment door and saw Tootsie at the top of the stairs. Slamming the door shut behind me, we took off running as fast as we could, never looking back until we reached the underpass near Levine's. Overhead, a Lackawanna train rumbled by, clanking and screeching its way west.

Up ahead the crowds that once filled the streets were gone; the traffic moved at its regular pace. Coming out of the underpass, I looked for the Zero.

"Where's the plane? I don't see it," Tootsie said.

TOP: Two dozen 17-year-olds to leave for Albany for the Navy for assignment to training stations. *BOTTOM*: The Marsheski and Sejan Families say goodby as their men leave for Army service.

TOP: Negro Company from community parades down Main Street. *BOTTOM*: National Guard unit gets rousing send-off as it leaves for war.

TOP: Theresa Monica Vrabel Capalaces, "Tree", our mom. *(Private)* *BOTTOM, LEFT:* Older sister Frances Ann (Frannie) working at Jumbo's Market. *(Private)* *BOTTOM, RIGHT:* Younger brother, Richard John (Richie), unafraid of heights or obstacles.

One of the alleys off Clinton Street where we lived and played.

TOP: Cigar shop—the kind where Grandma Vrabel worked as a young girl making cigars for 5 cents an hour. *BOTTOM*: Sokolovna Hall on Clinton Street—the social club for Slovaks in the First Ward.

TOP: Daniel S. Dickinson Elementary School on the hill at the end of Dickinson Street.
BOTTOM: St. Mary's Home where problem kids were sent to live and learn.

TOP: East Clinton Street Bridge where ice and snow were hand-shoveled over its concrete railings during winter storms. *BOTTOM*: Cutler's Dam spanning the Chenango River, the scene of summer's sun and fun.

TOP: Endicott-Johnson Shoe Factory where mama worked making shoes. During the war, she made boots for soldiers. *BOTTOM*: Tent ready to go to our guys made by Eureka Tent and Awning Company.

TOP: Link Aviation Flight Simulators used to train pilots. *BOTTOM*: General Electric Plant producing military weapons.

TOP: Boys turn to club for activities with friends. *LEFT*: Some boys wait and wonder what is keeping their pals.

TOP: Main game room where the action is non-stop. *BOTTOM*: For a penny, boys throw darts at Hitler. Proceeds go to the Broome County Red Cross War Fund.

RIGHT: Climbing the rope to reach the ceiling takes strength and determination. *BOTTOM*: My friend, Walter "Bucky" Bonsell, a happy guy with a big smile.

FACING PAGE, TOP: Back row, L to R: George Meade and my closest buddy Francis "Tootsie" Kolosna hold up 1946 seals exchanged for 2600 pennies collected by the Boys Club for the Broome County Tuberculosis Association. Donald H. Swartwood, left, hands check to Joseph E. Sparks, seal sale chairman. *FACING PAGE, BOTTOM*: 14 year old George Gerolmo poses as the healthiest boy at the Club.

ARMY
2000
1000
500

AIR CORPS
2000
1000
500

NAVY
2000
1000
500

MARINES
2000
1000
500

BOYS' CLUB
WASTE FATS CAMPAIGN
Victory GOAL Volunteers
8,000 lbs.
BLOCK BUSTING THE AXIS

CHARTS SHOWING THE AMOUNT
OF FAT COLLECTED BY
THE VICTORY VALUNTEERS

WARD 11

WARDS 8 & 9

POLIO INTER-WARD CONTEST

QUOTA	25%	50%	75%	100%
$14.00				
$5.00				
$5.00				
$4.00				
$5.00				
$3.00				

RIGHT: Boys Club Boxing Team warming up to entertain wounded soldiers at Rhoads Memorial Veteran's Hospital in a full program of bouts against the Utica Boys Club. *BOTTOM*: Never lead with your nose against a stiff left.

FACING PAGE, TOP: Campaign goals are set to collect waste fat for use in making ammunition. *FACING PAGE, BOTTOM*: Boys collect money for the campaign against Polio.

ABOVE: Boys' Club members eager to sign up for new programs. *BELOW*: Victory Volunteers line up for first march. George Dubock is at left. I'm on the right, leading the platoon. Fourth and fifth from the right front is Sammy Parisi and John Cleney, Further back is Bucky Bonsell.

VICTORY VOLUNTEERS
GETTING READY FOR
A HIKEING TRIP

LEFT: Sammy Parisi inspects the new Victory Volunteers uniforms on Bobby Franks, me and his brother Joe. *BOTTOM*: Victory Volunteers reached their quota of 500 pounds of waste fats in their drive to raise money for the Memorial Auditorium Fund. Bucky is on the left; that's me on the right.

TOP: Christmas Party at the club attended by 450 members. *LEFT*: Friends on home leave posing in front of Freije's Bar on Clinton Street. Back row, L to R: John Gaylo, Jr., Andy Rabey, Bill Rabey; Middle Row, L to R my pal Mike Cleney and me; Front Row, L to R: Mike Rabey, John Rabey. *(Private)*

Levine had covered the Zero with a huge piece of canvas, the kind that carnival tents are made of. In front of the cover Levine put up a sign: KEEP AWAY! NO TRESPASSING!

"It's there, underneath that big canvas. See the outline? There's the front end and that's the cockpit sticking up in the middle, and there are the wings and way in the back is the tail sticking up!"

"Christ, I wanted to see it!"

"Yeah, I know. Old man Levine was probably pissed-off with everyone gawking at it."

"Do you think he's going to take that cover off?"

"Who knows? But, hey, I got an idea! Let's come back here after dark and we'll get under that canvas and check it out."

"Do you think there's anything there to find?"

"Who knows, we might even find a dead Jap in there."

"Dead Jap? Oh, yeah, like there's gonna be a dead Jap!"

"Well, probably not, but we might find some blood or something!"

"We'll come back later, for sure!"

Tootsie and I made our plans for that night. We couldn't take the chance that Levine might reposition the Zero. We had to move fast and we had to keep our plans a secret. If any of the other guys heard what we were going to do, they'd want in and if too many guys got involved, we'd either get caught or have to make a run for it. And if you tried to make a run for it at Levine's, you never knew what you might run into. The whole place was filled with busted, jagged metal and all kinds of junk. If you got nicked, you could end up leaving a trail of blood all the way home for the cops to follow.

After the sun went down, we got the perfect kind of night we were hoping for—all dark and clouded over. When the moment was just right Tootsie and I slipped onto Levine's lot. Moving carefully, we made our way to the back of the plane, as far away from the street and the streetlights as we could.

I could see Tootsie waiting for me to lead the way.

"Toots, a little warning. Make sure you don't let go a cabbage fart when we're under that cover. You fart and I'm out of here."

"Yeah, don't worry about it. Let's go."

I lifted the edge of the heavy canvas cover and with Tootsie close behind, we slid underneath. In the darkness, I could feel Tootsie near my side. The air underneath smelled bad, as if someone peed all over the canvas.

"Jesus! It stinks like piss!" Tootsie whispered.

"It's also hot as shit under this thing! Give me the flashlight."

I felt Tootsie shoving the flashlight he got from his Uncle Ambrose's toolbox into my shoulder. I reached over and grabbed it. The flashlight seemed smaller than I thought it was, but when I turned it on, a big stream of light lit up the darkness. I was afraid the light could be seen through the canvas. I turned the light at Tootsie and saw his face dripping with sweat.

"You're friggin' blinding me with that light, for Chris' sake!" Tootsie said.

"I just wanted to see if you were sweating as much as I am. It's hot as hell!"

I beamed the flashlight toward the plane and when the light fell on the tail section, I heard Tootsie mutter, "Oh, my God!"

"Did I tell you this Jap Zero was here? You thought I was shitting you. Well, here it is!"

Tootsie and I climbed carefully onto one of the bundles of scrap metal surrounding the plane. Pushing up the canvas as we walked, we made our way closer to the Zero. Shining the light on the tail section, Tootsie and I reached up and put our sweaty hands on the tail's surface, moving across it to feel how smooth it was. Pushing on it, the metal gave a bit but it was plenty strong. When Tootsie began to move the flaps on the tail with his hand, a rusty metal sound came out. It scared us.

Slowly, we pushed our way forward toward the cockpit, where I hoped we'd find a souvenir—something to take home with us. Climbing onto the wing, we were careful not to push the canvas too hard so that someone passing by Levine's might see us. In the darkness, I reached up to feel for the cockpit and when my hand found the opening, I reached in and felt the hard leather seat fastened against the back of the cockpit. Lifting myself up against the canvas overhead, I reached in with the flashlight and turned it on. The beam lit up the control panel. I felt as if I were starring in a war movie at the Ritz.

I ran the flashlight over the cockpit and gazed at all the gauges and controls with their tiny signs printed in Japanese. *So this is where the sneaky bastard sat*, I thought.

"Man, this is unbelievable!" Tootsie said as he came up beside me and looked in.

"Move that thing around!" Tootsie said, eager for me to move the light all around the cockpit.

"Can you believe how small it is in here?" I said, looking carefully for anything we could take from the plane.

"They must be really little people."

"Yeah, but they know how to kill."

"Do you see any blood?" Tootsie asked.

"Naw, I don't see anything. Maybe the Jap pilot chickened out and jumped out of the plane with his parachute."

"See if there's anything we can pull off this sucker!"

I reached in and tried to grab anything around the control panel, but nothing would budge. I looked around the sides and the back and everything was bolted down. I pulled and yanked, but nothing moved.

Then I saw the stick the pilot used to steer the plane and on top of it the trigger he used to fire his wing guns. I knew I had to climb into that seat to feel what it was like to be at the controls of a Jap Zero.

Heading in feet first, Tootsie boosted me up and into the cockpit. I twisted myself into the seat and leaned back to catch my breath, trying not to think about how much hotter it had gotten and how much my dry mouth was dying for a cold drink.

Handing the flashlight to Tootsie, I told him to go check the propeller to see if we could get it off the plane and take it home. Tootsie worked his way across the Zero toward the front section.

In the darkness, I reached up and gripped the steering stick with my right hand. *So this is how it feels to be at the controls of one of these babies.*

I wrapped the lucky silk scarf around my neck and pulled the sunglasses over my eyes and pushed the stick forward, sending the plane into a deep dive. Looking to my left, I saw the clouds race by until patches of blue broke through and I spotted them, in formation, below me. A squadron of Jap Zeros roared toward one of our battleships streaming crisply through the Pacific waters. They'd never know how I got hold of this Levine Zero and by the time they figured it out, it would be too late.

My engine was deafening; I could hardly hear myself think. I concentrated on the Zeros below. Closing the distance, I could see the Zeros against the blue water below.

They spotted my plane overhead, but they thought it was one of their Zeros joining in. They never broke formation. I planned to attack the back of the formation first and then work my way to the front. Pushing the stick forward with my sweaty hand, the plane began to dive. I reached my thumb up to the trigger and squeezed off a burst, rat-a-tat-tat, which raced across the sky and ripped across the cockpit of the last Zero. I could see smoke and the pilot fighting to keep control when the plane burst into flames and exploded into a million pieces.

Seeing this, the Japanese squadron broke formation, racing to get an angle to take me down. It seemed like the battle went on for days: Zeros on my tail, one at two o'clock, one at nine. I yanked the stick back, pulled to the right and climbed straight up before banking to the left and at full speed attacking with my guns firing nonstop—Rat-a-tat-tat! Rat-a-tat-tat! One Zero hit and then another. I caught only a glimpse of them plunging into the sea.

One by one the Zeros began to disappear from the sky. The muscles in my right arm burned from the strain of keeping my Zero aloft. I checked the instrument panel and saw the fuel gauge heading toward empty. I was running out of time. There was one Zero left and as we streaked toward each other I could see the pilot's ugly little face and his narrow eyes focused on me. He probably thought I was a Jap pilot who went crazy and had changed sides, but when I pulled off my scarf and sunglasses, he saw I was a Yank. His eyes lit up and from the way his lips moved, I knew he was cussing me up and down in Japanese.

He sent a burst. I returned the fire—Rat-a-tat-tat! Rat-at at-tat! Rat-a-tat-tat! Patches of black smoke filled the air. I watched the Jap pilot slump forward against the windshield and with blood spurting out of his mouth and ears he raised his hand and gave me the finger as he rushed by and exploded in a big ball of flames. Screw you too, I thought.

Down below our ships slid safely on through the gently rocking sea. Having just seen the greatest air battle of the war, the guys below wondered just who I was.

SOMEDAY THEY'D KNOW. *But right now I had to get this baby safely back to Levine's Junkyard.*

The sky was clear coming in except for a cloud up ahead. As I passed through it, an almost disorienting smell of rotten cabbage hit my nose. My throat tightened. I gagged. I felt weak. My hand slipped off the stick; the Zero began to wobble. The nose tipped toward the earth. Sweat poured out of me. I felt myself blacking out. Suddenly a voice spoke.

"Cap. Cappy. I can't budge that damn propellor."

"Tootsie!!!"

19.

YANKS IN ALSACE, REACH BELGIUM; VERDUN, DIEPPE AND ST. MIHIEL FALL

CITY BATHHOUSES, PLAYGROUND CLOSED THREE DAYS AHEAD OF TIME BECAUSE OF POLIO EPIDEMIC

Girls Are So Dumb

The slapping sound of the morning newspaper landing on the back porch signaled the start of a new day. The smell of chicory perking in the coffee pot on the coal-fired cast-iron stove next door meant Grandma was up and in the kitchen. I stayed in bed, pretending to be asleep, until Mama left for work. She always worried about me getting into trouble, and knowing I was still in bed gave Mama a little relief to start her day.

When the apartment door closed, I listened till Mama's footsteps faded on the stairway and the front door slammed shut sending an echo throughout the Kelly block. Crawling to the window, I pushed back the worn green shade and watched Mama trudge off to another day of work at the E. J. Shoe Factory. I watched her cross the empty street and turn left on Murray Street, where she would climb a steep grade to the bus stop on Clinton Street and wait there for a Triple Cities Transit bus to take her to work. By the time the bus pulled off Clinton, on its way to Main Street, it would be mostly full of First Ward mothers and daughters going off to the factories in Johnson City and Endicott.

Real coffee was hard to get during the war, so a hot cup of Grandma's chicory would have to do. Having a piece of buttered rye bread with it took away some of the bitter taste.

I liked to sit and look at the comics in the morning *Sun* newspaper while I sat at the gray metal table in Grandma's kitchen. Blondie and Dagwood's son got a hundred on a geography test at school and he complained that if he had been on the radio, he would have won sixty-four dollars for knowing the answers. Smilin' Jack looks like he's going to get married, although he doesn't look too happy kissing his girlfriend.

Grandma swept the linoleum floor in the kitchen while singing songs from Slovakia. Although on the frail side, she was always happy as if every dream she ever dreamt came true. I would sip my chicory and read the paper, and be happy to be with Grandma.

Shoveling out the stove and putting the ashes in the can next to a pail of coal near the stove always left some of the ashes on the floor. She often missed sweeping them up, and when I pointed to the ashes on the floor, Grandma still seemed as if she didn't see them. I mentioned this to my Aunt Irene and she told me that Grandma was going blind, but she didn't want the operation the doctors were pushing for.

Unschooled, Grandma couldn't read or speak English, even though she had been in America for forty years. She had taught me a little Slovak, her native tongue, and it was all we needed to get by. She always asked me if it were time for the mail to come and if she should go and watch for the mailman. She was waiting for any news from her boys and praying for them to get safely home from the war. Now she was going blind.

Since Grandma couldn't read, she rarely looked at a newspaper. Even so, she was the first one to get the mail from Mr. Ed Rhodes, our mailman. He delivered the mail twice a day, and all the women on the street would be outside waiting for him as he trudged down Dickinson Street. If he knew he had a letter from someone in the service, he'd wave the thin, light- blue V-Mail letter high over his head and point to the woman it was for. If Grandma got a letter, she'd hold it till Mama or Aunt Irene or Aunt Virginia could read it to her in Slovak or broken English. Mr. Rhodes, the mailman, was so popular that he needed help from his son, Ed Jr., at Christmas time to carry the gifts he got from all the families on the street. The gifts were usually home-baked Kholachki's or bottles of wine. Ed and his son always ended up with a huge load to take home.

Today's headlines in the Binghamton *Sun* read: ALLIES ADVANCE ON PARIS: U.S. 3RD ARMY BREAKS THROUGH AT REIMS. An article lower on the page featured an upcoming visit to Binghamton by Hollywood actress Irene Dunne to promote a War Savings Bond drive in the Triple Cities, while another story mentioned a contract Link Aviation got to supply the Air Force with flight-training simulators. Lower on the page, in smaller print next to an ad for Fowler's Department Store, was news that Sergeant Jacob T. Hissin of Binghamton, a chaplain's assistant, was killed in action in France on D-day. The War Department notified his wife, Electa Mae, of 24 Lisle Avenue. Sergeant Hissin served with an amphibious unit of the 299th Combat Engineers when he was killed. I was glad Grandma couldn't read.

Turning the page, I spotted a story with a picture of five women joining the Women's Army Air Corp. The headline read: THIRD BLASKO SISTER ENLISTS IN WAAC; FOUR OTHERS JOIN UP. Elizabeth Blasko from Gerard Avenue was leaving as did her two other sisters, Margaret and Anne, before her. *What do women do in the service?* I guessed some were nurses, but I figured most were young and they just wanted to serve and do whatever jobs the troops needed doing.

Looking through the newspaper every day you could see that the women at home seemed to be doing a lot. Betty Pembridge from Union Center worked fifty hours a week in a war plant, but still made time to write letters to one-hundred-and-sixty-three servicemen and women every month. The E. J. Workers Chorus sang for eight hundred wounded veterans at Rhoads General Hospital. Bed patients heard the entire concert over the hospital's public address system. E. J. women took gifts around to the patients' bedsides and talked with them. This was tough work. I don't think I could have done it.

All this started me thinking about my sister, Fran. I was glad she was too young to join the service, but the idea that it could happen some day scared me. I never wanted Fran to leave us, ever. She always watched out for Richie and me and if she weren't here I would miss her too much.

Summer days on Dickinson Street were filled with the noise of kids playing on the sidewalks in front of the Kelly block. Worn-out sneakers screeched on the chalk-lined concrete and danced in the hopscotch squares. Girls skipped rope and sang songs with squeaky voices while some kids rode handmade wooden carts with roller-skate wheels nailed to the bottom of old wooden milk boxes. Older kids flipped bubble-gum baseball cards, matching heads or tails in winner-takes-all battles. Guys holding bulging old socks filled with marbles took turns leaning over a marked line in the dirt, rolling their marbles in hopes of hitting a winner and taking the pot. Some kids ran wildly at others, taking aim and then squeezing the triggers of handmade wooden pistols, sending "bullets" made from strips cut out of old rubber inner tubes. On occasion a fight would break out, sending kids rolling in the dirt until someone got hurt enough to scream for his mother. Arrows pierced chalk-drawn hearts on the cement sidewalks while kids pointed at the lover's initials etched inside the heart.

The older guys in the block showed up on the street later in the morning. They liked to mess around, spoiling games, while enjoying the sight of kids crying. Often their taunts or slaps brought tears to any kid who got in their way.

Most all the boys played war with plastic guns and rifles, fighting from sunup to sundown in the vacant lot next to the Kelly block. Hiding behind bushes and cardboard boxes, they took turns being GIs and Nazis and Japs. They threw small rocks for hand grenades and the "wounded" often lay crying in pain. The "dead" didn't move until the next battle. Then they rose up and reloaded.

Richie played among the kids of the Kelly block; Fran hated being around there so she usually rode off on her two-wheeler to meet up with her girlfriends in another part of the Ward. If I didn't make plans ahead, I always knew I could hook up with guys at the schoolyard at Dickinson or up at Cutler's Dam. It was too hot a day to go to the Boys' Club.

Today, with no plans in hand, I decided to go to the river. With my bathing suit on under my Levis, I stretched my legs and ran to the end of Dickinson Street, darted across Front Street, and snaked my way down McDonald Avenue toward the river. I climbed over the small stone wall that led onto the path that stretched a half-mile to Cutler's Dam.

I slowed to a walk to catch my breath and to look at the river below. Trees and bushes swayed gently on the river bank. It was a little on the cool side for a summer day. Every now and then the sun came out from behind a cloud and felt good when its rays touched you. For a half-mile, a concrete surface rose fifty feet on a steep angle from the river bank below to the path I was walking on above. They called this fifty-foot embankment *the viaduct;* it was built to keep the waters in check if the river flooded.

So far, I thought, my day was off to a pretty good start. I hadn't gotten into any trouble yet, but then I knew I wouldn't have to find trouble, it usually found me.

When I reached the end of the path I could see guys lying out on the dam. I climbed down the viaduct onto the boulders to the white concrete dam. Walking the dam, I said a few *Hi's* to the guys I knew and picked out a spot to sit. Although we made no specific plans, I was sure my friends would show up. I watched a guy fishing in the calm waters that were protected by the dam from the river's main currents. This wasn't a good spot to fish; this was where most guys swam. Even though his chances weren't good, I still kept an eye on the guy's tight line in the water on the slim chance he might get a bite.

It was still early, maybe too early, so I figured it best to just wait awhile to see who in our gang shows up. I waited some time and guys did show up; but they were some of the older guys already in Central High School, along with some guys I really didn't know. They probably had either quit school or were thrown out. With the war still going on, they could be the next ones to go. Scattered here and there were a veteran or two who got home early. You could tell they had been in the war because you could see their wounds as they lay in the sun. One of them had a large piece of bone and muscle missing on one of his legs. The other one had scars on his shoulder where it had been stitched up.

Except for the vets, being on the dam meant the guys were adventurous—some even wild, their exploits well known to the cops. Sometimes, older guys liked to use the younger ones to test their schemes. They would make you do risky things and if you got caught, the punishment would probably be less severe, because you're just a kid. If you didn't get into trouble, then the older guys got what they sent you after. I learned this lesson when older guys from around Dickinson Street took me to the carnival that was in town one day and made me steal cigarettes that were prizes at some of the games of chance. I'd have to bring the cigarettes to them and then they used them to trade for rides on the midway. I never got caught, but if I did, the carnys would have probably killed me. As it turned out, we rode so many rides I got sick and heaved from not eating all day.

Oftentimes you'd hang around with the older guys because they taunted you with, *You got any guts?* or *You wanna be a man?* They made it tough to walk away. They were trouble. You tried to steer clear of them, but here I was, sitting close enough to smell their cigarettes and hear them talking. They liked to use guys like me to steal candy and cigarettes and drinks. *Where the heck were our guys? They couldn't all be busy.* I was feeling nervous.

I decided to leave and head over to the schoolyard, but a tough-looking guy I never saw before stood up from where he and his pal, Whitey Liberacki, had been sitting and asked where I was going.

"To the schoolyard," I said.

"To the schoolyard, he said. Did you hear that Whitey? What's goin' on there?" the tough guy asked.

"I'm gonna look for my friends," I answered.

"Gee, I thought we was your friends. Stick around. There's nothing going on at Dickinson!" Whitey said, as he took out a pack of cigarettes and carefully lifted one and offered it to me.

I reached out and took it and lit it off his smoke. I sat down and puffed on my cigarette and wondered what he was up to. I sat at some distance from them, turning my back and pretending not to listen to what they were saying. They talked about girls, all about girls. They called them *broads*. They talked about shapes and sizes and lips and eyes and hair. They brought up a list of girls in the Ward who were ready; girls who were hot. They mentioned names of broads from Binghamton, Johnson City, and Endicott and what they wanted to do with them. All of the names mentioned were new to me, except for some in the Ward. When I heard any name I recognized, I listened to see what they were saying.

When the talking stopped suddenly, I turned to see them passing a small book around. Whitey saw me looking and handed it to me. It had a gray paper cover with two fasteners holding the little white pages inside. On the cover was a drawing of Popeye and Olive Oyl. Turning the pages, Popeye was standing with his fly open next to Olive who was naked. I turned the page and saw . . . .

"Gimme that," the tough guy said, grabbing the book from my hand. "You're too young for that stuff. A book like this could give you ideas."

Out of nowhere the tough guy mentioned the thing some guys do to themselves. He said if you did it too much, hair would grow on the palm of your hand. The talking stopped suddenly. I felt all their eyes on my back to see if I was checking my palm, but I just kept looking out at the river as if I never heard them. All this talk was new to me, but I didn't fall for his trick. Then the talk continued about girls.

The time passed and the talking went on. I bummed another cigarette from Whitey and after grabbing a light, I turned my back but sat a little closer to the guys. I listened intently as they talked and laughed. Next chance I got, I'd try to grab a peek at their palms. For all the talk, I couldn't remember any of these guys with a *broad*.

The sun stayed behind the clouds for a long time. From time to time, I stole a look to see who else had come to the dam. The empty feeling in my stomach told me to leave. I hadn't thought about my friends or why they hadn't shown up; my mind was busy thinking about the many girls I had heard about. I was getting real hungry, too. I wanted to leave, but I wanted to stay to hear more. I knew though, the longer I stayed, there was a good chance something bad could happen. Today, I didn't feel like any trouble. I stood up while the guys were still talking and flicked my cigarette butt into the river.

"Where you going?" Whitey asked, interrupting the talk about girls briefly.

"I gotta go. I'm hungry."

"You're hungry?" the tough guy asked.

"Yeah, I'm really hungry."

"You got any dough? asked the tough guy.

"Naw. I'm flat broke."

"Aha! Then you're going to Izzy's, you thief." Whitey said.

Just then I saw some older guys picking up their stuff from the dam.

"Hey, John!" I yelled. "You guys leaving?"

Johnny Baron nodded. "Hold on! I'm going too." I answered.

This threw Whitey and the tough guy off me. I quickly joined those guys to head off the dam and away from trouble. Even though I didn't know the three other guys, I knew Johnny, who was at Central High, and was an OK fun kind of guy.

We climbed the rocks alongside the viaduct to the top of the path. On the walk back, the worn path was narrow and we walked single file. We neared the far end of the path when Johnny, in the back of the line, spoke quietly, but loud enough for us all to hear. "Don't turn around," he said. "There are two broads behind us back at the dam coming this way."

Suddenly the guy behind me made a sudden left turn and said, "Follow me,"as he led us off the path and down the steep concrete viaduct to the river bank below. One by one we peeled off like fighter planes going in for the kill.

Another guy looked quickly at the girls on the way down and said, "Holy shit. Where did they come from?"

"They probably came up over the wall on Front Street near the miniature-golf course," Johnny said.

When everyone reached the river bank below, I asked, "What are we doin' down here?"

"See those two broads?" A guy said, pointing at the viaduct path and looking at me.

"Yeah," I answered after a long look at the two girls in the distance.

"Everyone's going to hide," he said. "And when they get right on top of us, you're going to yell up at them. Can you do that?"

"Yell what?" I asked.

"You yell up to them, *C'mon down, we've got something special for you* as loud as you can!" he said, looking me straight in the eyes. He had this *better-do-it-or-else* look.

"Why do I have to yell at them? I asked, glancing at Johnny.

"Because this is a test to see if you've got any guts," the guy answered. I looked at Johnny and he nodded and smiled.

"What if they say OK, what happens then?" I said hoping they would forget the idea.

"What do you think happens? We'll invite them down."

"Hey, what's the matter? You can't do it? Johnny asked.

"What are you, a sissy?" Another asked.

"No, I'm no sissy," I answered.

"C'mon, they're coming. You gonna do this or not?"

I turned to look at the guys and could see from their faces that this was no longer a time for any more talking. They had funny looks on their faces, the kind you see on the cowboys wearing the black hats on Saturday afternoon matinees at the Ritz.

"Yeah. OK." I answered.

Far down the path you could see the girls' dresses fluttering in the breeze as they made their way toward us. You hardly ever saw girls by the dam, so whoever they were they were probably looking for trouble. In a short time they were going to find it.

With all the trees and bushes along the river's edge, I was glad we had plenty of places to hide. I crouched behind a thick bush and watched the other guys take cover. I was satisfied that no one could see me from above. I felt like a Jap sniper in Bataan. Only I wasn't taking aim at Robert Taylor and I didn't plan to hurt anyone.

Spreading the branches of the bush, I peeked to see how close the girls were getting.

"Cappy," Johnny whispered. "Make sure you yell loud enough."

"Yeah, yeah." I whispered back, thinking time was running out for us and those two girls. I didn't know what was coming.

Maybe I was better off staying at the dam. I was scared, but I had to act like I could do this. I didn't really ever hang out with strange guys like this, but I didn't want them pissed off at me either. You never knew what they might say or do. I didn't understand how Johnny got involved with these weird guys.

"Don't yell too soon. Wait till they're right above us," Johnny added.

"OK, OK," I answered, thinking: *Why don't one of you yell up at them?*

Pulling a few branches back, I could see their hair and dresses blowing wildly in the wind in the distance. They looked tall and dressed up. Letting the branches go carefully, I kneeled down on one knee and waited quietly. I couldn't risk another look because I didn't want to take the chance the girls might see me. I wondered what was going to happen after I yelled up at them.

The only sound now was the wind in the trees and the river with its gurgling water running behind us. I started to go over the words in my mind, how I would yell to them and how I would make myself sound older.

I couldn't see or hear any of the guys hiding. It was like I was all alone. *Girls are so dumb*, I thought. They're only looking for trouble by going anywhere near Cutler's Dam. Now they're only a few minutes away from getting it.

From time to time, a breeze picked up and rustled through the trees making it harder to hear the girls coming. My knee hurt from kneeling, but I didn't move a muscle for fear I might be seen.

When I yell up to them, what if they yell back, "Sure boys, we'll be right there."

What will really happen when they come down and we all crawl out of the bushes? What happens then?

The sound of girls' voices was getting closer. I looked back at the guys . . . nothing moved. Practicing the words, over and over again, I knew that once I yelled them out, everything would be settled, one way or the other. From where I was, I didn't care, because it was just a voice coming out of a bush. Chances are the girls would pretend not to hear anything and they'll just keep walking like nothing ever happened. And Johnny would say, *At least you tried, Cappy . . . maybe next time,* and this would all be over.

My stomach hurt from not eating. I wished I were on Clinton Street stealing one of Izzy's big, juicy apples.

The voices on the path above were getting louder and clearer. I planned to wait until I could catch a peek at them through a tiny opening in the bush. Mosquitoes buzzed around my head. A huge bug was biting into my skin. I flicked my finger and sent it flying. *Son-of-a-bitch,* I thought, *what a lousy-ass time for these friggin' bugs to start screwing with me.*

Then a piece of white streaked through the opening in the bush. They were passing right above us. The sweat began to drop around me. My mouth was dry. I could hardly swallow. Then the bushes around me began to shout . . . *yell up, you idiot! . . . you're gonna lose them! . . . they look hot, you jerk!* The voices were strange. For a moment, I thought I was in an evil forest. Then I remembered, *I am in an evil forest!* I took a deep breath and crouched deeper inside the thick bush, bugs and all. I could hear them right above. It was now or never: *Hey, you two . . .* I yelled as loud and as deep as I could. Just then, a bug flew into my mouth and I started to choke.

"Hurry up, Cappy," Johnny hissed from out of a bush.

Clearing my throat, I took a deep breath. Before I could shout, I felt the bug moving in my throat. Almost gaging, I hawked out a lunger of spit.

"They're getting away," an angry voice whispered loudly from a bush.

Determined to get this over, I filled my lungs with air and let go, *Hey you two, how about a fuck?* The words came out like a little girl's, just like a sissy's. Still, for a quiet moment, my mind flashed with crazy excitement. Just . . . maybe . . . the girls might come down and . . .

Their answer came back loud and clear. "Wait till I tell your mother, Ronnie!" a sweet but angry voice said. Suddenly all the bushes around me started to shake and laugh.

As the two girls passed beyond the bush I was hiding in, I slowly moved a branch to see who they were, how they had known that voice was mine. It turned out they were the Jones girls, two nice, good-looking sisters, who lived together in a basement apartment of the Kelly block right where I lived. I watched them hustle down the path knowing they were heading straight for Mama.

A VOICE CAME from a bush, *Boy, did you just get screwed.* All the other bushes began shaking again with laughter. All the bushes except mine.

20.

BINGHAMTON SUN   SEPTEMBER 28, 1944

LIEUTENANT W. E. WILLS KILLED IN ACTION ON FRENCH FRONT, PRIVATE S. A. TRAVIS ALSO VICTIM—MISSING WOUNDED LIST GROWS

Night Sweats

The light from the marquee faded behind us as we walked away from the Ritz. Only the sound of an occasional passerby could be heard in the twenty or so steps it took us to be in the total darkness of night. My tongue was temporarily busy trying to dislodge one of Mr. Lalley's popcorn kernels stuck between my teeth, but soon I'd be needing my tongue to stand up to what was coming.

With Mike, the walk home from the movies at the Ritz always started innocently enough.

"Sergeant York was something," he said.

"Yeah, he sure was," I said as we began the walk from the top of Clinton Street down Murray on a starless and windy fall night.

"I mean the way he took his rifle and wiped a little spit on the gun sight and fired away, knocking off all those Germans."

"Yeah, and then the way he got them all to surrender, that was something," I said, glancing down the street, dark and deserted except for a dreary streetlight awaiting us at the next corner. Its gloom stood in contrast to the bright and warm lights we had just left only moments ago at the Ritz.

Like a beacon from a lighthouse, the Ritz marquee guided First Warders from every direction to a place where, for a couple of hours, they could forget the war and their worries and their loneliness, and dream about happy endings. Women came with their children and old ladies and old men came, many who only understood Slovak and Polish and Russian. The young people came, from high-schoolers to little kids eager to watch the movie stars and learn about life and death and crime and punishment and justice and mercy and heroism and sacrifice and love and hate.

But there were still things even the movies couldn't teach you. Things that made no sense, where all the pieces don't always fit and you can't guess the ending. Things like my buddy, Mike.

We had known each other since third grade. I first spotted him walking in the hallway between classes and noticed everyone making fun of him behind his back. His shoulders sloped and he walked hunched over with his arms swinging by his side in a strange rhythm. He looked like a gorilla, but no one dared to make fun of him to his face, because Mike was as strong as a gorilla. Still, when we passed in the hallway, he looked scared and alone.

Mike and I were put into the Fresh Air Program at Dickinson, where we and other kids got milk and snacks before school started to make sure we put some meat on our bones. Being skinny and poor, I kind of knew why I was there, but I never really figured out why Mike was, unless it was to get him to stop swinging his arms like a gorilla. Whatever the reason, Mike and I became friends. On the Dickinson playground, I struggled to outrun and out-jump him and failed, all the time. He was strong and quick; you took on Mike at your own risk. He played rough and he played to win. Behind his back, guys called him the "hotheaded Russian." With Russian parents and a no-nonsense, Uncle

"Struk" living with them, Mike towed the line, and whatever he took at home he dished out to anyone who got in his way.

"Gary Cooper was great," Mike said, eager to relive the movie.

Finally dislodging the shred of popcorn from between my teeth, I spit it out to tell Mike, "Yeah, he's always good."

"The place was packed. I couldn't believe it, the noise and the crowds around the candy," Mike said.

"You couldn't get anywhere near the toilet. I thought I was gonna pee my pants."

I remembered how we had pushed our way to the Ritz candy counter, finally getting waited on and hearing the cock crow to signal the start of the Pathé Newsreel. I recalled how the screen flickered inside the dark theater as Mike and I walked slowly down the aisle looking for seats while keeping an eye open for smart-asses trying to trip us on the way down.

The only seats left were in the front row, where we had to stretch back to look up at the screen and watch our guys fighting the Japs on an island in the Pacific. We all sat quietly as a booming voice told us that U.S. Marines were fighting fiercely on Corregidor. Bullets cracked, bombs burst, and grenades exploded; flame-throwers shot sprays of fire into holes hiding Japs while in the background march music played as our guys fired away at an enemy only they could see. Stretchers rushed the wounded to safety while a few Jap prisoners stood with their heads bowed. The voice on the screen ended the report by telling a tired but smiling Marine with a cigarette hanging from his lips, *Keep up the good work and this war will soon be over.*

I could still hear the Ritz crowd cheering and stomping their feet when the war story ended. We next sat through a fashion show on the screen where, from our angle, the models looked eight feet tall. Pathé cameras switched to Captain Clark Gable in his Army uniform flying around the country to get people to buy War Bonds. You could hear women in the Ritz making weird

sounds when Clark Gable smiled. The guys answered with whistles and shouts at the screen as various girls dressed in bathing
suits showed their stuff for the judges of the Miss America contest in Atlantic City. The winner, Miss Texas, cried while the
other girls gathered around for her crowning. The sports story
showed Heavyweight Champion Joe Louis taking the oath to join
the Army. It showed him getting his uniform and Army equipment handed to him. All dressed up in his new uniform, he smiled
and saluted at us. A lot of the guys in the Ritz stood up and saluted him back. Hitler was warned by the voice on the screen that,
*Your days are numbered now that the Champ, the Brown Bomber,
is fighting for us!*

The cock crowed again and Pathé News ended. Charlie, the
owner of the Ritz, threw in a Tom and Jerry cartoon and the kids
jumped out of their seats cheering for little Jerry.

Charlie patrolled the aisles like a prison guard in a James
Cagney movie. Instead of carrying a club, he carried a big silver
flashlight, and if you made too much noise, Charlie's flashlight
became a club. When he used it on a noisy kid, you could hear the
bop on the head all through the Ritz. The greater the number of
bops usually meant Charlie's movie wasn't too good, because the
kids would rather fool around and make noise than watch it.

If the movie was especially bad, we started to make up games
to entertain ourselves. It was fun to make noise, but you had to do
it in such a way that another kid would get bopped by Charlie. We
even invented a game called "Charlie." The object was to make
noise and wait for Charlie to get within striking distance. Then,
just before he flashed his light on us, we would put on our best
angelic faces and act interested in the movie. Charlie would
swing his light across our faces like a spotlight on a prison-yard
breakout to find the guilty one. Sometimes, out of frustration,
he'd just grab any guy who looked suspicious and throw him out
of the theater. That sight, the slow walk up the aisle, the convict
followed by the law, always looked like the warden walking

Jimmy Cagney to the Chair in *The Public Enemy*. Charlie never caught on; the more he beat on us, the more trouble we caused.

Mike and I didn't live too far from the Ritz, but I knew from experience that walking home with Mike always came with a price.

A cool autumn wind made the trees beneath the streetlight at the corner of Murray and Dickinson cast their moving shadows on the sidewalk below. Every so often the wind whistled and the leaves danced in the air as they fell to the ground. Dickinson Street is where Mike and I were supposed to go our separate ways.

"Did you see what's playing tomorrow?" Mike reminded me as we approached the corner.

"Roy Rogers and Hopalong Cassidy."

Fist-fights and gunfights and a posse ridin' out after the bad guys highlighted Roy Rogers and Hopalong Cassidy's next stop at the Ritz. Roy and Hoppy's pearl-handled six-shooters spit fire as the bad guys dropped like flies. The coming attractions showed Roy saving a pretty girl and then singing about the Wild West. I liked Roy and Hoppy but my favorite was The Lone Ranger and Tonto and the opening music and the Lone Ranger yelling *Hi-yo* to his horse, Silver, to get him moving fast. Nobody knew what *Kemosabe* meant when Tonto said it, but you knew it meant business. No matter who was playing on Saturday you'd have to get in line early because every kid in the First Ward would be there pushing and yelling to get in for a good seat.

"We better get there early or we'll end up sittin' down front looking straight up again," Mike said. "My neck is killing me."

"Yeah, I know what you mean," I said, knowing the movie talk was coming to an end. I planned to make it quick, but I knew what was coming.

"Mike, I'll see you tomorrow."

"Cappy, wait a minute. Just walk me to the next corner."

I looked up the road and there were no street lights up ahead. I started to turn and said, "No way, Mike. You can get home OK. You don't need me."

"Just up to the next corner. It ain't that far," he begged.

"If I do, that's it. No more."

"That's all."

"I mean it. That's as far as I'm going."

I set out with Mike at a brisker pace, knowing the sooner I got there the sooner I'd be on my way. Along the way, we listened, we watched. Trees swayed and dogs barked as we passed dark houses. People had gotten used to the blackouts during the war, and houses appeared vacant at nighttime.

Even in the cool night air I could feel my shirt getting sticky from sweat. I sensed Mike bumping against me and wondered about him. How could someone so tough and strong enough to beat up any kid around be afraid of the dark? Maybe I could understand it if we saw *Frankenstein* at the Ritz, but *Sergeant York?* I just didn't get it.

We walked by the dark, weed-filled lot that was used for revivals in the summer. We would sneak in the big tent and watch the people singing and praying and clapping to church music. Preachers yelled to God with loud, strong voices. People fell to their knees and followed with, *halleluja, amen, praise the lord, I have sinned, mercy Lord, forgive me, save me, heal me*. It was hot inside that big tent under lights that filled those summer nights. Oh, how I wished for a revival tonight to light my way, but the dark and cool night wind carried my wish away.

"Shove over, for Chris'sakes. Give me some room," I said.

Mike moved over a bit. "Oh, shit," I muttered as I tripped over a bump in the sidewalk.

"What the hell is wrong with you?"

"I can't see shit, Mike."

We paused when we reached the corner of Meadow Street. "OK, this is it," I reminded Mike.

He reached up and grabbed my arm. "Just walk me to the corner of Lydia."

"No way."

"It's not that far," he said, tightening his grip.

"Lydia is where you live."

"I've still got to go around the corner and halfway down Lydia."

"That's only about seven houses from there."

"Yeah, but that's the darkest part."

"If I walk you to Lydia, who walks me back to Dickinson?"

"I'll pay for the movies tomorrow."

"I can sneak in."

"I'll buy the popcorn and candy."

"This is it. I walk you to Lydia and that's all. That's as far as I'll go."

"It's only one more block."

Looking up ahead, darkness was everywhere and the wind howled high in the trees. Mike moved around me to get away from the houses and closer to the open street. On this block, the thickness of large trees could easily hide someone. Our eyes shifted back and forth, from the houses to the trees, as we walked carefully in the blackness of the night.

"Jesus!" I yelled when the wind caught a screen door and slammed it against a front door of a house on our left. Mike grabbed my arms and held me like a shield.

"What the hell are you doing?" I yelled at Mike.

"You yelled and I . . . ."

"Don't grab me. I need to be able to take off. Let go."

Mike's grip eased on my arms and I jerked away.

"I'm gonna head back."

"You promised me you'd go up to the corner."

"Don't ever grab me like that."

"Don't yell."

My legs stretched out to cover more ground. I felt Mike keeping pace as he bumped up against me again. Only a few more steps and we would hit the corner of Lydia Street, where Mike would turn left and I would back track to Dickinson.

I remembered when Mike got a paper route, delivering the morning paper, the *Sun*, and how he would come by the Kelly block early in the morning and throw pebbles at my window to wake me up and beg me to come with him to help deliver his papers. Even though it was daylight, Mike hated being alone. I went a few times, but when Mama found out I didn't get paid, she yelled at Mike to take a powder the next time he showed up at my window. I got up early one morning just to see how Mike was doing on his route and I couldn't believe my eyes when I saw him and his mother delivering the papers together. He was that scared he had to have his mommy with him. And Mike didn't even care if anyone saw them together walking down the street pedaling papers.

"OK, I walked you to Lydia. I'll see you tomorrow and remember, you're buyin' at the Ritz."

"Cap. Wait a minute."

"What?"

"See that tree?"

"What tree?"

"That big one down there."

"I can't see anything down there."

"There's one there, only a little way down. Just walk me to it."

"Are you crazy? If I walk you down there, you're almost home."

"Then just walk me fifty steps. You can count them."

"No I ain't doin' it. That's it."

"Walk me ten cracks in the sidewalk."

"No way. You're nuts. Who's gonna walk me home?"

"OK. Just five cracks. Just five."

I didn't answer. I didn't move.

"Just take three more steps with me, please," Mike pleaded.

I stood with my arms folded on my chest and offered no response. We looked at each other sensing what was about to happen. Without saying a word, Mike and I took a step back from each other. We each took in a deep breath and in a flash, spun in opposite directions and tore our separate ways.

I never looked back. I ran into the middle of the deserted street, my legs pumping as fast as they could. I strained for more air as the wind whipped my face and leaves swept across my path. I knew that Mike was already home and I was angry that I was still on the street in the pitch black, all alone. I wasn't afraid of the dark; I was only afraid of what Mike was afraid of, and he never told me what that was. That scared me more than anything. So, I ran as fast as my legs would carry me.

Up ahead a car turned the corner, its headlights sweeping across Dickinson Street. I raced to catch its light to lead me home, but darkness swallowed the car as it drove off. A mean-sounding dog barked in the darkness. My lungs began to burn as my heart pounded in my chest.

TURNING THE CORNER, I saw a dim light shining outside the Kelly block. I was almost home, but I knew I'd still have to swing open the front door and walk up those dark, creaky stairs.

21.

EXTRA
ROOSEVELT DIES

The President's Death

News that President Roosevelt died stunned the Ward and the city. Clinton Street looked deserted. If you weren't buying a newspaper from a kid on a corner yelling, *Extra! Extra! Read all about it! President dies,* you were glued to a radio or praying at church. Suddenly the outlook for our country turned from upbeat and confident to uncertain and gloomy. With the only president us kids ever knew and loved, it now seemed that we all had more to fear than fear itself. Who would lead us now? Who would carry on the war and win it? Could it go on longer—long enough to take my buddies and me to fight?

All during the war, we crowded around the Philco radio that Uncle Joe bought before he went in the Army to listen when President Roosevelt scheduled one of his Fireside Chats to talk to us. It was always important. We listened to him tell us about how our guys were doing and what we could do to help them. He praised our troops and the people back home buying War Bonds and Victory Stamps to support our guys. On his last Fireside Chat during the war, he finished with, *We are now in the midst of war, not for conquest, not for vengeance, but for a world in which this nation, and all that this nation represents, will be safe for our children. We expect to eliminate the danger from Japan, but it would serve us ill if we accomplished that and found that the rest of the world was dominated by Hitler and Mussolini. We are going to win this war and we are going to win the peace that follows. And in the difficult hours of this day—through dark days that may be next to come—we will know that the vast majority of the members of the human race are on our side. Many of them are fighting with us. All of them are praying for us. For in representing our cause, we represent theirs as well—our hope and their hope for liberty under God.* He sounded strong and it made us all feel safe. Now he was gone—we would not hear his voice again.

Walking out of the ward to the Boys' Club with Bobby Franks, Johnny Cleney, and Joe Parisi we wondered why Mr. DuBock called this meeting with the Victory Volunteers. We were all kind of worried. When we entered the crowded meeting room, Mr. DuBock called roll: *Capalaces—here sir! Cleney—here sir! Franks—here sir! Parisi—here sir!* . . . and on it went. Not one guy missed this meeting.

Mr. DuBock asked us to sit and make ourselves comfortable, while he sat down on top of a small desk. We didn't know how long the meeting would last, it always depended on the number of questions that might come up. Mr. DuBock seemed especially serious and before he started to speak, it got so quiet, you could have heard a pin drop.

"Starting with this meeting I will address you as men," Mr. DuBock said. "Because of what you've all been through during this long and difficult war, you have earned the right to be called *men*. I've watched you from the very beginning—going from boys to young men. You've grown up fast—too fast. Every one of you has worked hard at your assignments. You did your duties without complaining. You've accomplished a lot to help our guys fighting overseas. I'm proud of you all. We're meeting to talk about President Roosevelt—and our new President and Commander and Chief, President Truman. Everyone is sad that we lost President Roosevelt. He was a great man who led and served our country during some of its darkest days. It was a big load and it wore him out. When he was thirty-nine, he got polio. You know what that is." Mr. DuBock said, pausing to look around the room for any questions. None came.

"It's the disease some of our own school kids have gotten. It cripples you and it can also kill you. President Roosevelt lost the use of his legs when he was thirty-nine. Even though he struggled and was in pain, it didn't stop him from holding the highest office in the land. Now, this man of courage is gone. We thank him for his service and pray that he's in heaven," Mr. DuBock said, bowing his head for a moment. "His work is over, now Vice President Truman's begins. He takes over as our new President. We don't know much about him. He's from Missouri. He looks like he's a little man, but as we've learned from some of our Boys' Club members that doesn't mean he's not tough. Truman takes on a big load. We've got to get behind him and help in every way."

"Finally," Mr. DuBock said as he stood up, "I've never been prouder of anything I've done in my life as I have in leading the Victory Volunteers and you men. We're all going to be sad for awhile, but we have to stay strong. We have to keep working till we get all our guys back from the war. When we do, all our sadness will turn to joy. Are there any questions?"

He looked around the room with a look that took everyone in—a look we never saw before—like he wasn't going to see us again.

NO ONE MOVED. No questions came. It was quiet for the longest time.

22.

EXTRA
GERMANY QUITS

EUROPEAN WAR COSTS 269
BROOME LIVES, 520 WOUNDED

**Even Greater Toll in Pacific Grim Outlook
Casualty List Reminder Tempers
Celebration of V.E. Day**

Our Guys Did It

When the news came that the war in Europe was over, excitement spread throughout the Ward and beyond. People waved flags and shouted and danced in the streets. I pounded on an old pot with a wooden spoon while I sat outside on our Kelly block steps as people walked by waving and smiling.

The radio brought news that General Eisenhower had gotten the unconditional surrender of the Germans. The Extra Editions of the newspapers on May 7, 1945, hit the street with big letters that read: NAZIS QUIT.

All around town, people were asking when the men would be coming home. No one seemed to know for sure. Mama thought it would be soon, but our men were still fighting the Japs and nothing was definite. I watched the smile on Grandma's face when she was told the news. It looked like her sons, John, Joe, and Bill, would return home soon. But fighting in spots was still fierce in Germany and it took time for the news of those killed or wounded to be reported. Just a few days before the good news of the German surrender, the *Binghamton Press* printed: *3 More Area Men Give Their Lives, Pvt. James E. Crawford, 23, Infantry U.S. 7th Army; Sgt. Rudolph Stary, 22, U.S. Infantry; and PFC George G. Seeley, 35, Infantry U.S. 5th Army. They were killed in action in Germany and Italy.*

The next day, the newspapers reported that Draft Board 448 ordered 62 area men to report to Syracuse on May 18, for their pre-induction examinations. This was the same day that the *Binghamton Press* reported the death of Private First Class Lawrence Reynolds, 22, American Division, 132nd Infantry, killed in action on Cebu in the Philippines. Men from the Binghamton area were still leaving to fight in the Pacific.

No one knew exactly what to expect when the men got home. They had been gone a long time in a tough war. Captain Marvin M. Alderman, a dentist serving with the medical corps in the Philippines, wrote to his sister Molly and it appeared in the *Binghamton Press* on May 8. In the letter, he wrote about what the people back home should expect when a soldier returns home from the war: *Men returning from overseas have undergone privation, miserable living conditions, bad food and loneliness. . . . He'll be coming home to the things he has been dreaming about for months. For awhile he will be in a dream—he will be satisfied to merely sit in a room with a real chair and furniture. . . . He doesn't want to see people or talk—he wants to absorb the full pleasure of his return, perhaps in silence, perhaps by talking, perhaps by doing nothing but sitting. I would be very much surprised if I act any differently from the ways I have set down here in this letter.*

That night I found an unused V-Mail letter, and sat down and wrote Uncle Bill a letter. There wasn't a lot of space to write on it, so you couldn't say a whole lot. I didn't know exactly where he was, but I knew from his last letter home he was somewhere in Germany. In the letter, I told Uncle Bill that everyone was happy about beating the Nazis. But when the news hit that President Roosevelt had died on April 12, it seemed as if we lost the war. The flags flew at half-staff and people cried. Everyone talked about his great leadership and now he was gone. I never saw so many sad faces and people wiping their eyes for days and weeks. I heard people say they were scared without him. Nobody seemed to know the new President, Harry S Truman. In the newspapers he looked like a tiny guy with thick glasses. He always wore a bow-tie. He looked like a sissy, not tough and strong like FDR.

I SEALED THE letter, put a stamp on it and gave it to Mr. Rhodes, our mail-man. I didn't know if Uncle Bill would ever get it. But I hoped he would.

23.

BINGHAMTON PRESS   JUNE 23, 1945

MISSING SINCE BATAAN, SOLDIER LISTED AS KILLED; ANOTHER DIES IN CAMP; 2 OKINAWA CASUALTIES

5 Area Men Are on Day's List; Marine, Sailor Are Wounded

The Wooden Box

Men began coming home from the European Theater, but here at home no one ever knew for sure when any of Grandma's sons, my uncles, the Vrabel boys, would be among those arriving. It was tough getting any news. All you could do is wait, hope, and worry . . . about things . . . like pigeons.

What is there to like about pigeons? They make noise, they poop everywhere, sometimes even on your shoulder, when you least expect it. They're always hanging around for a crumb to hit the ground. You can't eat them. So, what's to like? None of this mattered to my brother, Richie. In his eyes they were beautiful and he loved them.

The pigeon-cooing drove everyone nuts and even though Richie knew we didn't like them, he didn't care. His pigeons came first. On the outside porch, off Grandma's kitchen, Richie kept his pigeons in a large wooden storage bin. He didn't have one or two, he had a flock. And every chance he had, he was out searching for more to add to his pigeon empire.

If Richie had been gone too long, Mama always sent me out to find him. I usually started my search in the abandoned warehouses down by the railroad tracks where he liked to crawl inside, climb to the highest points and search for pigeons. Whenever I spotted him walking on a narrow beam, I was always careful not to scare him for fear he might fall.

"Richie!" My voice echoed inside the empty shell of one of the buildings. He didn't answer even though I could hear him up there. "Richie, it's time to go home. Mama wants you home right now."

Once again, no answer. "Richie, you better get down here or you're gonna get it."

Richie peeked around a wooden post and looked down at me. He must have been a hundred feet in the air. "Shut up you jerk . . . you're scaring the pigeons!"

"Then get your ass down here, right now," I yelled back.

"What do you want?"

"You've gotta come home."

"I'm not ready yet."

"You're gonna get your ass kicked if you don't get down."

"Yeah, by who, you?"

"No, by Mama."

"Yeah, I'm scared."

"Let's go, I don't have all day."

"Just go. Leave me alone."

"You know I can't do that. C'mon. C'mon home. You can do this tomorrow."

"No I can't. I'm doin' it now."

"Are you gonna come down or do I have to come up and get you?"

"C'mon, just try and you'll fall flat on your ass."

"Hey, Rich, how did you climb up there?"

"Wouldn't you like to know."

"C'mon, there aren't even any pigeons up there."

"Oh, no? How's this?"

Richie banged the roof with something and the loud sound that followed suddenly set off flapping wings exploding as hundreds of pigeons scattered to new perches.

"Are you crazy?" I yelled up at Richie.

"Yeah, what are you gonna do about it?"

"I'm gonna kill you when I get my hands on you. Now tell me how you got up there."

Richie didn't answer. A moment passed and I could see and hear him begin to move.

"I'm coming down. But you promise you won't hit me?"

"Yeah, I promise. Be careful coming down."

I never knew what Richie would get into and no matter how innocent it seemed, I never rested easy. Like the time I swiped some rifle shells from Sears Roebuck and I thought I hid them real good, until early one Saturday morning I heard a gun-shot ring outside our window that woke me up. The next thing I knew Richie rushed into the apartment holding his dirty T-shirt against his stomach. Blood was on it. He cried as he tried to tell me he was banging on one of the bullets with a rock on the street outside and it went off and a small piece of the bullet hit him in the stomach. He begged me to help him and not tell Mama. I got a little Vaseline and a bandage and some tape from the bathroom, and after cleaning up the blood around his stomach I put the Vaseline on the cut and taped the bandage down on top of it. It stopped both the bleeding and Richie's crying. I warned him never to fool around again with bullets. He was so scared; I think it was the only time he ever really listened to me. But I still had to keep a close eye on him.

Now here he was crawling down a rickety old building like a

monkey. He was carrying a burlap bag in one hand and holding on to the beams with the other. In short time he was on the ground, heading out of the semi-darkness toward me.

"Why do you come here? Do you want to kill yourself?" I asked, shielding my eyes as we walked into the bright sunlight from the abandoned building.

"For the birds. For the birds."

"It's dangerous to be in those buildings. Those freakin' birds aren't worth it."

"You don't know what you're talkin' about."

"Oh, yeah, what's in that bag?"

"A bird."

"A bird? Show me."

Richie stopped and loosened his grip on the bag and reached his arm deep inside, swirling it around until he located what he wanted. He pulled out a newborn pigeon and held it toward me.

"You went all the way up there for that?"

"It's a beautiful baby."

"It looks like a naked scarecrow. It's all skinny and stupid-looking."

"That's what baby pigeons look like when they're young, and then they grow into beauties."

I took a closer look at the wrinkled, featherless bird snuggled in Richie's hand and said, "Yeah, if you say so."

Richie thought I didn't know anything about his pigeons. I pretended I wasn't paying attention, but I had listened to him tell his friends about his birds when they came over to see them, and I learned about the different ones he had—the Rollers that flipped over and over when they flew; and the Tumblers that did back flips when they flew; the Homing pigeons that he let fly away and they'd come right back, and the Trumpeters with their big fantails and puffy chests and big hoods on their heads.

Richie didn't have the money to buy the corn seed he fed them, so I wondered how he was doing all this. He worked really hard to find the pigeons. He went way up inside old abandoned buildings, climbing and crawling his way under the roofs where pigeons built their nests. In his hunt for pigeons, he was guided only by shafts of light coming through broken windows. Then he'd snatch little babies away without ever caring about the baby pigeons' mothers and fathers. If Richie wanted something, he got it, and you were smart if you didn't get in his way.

Sitting on the steps that led to the street outside our kitchen, I watched Mr. Rhodes, our mailman, go on his way after he made his delivery to the Kelly block. After checking the mailbox, I didn't want to tell Grandma that nothing came today from her boys. She hadn't heard from them in a long time and this would be another day without any news of when they would be coming home from Germany now that the war there was over.

The summer of 1945 was ending, and with the return to school coming, I didn't want to waste the last few days of this summer, especially this day with its beautiful blue sky and hot sun. But there was no sign of the gang anywhere, so I sat on the steps listening to the cooing of Richie's pigeons while he fed them. I was thinking that if one of the guys didn't show up soon, maybe I'd take Grandma's dog, Pudgy, to the river where she loved to swim and get a bath.

Before long, a big brown truck stopped on the street in front of our steps. A man got out and yelled up at me, "Is there a Vrabel, Elizabeth Vrabel, living here?"

"Yeah," I yelled down. "She's my Grandma."

"Got a package for her."

I ran down the steps with Richie close behind. We stood on the side of the truck as the man opened the back doors and reached in and dragged out a big wooden box and laid it down on the sidewalk. Richie and I saw Grandma's name and address written on it, printed in big letters in dark ink. In the corner was Uncle John's name, but with no real address other than the way it was on all his letters.

"Just take it?" I asked the driver.

"Yep, it's your Grandma's."

Richie and I each grabbed a side of the box and tried to lift it. It was heavy and its thick solid wood made it hard to grip. We set it down and decided to wait for the truck to pull away.

"You boys got that? It's really heavy," the driver said.

"No problem," I answered. "We got it."

Richie and I maneuvered around the box to figure out the best way to grab it. We paused for a minute and watched the brown truck jerk onto the road and go off down the street.

"Hold on tight. You go first and I'll lift from the back," I said. Together we lifted the big wooden box and took it up the steps. Halfway up I had to set my end down. My arms hurt. Then we started up again, straining to move the box without dropping it. As soon as Richie made it onto the porch, I pushed with all my might to get my end up onto it. Then we dragged it back across the wooden planks of the porch floor to the door outside Grandma's kitchen. Even though she was blind now, we turned the box so Grandma's name faced the door.

Ma. Ma. Te mash box, we yelled into her ear as she lay in her bed. We knew a little Slovak, but not the word for box.

Shtow? she asked.

Box, Ma. Box. Packagekoo, from Johnitchkoo.

She smiled and pushed herself up and we took her hands and walked her from her bedroom through the kitchen to the back door. We pulled her arms down toward the box, and when her hand touched it, we looked at her and saw how happy she was.

We asked Grandma if we could open it and she nodded her head, so after we took her back to bed, we looked for anything to open the box that was nailed shut. We tried a shovel, a screwdriver, anything we could find but we couldn't even budge the lid.

I ran next door to Mr. Ruggerio, our neighbor, and asked him if he had a hammer I could borrow. He had a nice big hammer and he asked me to be sure to bring it back.

Now I had a real tool. I tried to wedge the claws of the hammer into the small line that ran the length of the front of the box, and tried to jerk it up and pry the lid open. It was difficult getting the hammer claws inside where the top was nailed, so I began to raise the hammer and strike the claws at the opening, hoping that one swing would hit the mark and lodge the hammer claws deep into the wood and wedge it open a bit. The box was nailed so tight into the thick wood that none of my tries hit the mark. Richie told me to keep going, but my arm was getting tired. I told Richie to back up and I stood on top of the box and raised the hammer high with both hands and slammed the claws against the wood. On one swing I felt the hammer claws stick and from the look on Richie's face, I knew I had finally sunk the claws into the lid.

Richie and I took turns prying the top off. He had freed one end and it was my turn again to work the other. Little by little, the lid came up and soon the nails holding it could be seen. Long and thick, they were set deep into the wood. We now knew how much farther we had to go to get the lid off.

With one final pull, the front of the lid was free. Richie and I got our hands under the lid, making sure we gripped between the nails and lifted as hard as we could. As the nails loosened, the wood made a sound like a baby squealing and we pushed all the harder. The lid was finally sitting up now for us to get to see what was inside.

Richie and I dropped to our knees in front of the box. Our eyes opened wide as we stared inside. Richie reached in and grabbed a dark steel combat helmet with a Nazi ensignia on it. I picked up the beautiful handle of a knife with a Nazi Swastika on it and pulled it out of its holder. The blade was polished. Carved into the shiny silver blade was *Der Deutschland*. Richie pulled out a pair of Nazi soldier's boots. He took his sneakers off and put them on. I pulled out a Nazi flag that was so big, Richie and I couldn't hold it up. There was a big red-and-black Swastika on it. We threw it on the storage bin with the pigeons inside and they began cooing. Richie pulled out more knives, each one spotless and official-looking. I went to the bottom and ran my hand over what seemed like a half-dozen pistols. I pulled one out and Richie and I looked at a real Nazi pistol. We rubbed our hands over the pearl-like handles and polished steel. *Wait till Tootsie and the guys see this!*

You couldn't help but wonder what happened to the Nazis who had this stuff and how Uncle John got it. Maybe he had killed them or took them prisoners or just stole it. If that's what it took, we didn't care. Wherever or however Uncle John got this stuff, this was real and now it was ours.

Richie and I continued to empty the wooden box and with each new piece we pulled out we were amazed. We couldn't wait to tell Mama and sis and our aunts. We knew we'd have to wait for Mama to tell Grandma in Slovak what her son, John, had sent her.

This box was like a pirate's treasure-chest full of shiny and sparkling loot and, like fellow pirates, we'd hide this box and everything in it and not tell anyone about it. And when it was safe, we'd take it out, every day, and look at it and touch all the things inside while knowing the other kids in the neighborhood were playing with plastic guns and knives and rifles from Philly Sales.

RICHIE AND I had to really be careful with Uncle John's stash. The Kelly block was crawling with thieves.

24.

MORE SOUTHERN TIER FIGHTING MEN AMONG 10,000 YANKS DUE TO REACH THEIR HOME SOIL TODAY

8,000 of Veterans Salute Statue of Liberty at N.Y.C.

We Gotta Help Those Guys

I remember how noisy it was and then how quiet it got when some of the factory workers boosted me onto a table and I stared at the big crowd waiting for me to speak. Nobody knew how bad my legs were shaking or how fast my heart was pounding or how scared I was or that I didn't want to be there. None of that mattered. This is something I had to do, because Charles R. Messier, the Executive Director of the Boys' Club, gave my name to the Community Chest Speaker's Bureau. Mr. William W. Driver, Chairman of the Community Chest Industrial Division, told me I'd be going around to the different factories in Binghamton to talk to the workers about giving to the annual Chest Drive. I was to tell them especially how much the money helped our Boys' Club.

There were a lot of factories doing war work in and around Binghamton. Endicott Johnson Shoe Company made combat boots for the Army. Link Aviation built flight simulators to train pilots. H&R Manufacturing made machine-gun coolers. The Atwood Tent & Awning Company made tents and ponchos for the soldiers. IBM made rifles. And here, at Drybak's, workers sewed around-the-clock to make uniforms for our troops.

I stood in front of the workers of Drybak's Manufacturing Company wearing a new white shirt, necktie, and pants with suspenders that Mama bought me at Fowler's Department store on Court Street. Mama worked hard on her job at the factory, but she never had enough money to pay all the bills. It didn't matter to her how broke she was. She would use any credit she could put her hands on to make her kids look good if we were out in public. And if the stores told Mama her credit was all used up, she would fight, argue, and beg until she got what she wanted for us.

Hundreds of workers packed tightly around hundreds of sewing machines scattered on the large main floor of the factory. Most workers were women whose sons, brothers, husbands, and even some fathers were fighting overseas. I was scared to speak in front of total strangers. It was hard for me even to look at the people there. Who was I to talk to them about sacrifice and support?

Before coming up, Mr. Edwin V. Chandler from the Community Chest picked up a microphone and told the crowd that my father was killed in the war. While he was speaking, I could sense all those eyes on me and my face turned hot. I felt on the spot. It was like the time I got caught stealing at Kresge's Five & Ten Cent Store, and the manager took me into the back room and said he was going to call the cops and tell my mother. When I faked crying, he gave me a break. That wouldn't work here.

Just as I was about to squeeze the first word out of my dry and tight throat, Mr. Chandler added, *You might want to know Ronald recently received the Kate Smith Award for Community Service*

*for his work with the Boys' Club's Victory Volunteers. He collect-
ed the most fat for the war effort. It's used to make ammunition.
So, if Ronald looks familiar to you, he may have knocked on your
door when he was out there collecting.*

The crowd applauded and my face turned red hot and then it
got real quiet. Mr. Chandler handed me the microphone and
smiled.

I looked out at the crowd and saw women standing under big
lights shining down from the ceiling. Others stood in the shadows. Wearing their work aprons, they looked tired and serious. I
could feel the sweat rolling down my back and the microphone
shaking in my hand.

"Ah . . . thanks a lot . . . ah, for letting me speak to you."

"Speak up a little louder!"

"Uh, uh, thanks a lot for letting me uh . . . speak to you," I
repeated into the microphone, pausing a second to see if anyone
was about to yell out again. "I'm in the fifth grade at Daniel S.
Dickinson Junior High School and I'm a member of the Boys'
Club. I'm proud to say I'm in the Victory Volunteers . . . maybe
you've seen us in the parades and other stuff. Anyway, we gotta
help our guys over there. They're fightin' for us and they want to
win this war for us. If you give to the Community Chest, it'll help
all the boys at the Boys' Club help support our troops by doin'
what we can. Remember, we gotta help those guys. From all the
guys at the Boys' Club, thanks a lot for your help."

No sooner had I finished when I heard a few hands clap and
then others joined in and it got louder. My knees shook as I
stepped off the stage and stood next to the table when Mr. Driver,
the chairman of the Community Chest, took the microphone and
got up to speak. He spoke like President Roosevelt, his voice
echoing around the room clear and strong.

"We have much to be thankful for. Our men are still fighting
a war in the Pacific and are winning. All of us in this room have
someone or know someone who is in uniform serving our coun-

try. Some have been wounded. Some have paid the ultimate price. It's been work like yours here in this factory that has helped to keep our fighting men fit for the struggle. It's your love and your support that has let our men in foxholes and jungles and ships around the world know how much you care. We know times are tough. We know how hard it is to make ends meet. But please, for the sake of our fighting men, give to this year's annual Chest Drive. For when you do, you'll be helping young people like Ronald here at the Boys' Club grow up to be decent citizens. Remember, the boys at the Club belong to our service men abroad. They're the sons, brothers, and nephews of our fighting men. And when you help these kids, you help those fighting for them. And when this terrible war is over, our men will come home knowing we took good care of their kids. You'll be receiving information in your paycheck on how you can give. Please help, and may God bless you and may God Bless America."

Everyone clapped and then someone shouted, *Let's get back to work!* And the hum of the sewing machines began to sing around the room. A man from the factory wearing a shirt and tie grabbed my arm and asked me to come with him to his office. The men from the Speaker's Bureau said it was OK. I followed him as the noise of the machines reached a dull roar. Every now and then one of the sewing women stopped long enough to give me a smile as we passed by rows and rows of workers hunched over their machines.

There were two women in aprons waiting for us as we entered the office. The man closed the door, shutting out some of the noise of the factory.

"Ronald, the workers and I would like to give you a gift for speaking to us today. Have you ever heard of the "Ike Jacket?"

"No, sir, I haven't."

"Well, this is an Army jacket that was specially made for General Dwight D. Eisenhower, the top general in the Army. I think he's got four stars, maybe five. Anyway, they call General

Eisenhower, *Ike,* and the jacket was named *The Ike Jacket.* Here's a picture of him wearing it. Looks pretty nice on him, doesn't it, Ronald?"

"Yeah, it sure does."

"Well, we make that jacket here and we're going to make one for you. What do you think of that?"

"Thank you very much."

"The ladies are going to measure you now and then we're going to make the jacket exactly to your size. Go ahead, girls."

"Just stand perfectly still," one of the women said as she stretched a cloth measuring tape from my shoulder to my wrist and shouted out numbers that another woman wrote down on a piece of paper. Then the tape went around my chest, then around my waist and finally down my back from the bottom of my neck to my waist.

"That wasn't so bad now was it, Ronald?" the man said after the last number was written down and the worker had rolled the cloth tape up and put it in her apron.

I nodded.

"Well, I'll take you back to the people who brought you," the man said. "After we make this jacket, we're going to send it to you. It'll take a day or two. This is a gift from us. We hope you like it."

"Thank you," I said just before we walked back through the factory with the women pushing brown cloth through their sewing machines, working like machines themselves.

That noise of Drybak's Factory never left my head for the next two days, and on the third day a package came to Dickinson Street for me. I took it into my bedroom and opened it. Inside was the Ike Jacket from the Drybak workers. I took it out and slipped it on. I buttoned up the front and then the sleeves. Then I pulled the beltlike tab and buttoned it at the waist. It fit good and snug. I went to the bathroom and looked at myself in the little mirror on the wall. I threw my shoulders back and stuck my chest out. There

I was in a brown wool Ike Jacket. It fit great, but I knew wearing it outside was a problem. Too many kids would think I was showing off and would say, *Who the hell does he think he is wearing an Ike Jacket?*

The jacket was too beautiful to hang on a hook and too hot to wear inside our apartment. So, I walked slowly out of the Kelly block looking like a little general. I tried not to look like a big shot and most of the kids seemed to accept me wearing it. But it didn't take long for "war" to break out. Joey Combs, a kid from the block, wanted to try the Ike Jacket on. When I refused, he grabbed it and popped a couple of buttons off.

A CROWD OF kids gathered as we fought in the dirt near the street and then onto the vacant lot next to the Kelly block. Joey fought hard, but you don't mess with Ike. When it ended, there wasn't much left of the jacket; but as bad as it looked, it still looked a lot better than Joey.

25.

BINGHAMTON PRESS   AUGUST 8, 1945

HIROSHIMA IS NO MORE

150,000 ARE "SEARED TO DEATH," CORPSES "TOO MANY TO COUNT"

Scary Times

J APS ADMIT AND U.S. PICTURES SHOW: HIROSHIMA IS NO MORE the headline read on August 8 in the *Binghamton Press*. As soon as the news hit, everyone was talking about the big bomb. The way people talked, it was like something out of a Purple Monster serial at the Star Theatre, except that for 150,000 Japs there was no escape from death in this episode.

The idea of an Atom Bomb didn't seem real until we saw it on the Movietone Newsreel at the Ritz. With our own eyes we saw the big ball rise into the sky. It still didn't seem real, but when they showed the ground flattened and only a few people left walking around in a daze, it was real enough. Nobody knew what it all meant or where this secret weapon had even come from, but we were all happy it was our bomb.

The newsreels also showed the Nazi concentration camps with U.S. and British troops freeing prisoners whose faces were like masks with skin stretched tightly over bulging bones. Their eyes seemed dead. Around the camps, dead naked bodies were stacked like white candles in trucks. Others were stacked in piles like mountains next to huge holes filled with more dead people. Death seemed everywhere. It was from the newsreels where we first heard of Dachau, Bergen-Belsen, Auschwitz, and others. Sitting silently in the dark in the Ritz, we first heard about gas-chambers, ovens, and the Jews. I didn't understand it all. Izzy Lipshutz, the grocery-man, and Jacob Eisenberg, the pharmacist, and Mr. Levine, the junk-man, and Bernie Shapiro, my funny friend, were Jews.

WHAT WAS WRONG with being Jewish?

26.

BINGHAMTON SUN   AUGUST 9, 1945

SECOND ATOM-BOMB HITS NAGASAKI

CITY PERISHES IN HOLOCAUST OF ATOM BLAST

Party Line

A second atomic bomb dropped by the U.S. destroyed the Japanese city of Nagasaki, killing 40,000 people and injuring thousands more, the newspaper reported on August 9. Everywhere you went, people were buzzing about this new weapon. All that people knew was just one of these bombs could kill lots of people. Nobody said much about the deaths. Nobody seemed to care. People were just happy it was them and not our guys who got it.

Now with all this atom-bomb news and with our guys celebrating in Berlin, every time you picked up the phone to make a call, some other party was already using the line. It was always tough using the phone next door at Grandma's because you could never get a free line to call out. This went on all hours of the day and night. No longer was it easy to get a free line to call the drugstore and ask, *Do you have Sir Walter Raleigh in the can?* And when the clerk answered, *Yes,* we'd shout, *Let him out—he can't breathe in there!* and hang up. We missed calling up girls and listening to them say, *Hello? Hello? Hello?* as we replied with dead silence. We couldn't call school pretending to be a girl to report that, *Ronald is sick and he won't be at school today.*

Sooner or later everyone in the Kelly block knew everybody else's business, thanks to the party line. It was a gold mine for finding out what your neighbors were up to. The party line was the cheapest service you could get, but it meant you had to share the same phone line with others. So when you made a call, someone else in the block might already be on the line and you'd have to hang up—or would you?

I only stayed on the line if what I listened to sounded interesting—like the time I heard a man with a strange-sounding voice telling Helen Searles, a beautiful woman who lived upstairs next to the Pudiak's, that he loved her. I noticed how the two of them sounded. They spoke softly about love. They teased each other and laughed and giggled at the things they said, like little kids. He said something in French to Helen and told her it meant: *I love you very much.* He said, *Someday I'd like to be in Paris with you.* Hearing this, I figured he must be one of the vets who just got home.

Helen and her boyfriend talked about meeting tonight at the George F. Pavilion where the big bands were coming back more frequently now that the war was turning in our favor. Every Friday and Saturday night, women put on their best clothes and their dancing shoes, perfumed themselves, and polished their fingers and toes. Then they danced into the early morning hours with the few men home from the war who bathed with Lux Soap and shaved close and splashed Mennen After-Shave on their faces and put Brylcream on their hair, and wore new suits with pegged pants they bought at Mo Garber's cheap clothing store on Clinton Street. The bands played swing and couples jitterbugged, and when Harry James played "You Made Me Love You" on his trumpet, men and women squeezed tightly against each other and moved slowly as if in a dream.

I soon got in the habit of picking up the phone carefully before I made a call. That way, if someone was on the party line, I could hang up. Most calls were short since you never knew if anyone was listening or sometimes, if you stayed on too long, someone might get on the party line and yell, *Stop hogging the line!* or *Get off so somebody else can make a call!*

If you wanted to keep something secret, you never said it over the telephone. So, when Mike Ganisin called and said to "come over," he had "something to tell me," I knew it was important so I rushed right over.

"I'm having a party Friday night at my house. Can you come?" Mike asked me.

"Yeah. I guess. What's it for?"

"Just for fun. My sister, Ann, thought it would be a good idea to start having parties and inviting people over to the house."

"Oh. Yeah, that's good."

"There're gonna be some girls, too."

"Girls? Real girls?"

"Yeah, real girls, stupid."

"Who's coming?"

"You know, the regular gang."

"I mean the girls."

"A few from Dickinson. Maybe one or two from Saint Cyril's."

"That's good. Which ones?"

"I don't know yet who's going to come. Just show up Friday night around seven and then we'll all know."

Walking home from Mike's, I came to realize I'd be going to my first party ever. And there would be girls there. I'd have to wear my best clothes if they were washed. If I needed anything special, I'd have to go to Clinton Street and grab something.

Friday night came and I took my Saturday-night bath one

night early to remove a week's worth of First Ward and Kelly block dirt. I scrubbed myself with a bar of scratchy Lava Soap, and the dirt peeled off me until the bath water was as muddy as the river after a hard rain.

On the way to Mike's, I could see the lights from his house all the way from the corner of Murray Street. In the distance, I saw people going into the house from the street. The closer I got, the louder the noise inside sounded. Even though I'd know almost everyone there, I was feeling nervous.

I opened the screen door on the porch and walked in to see all my buddies huddled together on one side of the room. On the other side were four girls talking to each other. Mike's sister, Ann, waved to me and said, "Come on in, Ronnie, and join the party." I rushed to my buddies, Mike, Tootsie, Peewee, and Yonkie. Vic and Jug-bug couldn't make it. We all talked to each other while keeping a steady eye on the girls. They were all in dresses. They had their hair fixed up and were wearing real lipstick. Donna Richardson, Patty Hrib, Barbara Grabosky from Dickinson, and Betty Ann Bederka from Saint Cyril's looked a lot more grown up than I remembered.

There was lots to eat and drink and the guys all talked a lot and looked at the girls, but things started to quiet down. That's when Mike's sister, Ann, suggested we play Spin-the-Bottle. Since none of us had ever played it before, Ann showed us how. We all sat down and formed a circle and Ann put the girls in different spots between the boys. She put an empty soda bottle on the floor and spun it. Whoever the bottle pointed to when it stopped had to kiss the person who had spun the bottle. The kiss took place in a small dark room off the living room where no one could see what was going on.

All four of the girls in the circle were pretty. I couldn't believe we were all sitting in a circle ready to spin the bottle. Ann let Mike go first and when he spun the bottle, we all yelled for Mike. The bottle stopped in front of Barbara Grabosky, and the two of them stood up and left for the kissing room. Everyone waited to see what they would look like when they came out. Quickly they came back into the room wearing red faces. We all let out a cheer.

When my turn came, it stopped on Tootsie and I reached over and gave him a kiss on the head. He pushed me away and I had to spin again. This time it slowed and stopped in front of Betty Ann Bederka. Everyone yelled as we stood up and walked out of sight. In the dimly lit kissing room, I realized I had never kissed a girl before. Not only did I not know what to do, but I really didn't know what Betty was going to do. We could hear everyone in the room buzzing while we slowly stepped toward each other. I watched Betty lean toward me and I closed my eyes. Her warm, soft lips touched mine. I could feel waves of her warm, soft breath hitting my cheek. The taste of her lipstick stuck in my mind. I never dreamed girls tasted this good. Out of all the games I learned growing up in the Ward, Spin-the-Bottle was now my favorite. The bottle spun all night and everyone got their share of kisses.

Ann did her best to show us guys how to be gentlemen. She also wanted us to think beyond the First Ward and about all there was to growing up. Soon, Mike had us going to new places and trying new things—even outside the Ward.

The YWCA on the corner of Exchange and Hawley behind the Courthouse began to hold free dances on Saturday nights for younger kids like us. We scrubbed ourselves clean and combed our hair and put on a shirt and pants. Then we shined our shoes and marched off to the Y to try to meet girls from all over Binghamton, not just the First Ward.

None of us knew how to dance too well. My sister Fran tried to teach me how to Jitterbug and slow dance. She played "Caldonia" by Louis Jordan and His Tympany Five on a little record-player she borrowed, but it seemed stupid dancing with your sister. Even though she and Mama were great dancers, I had a hard time getting my feet to do what they were supposed to do.

I'd do my best and hoped I wouldn't step on a girl's toes or look too stupid.

When we got to the Y, we always stayed in the back and just looked to see who was there. The first thing you noticed was a smell that seemed to be everywhere. The girls wore perfume and lipstick and rouge and it floated through the air.

Music came from a 45-rpm record-player through speakers on the small stage at one end of a large dimly lit room. The windows were open on warm nights, and even though a large fan whirled near the stage, the handkerchiefs stuffed in our back pockets would be put to regular use wiping the sweat off our faces. There were few girls there from Dickinson. Most were from other parts of the city. There were also a lot of guys from different parts of the city. Some I knew from the Boys' Club, but there were a lot of others I didn't know.

My eyes settled on one or two girls standing just off the dance floor. It was always scary to ask a girl to dance. The worst thing was to spot someone and then head out across the floor to ask for a dance, only to have her shake her head, *No, thank you.* Worse yet was the walk back to your friends. Everyone watched to see which girls might accept a dance and those who didn't. If a girl did accept a dance, you checked to see what kind of guy she seemed to like. We soon learned that it was always a big gamble asking any girl to dance. You just could never figure out what a girl would do. Some girls just seemed satisfied to dance with their girlfriends, especially the Jitterbug. One thing for sure, guys who were good dancers never got turned down.

As the music played and the evening went on, we all made our mental notes . . . who was there . . . who would dance . . . who wouldn't. And if they turned you down, what did the guy look like that you saw her dance with and how did you compare with him in looks and clothes? You tried to have courage and ask a girl who looked good to you, but the fear of rejection prevented your legs from taking that first step. Sometimes I'd try to get Mike or

Tootsie or Peewee to ask a girl to dance to test the waters. If they got turned away, then it saved me from making a mistake. I spent a lot of good dance time just looking.

I waited for a slow dance and finally got the nerve to go over and ask this girl for a dance. I had watched her dancing with a lot of different guys. Although I was nervous enough to feel my knees shaking, I made the scary walk across the floor and when I asked her to dance, she stood up and smiled at me. We stepped onto the floor and I held her the way Fran had taught me.

I put my right arm around her back and when she slid her hand into mine, it felt soft and warm. I didn't talk or even look at her as we danced at arms-length to "Candy" by Jo Stafford. I kept trying not to make a mistake. Little by little, we drifted closer to each other. Soon I could feel her hair hitting my face and when our cheeks touched, I could smell the sweetness of perfume mixed with her sweat. Her warm body moved against me and I began to sweat. I was hoping the song would end before I drenched her. When it did, we peeled our faces away from each other and I said thanks as I turned and pulled my handkerchief from my pocket and sponged off my face now dripping with sweat.

The dances always ended at eleven, with Glenn Miller's "Moonlight Serenade" the last song. This was the last chance to get, if you finally had the nerve, that final dance with the one you had your eye on all night.

If you didn't move fast enough she'd be gone, dancing the last dance, cheek-to-cheek, with someone else. Sometimes I wouldn't even try to dance the last dance. If for some reason a girl declined, I didn't want to go home with that on my mind. I'd rather sit it out and think about next week's dance and what my chances would be to dance with the one I had my eye on all night. She was the one who danced almost every dance with a different guy and her wet white dress was clinging to her tiny waist. I'll never forget when she passed by me, how her face glowed from all the dancing. And how the air around her reminded me of the smell of a Lamb's ice-cream sundae with syrup all over it. It didn't take long to learn that the most popular girls were the ones wearing the soaked dresses.

WE OFTEN WAITED outside the Y afterward to watch the girls leave and see if they would throw us a look. When the last one left and the rumble of their girlish talk and laughter faded, we started our walk back to the First Ward in the night air. As long as we got in one dance, the night wasn't a flop. It was always good when all the guys who came together got to go home talking about at least that one dance they got and how warm and soft girls were, and how clean and how sweet the air around them smelled.

27.

U.S. FORCES LINK UP NEAR YOKAHAMA

HOBBIE'S CAPTIVITY 150 DAYS OF JAP BRUTALITY AND TORTURE

Bamboo Rods Used to Flog Rescued Flier

The Magic Dice

We never knew when it was coming, we just knew it would.

The procession of brightly painted trucks moved slowly through town casting a magic spell on all in its path. Exciting yet scary, it always came at just the right time.

Kids chased after the colorful caravan, screaming at and taunting the strange-looking people inside. Old folks stretched from porch chairs to get a better look. Teenage girls broke into laughter as the weird men in the trucks waved at them with tattooed arms. A truck with a huge picture of a smiling woman with little clothing caught the eyes of the older boys. Her gloved arms extended skyward toward the three-foot letters of her fancy French name. Others on the sidewalk pointed to a truck going by with the picture of a figure who was half-man and half-fish, while others cringed at the sight of a passing truck with the image of a woman whose baby was born attached to her stomach, and according to the sign on the truck, *It's still there, alive, and well!* Veterans who had returned from the war watched the passing parade through smoke-stained windows in the beer joints along the route.

When the war started, the carnivals ended. During the war years, our town was dark and quiet. It seemed air-raid-drill sirens wailed night and day, testing city plans to get people off the streets and into shelters. Sometimes at night, flying aircraft would simulate an enemy attack by dropping bags of flour onto houses and buildings, and in the morning people would check to see if they were "hit" by a "flour bomb." If you owned a radio, it was turned so low that people used to gather around on the floor listening intently to find out what was going on in the war. Then to scare their worries away they tuned to shows like *The Shadow, Inner Sanctum,* and *Lux Theatre* or for laughs they tuned in *The Goldbergs, Amos 'n' Andy* and *The Jack Benny Show.* Grandma listened to polka music on a small radio and was happy to hear a Slovak-speaking announcer introducing the songs and talking about events in the Slovak community. Now with the war almost over, the carnivals were back in business and small towns all over upstate New York were returning to normal.

While it lifted the spirits of many, there were those who saw the carnival as trouble-on-wheels. For the next two weeks, mothers would keep a close eye on their sons and daughters' comings and goings. Kids would be on the hunt for money for the carnival. Money left for the milkman on back porches would have to be watched. The clerks at Woolworth's Five and Dime and the American Store kept a sharp lookout for young people and special merchandise. Cigarettes could be swiped and traded to carny workers for free rides and free shows. When the carnival was in town, the lines of people waiting to make confession at Saint

Cyril's Church got longer as did the time people stayed behind the closed doors of the confessional.

When the James E. Strates Carnival came to town, the show always set up on the same spot. It was away from the center of town on a big vacant lot called Stow Flats on State Street next to the city dump. The carnival had to be far enough away where there was room to set up, yet close enough for folks without cars to walk to. There was plenty of room at Stow Flats to handle the carnival's huge fleet of trucks and equipment.

When the carnival came to town, my pals and I liked to go out early to watch them setting up. Carny workers never stopped from early morning till late at night. Most of them were young; others looked as if they might have been in the war. They smoked Camels and swigged Genessee Beer, and hardly spoke to each other when they worked. They looked like a band of cut-throat pirates, the kind you'd see in an Errol Flynn movie. The carnys warmed up some if a young girl happened to pass by. They'd smile awkwardly, trying to hide their bad teeth. Girls were warned to stay away from them.

The carny people reminded us of the bullies we had in town who liked to hurt people and then laugh at them when they cried. We kept our distance from the carny workers. Still, we liked to watch them take a vacant piece of land and turn it, piece by piece, into a magical city.

Opening night of the carnival always drew a big turnout. But you learned quickly that the best time to go was the last night before the carnival left town. On the last night, the carnys put on *special* shows, on the side, with some of their women if people put up the money to see them.

Richie got wind of my plan early. He saw me making daily runs to the grocery store, returning deposit bottles for nickels and pennies. He caught me hoarding bottles and one day he saw me stuffing them on my body to take to the store. Because I couldn't find a paper bag or box to put them in, I stuffed deposit bottles inside my shirt, down my pants-legs, in my pockets, under my armpits, and in my folded arms. I even jammed my fingers into as many bottle-openings as I could to cut down on the number of trips to the store. Under a full load, I'd limp all the way to the store.

My brother knew I was raising funds for the carnival. What I didn't know was Richie had a plan, too, and it began unfolding late one night while I lay in bed.

"Ronnie? Ronnie? Are you awake?" Richie asked.

I wasn't in the mood to talk, so I answered wearily, "Yeah, what do you want?"

"Are you going to the carnival?" Richie asked.

"Yeah, probably," I answered matter-of-factly so as not to let him know my heart was set on it.

"Can I go with you?"

"Gee, you're too young. Maybe when you're older," I mumbled hoping this would end the talk.

"I'm gonna be nine soon," Richie responded.

"There's a lot of stuff there that's pretty rough."

"Yeah, like what?" Richie asked with heightened interest. "Like what? Tell me!"

"Just things you're too young for."

"Like what?"

"OK, like this guy, Mr. Finn, who's half-man and half-fish." I hesitated for a moment, then said, "You think that's bad? What if I told you that the carnival has a woman named Naomi who's got a living baby attached to the outside of her stomach."

"Alive? The baby's alive?"

"Alive and kicking."

"How does the baby eat?"

I offered no answer to the mystery.

"Does it talk? The baby . . . ?"

Again I said nothing.

"How does it go to the bathroom?"

"You find all that out when you buy the ticket to go in and see it."

"Wow, that must be something."

"I know it would scare me," I said trying to discourage him.

Richie seemed to be just getting warmed up. "What other weird stuff is there?" He asked moving closer to me.

"Lots and for Chris' sake, move over! Stay on your side of the bed."

"Like what else?" Richie asked.

"Like Monique."

"Monique? Who's that?"

"She's a French Lady who dances and she's very beautiful."

"So what's so weird about that?"

"Well, I can't tell you because they won't let you in anyway. You're too little."

"Too little for what?"

"Well, Monique dances and she . . . she . . . ."

"She what?" Richie asked impatiently.

Dropping my voice, I whispered, "She takes off her clothes."

"She takes off *crows?*"

"She takes off her clothes," I said raising my voice.

Richie got quiet. I thought he might be wearing down.

"How much?" Richie began grilling me again.

"How much what?"

"How much does the French lady take off?"

"Usually everything on top and most everything on the bottom. But on the last night, she could take it all off. She might show it all. You never know, it could get wild."

My brother got quiet again. I figured I needed to put a little fear in him so I added, "On the last night of the carnival the biggest worry is that sometimes carny people take young kids, young boys, and steal them for the carnival." To put even more fear in him, I added, "You could end up working from morning till night, traveling from town to town putting up the show. Or, they might turn you into a freak and Mama would never see you again unless she saw *your* face painted on the side of one of their trucks. But they'd probably make you so ugly, even Mama wouldn't recognize you anyway. The carnys are pricks."

Richie didn't say a thing. I could hear him breathing and hoped I had scared the hell out of him.

Over the next few days I noticed a decline in deposit bottles around our place. Even when I went to steal the neighbor's, I couldn't find any. I needed to have money for the carnival. There's no way to go there and sneak in or try to trick your way into a show or onto a ride. The carnys are too smart for that and if you get caught, the carnys enjoy making an example out of you in front of everyone. I knew guys who got caught. They never tried it again. So you need dough in your pocket and you'd have to do what you had to do to get it.

I borrowed a wagon from a little kid on the block and went around picking up any junk metal I could find. Tin cans were OK, but if you could find any copper wire, brass, lead, or aluminum, you could make out pretty good at Levine's Junkyard. Old man Levine was still taking it in even though the war in Europe was over, but he was paying less for it. I didn't find a lot of good junk, but I found enough metal to make the trip to Levine's. Every little bit helped.

On the way over, I stopped by the American Store and stole a pack of Lucky's. I had a smoke on the way to the junkyard and was glad it was still easy to swipe stuff from the American Store, even when they knew you didn't have any dough when you walked through the front door.

Inside our Kelly block apartment, I checked deep inside our worn sofa for any change. I don't know why I looked; no one ever came to our house with money. But I remember that once Fran found two quarters there. I reached way down inside but came up empty except for some old cracker crumbs.

Grandma lived in the apartment in back of ours and even

though she only spoke her native Slovak, she understood when I asked her for money in my rough Slovak. Grandma didn't work, but once in a while she had a little change wrapped in a knot inside the handkerchief she kept under her pillow. It was a magic hankie. I couldn't figure out how or where she got money, but one thing I did know, whatever she had, she gave—no questions asked. I watched her eyes now clouded over from glaucoma as her hands moved around her handkerchief searching for the knot. I watched her smile when she unraveled it and gave me the few dimes, a nickel, and some pennies she had stashed away. Most of the time, when I went to her for money, she would show me her wrinkled white hankie, without a knot in it. This was her way of letting me know she was broke.

If I were really desperate for money, I'd go to the E. J. Shoe Factory where Mama worked doing piecework, slapping pieces of cowhide together with glue. E. J. gave work to most of the women and men in Binghamton, Johnson City, and Endicott that wanted it. You didn't need an education or know anybody to get a job, all you needed was a strong back and a strong desire to put food on the table.

Climbing three flights of worn stairs littered with cigarette butts, I entered the factory floor through a pair of swinging doors and heard the roar of machines, and saw the floor full of workers keeping pace with the clickity-clackity-clunk of metal and belts and pressure.

Walking through the noise past workers bending and stretching to the clickity-clackity-clunk, I smelled the stale air filled with the stink of animal skin and glue and sweat, and it made me sick. I held my breath as I searched for Mama's work station. Usually, when I approached, I'd find her hunched over a small table taking leather cutouts and running them over a pasty glue, slapping them together like a sandwich and placing them on a rack. When she made her count, she took a hole-punch and clipped a coupon that she would later turn in for her pay. The more work she did, the more coupons she punched, the more money she made. Mama worked like a machine. Still there was never enough money to make ends meet, let alone to spend on a good time like the carnival.

I never interrupted Mama. Someone usually yelled, *Hey, Theresa! It's your kid.* She'd turn around and give me a hug while I was trying not to gag on the sick smell of glue splattered on her apron. She reached into her apron pocket and pulled out a dime and gave it to me. Then she'd proudly send me off to say *Hi* to her coworkers, which was another way of saying, *Go put the bite on them.*

Almost all of the workers were women and they'd yell to me and I'd stop and say *Hi.* I'd get another hug (and another gag) and I'd feel them slip something into my hand.

On my way out, Mama would ask me how I did and I'd pull what I collected out of my pocket to show her. If it wasn't much (and it usually wasn't) my mother would look at it and say, *Cheap bastards.*

Outside the factory, I sucked in the fresh air hoping to clear my lungs and the stink from my mouth and the clickity-clackity-clunk from my ears.

I always went right home and stashed my money in a secret place and scrubbed myself and changed my shirt. I really hated getting money that way; it was like begging and it left a different kind of stink on me, sometimes for days.

On Saturday, the last day of the carnival, Richie seemed to be everywhere I was. When night came, I went to my secret hiding place to gather up my money. I kept it in an old tobacco pouch under our pee-stained mattress. After counting out close to a dollar-and-a-half, I stuffed the change into my pocket.

"Can I go with you?" Richie asked coming into the bedroom.
"No, you can't."
"I won't get in the way of your friends."
Richie didn't know this was probably the only night I could

ever remember that none of my gang could make it. They either couldn't get any dough or they were in trouble at home. Even Tootsie, he had to work at his sister Helen's place and sleep there overnight.

"Hey, I can't take you."

"Why not?" Richie pressed.

"Look, I told you, you're too young. You'll have plenty of chances to go later."

"I don't want to go later. I want to go now," Richie pleaded.

"How can you go, you don't have any money, and what I got I need."

"I've got money."

"Where'd you get money?" I said.

"I got it, that's all."

"How much?" I asked, figuring he didn't have much.

"Almost two bucks."

"Two bucks! Where'd you get two bucks?"

"I saved it for a long time, 'cause I want to go to the carnival."

Having more money than me made me rethink my brother's request. I didn't want him with me, because he'd slow me down. I felt sorry for him because he never seemed to have any fun; he was always getting into trouble and I worried about him. With Richie, you never knew what to expect and you always had to be on your toes. But, what the hell, he had money. "OK, I'll take you on one condition," I said. "I hold the money."

"You hold the money?"

"Yeah, that's right. I hold it . . . all."

"But, you don't spend it all, right?"

"No, I hold it so you don't lose it. The carnys got all kinds of ways to get their hands on your dough."

The carnival lights lit up the night sky above the city. The music of the midway blared out on loudspeakers while kids screamed and laughed on giant rides slicing through the air. As soon as you paid and came in, the carny people manning the games of chance would point to you and yell out, *Try your skill right here, my friend! Knock down the milk bottles and win this giant teddy bear. Three balls for a nickel!*

I pulled Richie's hand and whispered, "Keep moving."

The carnys taunted, their smooth tongues lashed out like serpents hunting for prey.

You look like a winner. Get over here and just hit three balloons with the darts, any three and pick out any of the prizes. Four throws for a dime. Two nickels. Ten pennies. Whaddya say?

Easy as pie! Shoot out the bull's eye and you're the big winner. Hey, you, yeah I'm talking to you. You look like a good shot. Win a prize for your kid brother. Only a dime for five shots.

C'mere, kid. Take the hammer and ring the bell. Show your little pal how strong you are. Only costs a nickel. We've had a lot of winners tonight. I've never seen such strong guys before . . . anywhere!

Richie's eyes got bigger and bigger. I could see he wanted to play, he wanted to take them up on their challenges and win. "You gotta go slow here," I said trying to settle him down. "They're gonna take your money for sure and the quicker they get it, the better they like it and the sooner we go home."

"You could win those games," Richie said, eager to beat the carnys.

"Yeah, maybe I could and then maybe I couldn't. They make it look real easy till you put your money down. Let's look the place over, first. There's lots of time," I said.

Richie thought there wasn't anything I couldn't do. That's why he had no fear starting a fight with older guys, so I'd have to jump in. My brother knew I wouldn't let anyone hurt him. He got me into more fights, just to prove how tough he was. I learned I had to keep a close eye on Richie, because he had a way of getting us into trouble.

On the last night of the carnival, the crowds were big. It was tough keeping an eye on Richie as we zigged and zagged through the people. I was always amazed at how many people were at the carnival who I'd never seen before. They must have come from all over town. Being at the carnival made you happy, at least for one night. Little kids with candy-stained faces were pulling on their moms. Teenage girls whispered and laughed to each other. A boy pulled a kid's hat off his head and threw it in the air. Babies cried their lungs out and old people walked on the edge of the crowd, holding onto their purses and trying not to be run over. Some rough-looking guys burst a kid's balloon with a cigarette and the kid started bawling.

The war vets were easy to spot. Most were serious, with a nervous, uneasy manner about them. Some were with their wives and kids. Some were with other vets; a lot were alone, moving with the flow of the crowd, smoking cigarettes and staring ahead. I thought they'd be happier being home, but then again there was a lot I didn't know.

Richie and I decided to try a couple of midway rides. The Octopus went round and round with tentacles stretching way out from the center, spinning us up and around high in the air and suddenly plunging us toward the ground. Just at the moment we felt the crash coming the ride suddenly whipped us upward toward the sky. Our stomachs felt queasy. Richie held on tight, but he didn't scream like the others. He was having the time of his life.

He wanted the Rocket next. Suspended on a giant arm, we sat in a capsule as we rotated through the air forward, then backward. Even gripping the metal bar across your lap with all your strength, you were sure you would fall out and die. All you could see as you spun around at dizzying speeds were pieces: the blurred midway, the crowd walking, then the night sky, a piece of the top of the Tunnel of Love, your feet hanging upside down. You felt your stomach moving first toward your head, then suddenly down toward your feet. You felt like throwing up, but you held on till you sensed the rocket slowing down and the ride ending.

On the way to the freak shows, we stopped and bought cotton candy. It stuck to the roof of our mouths and our tongues poked at it until we tasted its fuzzy sweetness on its way down to our stomachs.

A crowd gathered around a freak show up ahead. Richie and I could hear the carny onstage telling the folks what was waiting for them inside the tent. *Ladies and gentlemen, step right up and get your tickets to see Naomi and her baby. You intelligent people probably think you've seen it all. Well, I'm here to tell you, you ain't. Tonight, you'll see a medical marvel like no other in the world—a live child attached to the outside of its mother's stomach. How could that be you ask? Good question, because we've been to the best doctors in Switzerland and Denmark, and even they don't have an answer! You'll be astounded, flabbergasted, and even shocked. And tonight, only tonight, because it's our last night in town, Naomi will let someone from the audience touch the baby. Our show starts in fifteen minutes. So step right up and get your ticket and go in and see for yourself. When you do, I guarantee you'll never forget Naomi and her baby!*

I noticed when carnys spoke, they always used the same words that are painted on the sides of their trucks. They seemed to know the people from Binghamton were easy to *astound, flabbergast*, and *shock*. No sooner had the carny stopped talking, the crowd rushed into line for tickets.

Richie and I watched the crowd move inside the tent. Richie looked up at me to see what I thought about Naomi and her baby.

"Not worth the dough," I said. "Tootsie's sister Undo told him she saw the show and she said you can't see much."

"How come you can't see it?" Richie asked.

"Because they have the lights low and the audience has to sit far away from Naomi and her Baby."

"How come you can't get close?"

"They won't let you. She's sitting up on a stage. Undo said there's something there, but you can't tell what's on her stomach, even whether it's a baby. I don't think it's worth our going."

"Then when are we gonna see something?"

"Hold your horses. We will."

"Well let's do it."

Richie and I had to be choosy about what we spent our money on, or before we knew it we'd be broke. Shaking my head to Richie, I began to walk toward the Mr. Finn, Half-Man and Half-Fish Freak Show. The canvas show-entrance was dropping shut and a man on the outside stage put up a sign: ALL SOLD OUT. NEXT SHOW AT 9:00 P.M.

As we walked the midway, we spotted a bunch of girls in the crowd who were different. With their nice clothes and clean faces, you could tell they came from the West Side where they lived in nice houses with fences and flowers. These girls had smooth, white skin and thick hair, their eyes seemed to dance, and they never looked down when they walked; they didn't need any luck finding a coin on the ground or a cigarette butt with some life left in it. When West Side girls passed by, the air around them smelled like a bar of Lux Soap. It was as if the night air was filled for a moment with lilacs. I liked to stare at them to see if they'd look at me. They had a way of looking at you without seeing you. I always felt invisible, like I wasn't there. I wondered why these girls came to the carnival; maybe it was to have a good laugh.

I waved at a few people I knew, and when I turned to check on Richie, he was gone. I began to panic. Maybe the carnys really did get him! I lit a Lucky and took a deep drag and said to myself, *Don't panic.*

Up ahead I could see a huge crowd standing around some of the attractions. Pushing ahead, I saw the man on the stage in front of the large sign that read: MONIQUE. Men and boys stood listening to the carny's pitch. *She's from Paris, France. What more do I need to say?* Moving from in front of the large picture behind him, he pointed to it and yelled, *Look! No, feast your eyes on this lovely being!*

My eyes went to the huge picture of Monique behind him. She wore a top and bottom made out of feathers that seemed to show more than the little outfit covered. Monique's long blonde hair and beautiful eyes and wet lips were like magnets. I wanted to stay and hear more, but I had to find Richie.

I was relieved when I spotted him standing right there in front of the stage listening to the carny tell about Monique. Slowly, I closed in where I could keep Richie in sight. He was slippery and could cause a lot of worry. But for now, it looked as though his feet were planted in the ground.

With Richie right where I could keep an eye on him, I looked back at Monique's picture and went over it from her toes to the top of her head. Every inch of her seemed perfect. I'd never seen such a beautiful woman. She was smooth and had an astounding body. And the fact that she was from Paris, made her seem all the more mysterious. No one in Binghamton ever looked like Monique, except for some of the babes in the movies at the Ritz.

I looked over at Richie staring motionless up at the stage, his eyes and mouth wide open. I jiggled the money in my pocket, thinking how much I wanted to see all that Monique had, but with my kid brother with me, there was no way we'd get in. I went over and tapped Richie on the shoulder and nodded for him to follow. He didn't budge.

"I want to go in there, to see the show," Richie said. I could see that he was serious.

"They won't let you in, you're too young," I answered.

The carny turned from Monique's picture and with a smile said, *Tonight, gentlemen, you're in for a special treat. Tonight, Monique will show you everything you want to see!* No sooner had the carny man said that, the crowd quickly rushed toward the ticket-seller's booth. There was a lot of pushing and shoving and even a scuffle or two as the line formed for the lovely Monique.

"C'mon, let's try. Go get two tickets," Richie ordered. "Hurry up or they'll sell them all. C'mon, do it."

Already he's barking orders. There was no way we'd get in, but I'd have to show him I tried or I'd never hear the end of it. *Don't move from here!* I yelled as I ran toward the line. I bucked my way into line and when my turn came, I put my two quarters down and raised two fingers at the carny ticket-taker. He gave me a funny look as if he were going to say something. Suddenly, I was pushed from behind and the force threw me against the ticket booth. The line was long and it was starting to get rough. Someone from the back yelled, *Let's move it!* The man in the ticket booth yelled back, *Take it easy! You'll get your tickets!* And with that he handed me two tickets through the window opening. *Have your money ready and it'll move a lot quicker!* He yelled to the others.

I waved to Richie and he ran to join me. "Just follow me and don't say nothin,'" I warned him. A young carny was taking tickets at the tent entrance. The line was moving fast and that was good. Suddenly it was our turn and the ticket-taker grabbed my ticket, then paused when Richie held out his ticket.

"Hey, kid! How old are you?" he asked. *Oh, no! I thought. This is it! We're out of here. Not only are we not getting in, but we're going to lose our dough! I'm going to kill Richie for this!*

"Old enough," Richie answered, looking the guy in the eye.

"Yeah, he is," I added, trying to keep up the bluff. "He's just short for his age. He smokes too much!"

"You smoke, kid?" The carny worker asked Richie.

"Yeah," Richie answered. "You want a smoke?" Richie reached into his back pocket and pulled out an almost full pack of Pall Malls. "Here, keep 'em. I got more." *Where the hell did he get those?* I thought.

The ticket-taker took the cigarettes and Richie's ticket. We were in and from the smile on my brother's face, I was beginning to see his plan must have included a trip to the American Store.

A cloud of cigarette smoke drifted over the crowd inside the tent. There were a few grownups from our part of town who were in the stands, and some war veterans who probably had met Monique in Paris.

I didn't look around much since I didn't want them to spot Richie and me and give us any disapproving looks. I knew they didn't really give a damn, except if we were their kids, but I still couldn't help feeling a little funny. There were a couple of spaces way down front near the stage, so Richie and I squeezed in. Everyone was eager for the show to begin. *Don't look around. Keep your eyes on the stage,* I whispered to Richie.

The stage in front of us was about five feet off the ground. Bright lights hung all over and the light spilled onto a curtain spread across the back of the stage. Nothing seemed to be happening for a long time and the men and boys in the stands started to stomp their feet and whistle and call out for Monique while French music played through a loudspeaker.

I wondered whether the women Uncle Bill told me he saw in Paris were as beautiful as Monique. For sure the road to seeing them was a lot tougher than buying a ticket at the Carnival. Toward the end of the war, it turned out all three Vrabel brothers were somewhere in the "Ruhr Pocket," the area called the "Armory of the German Reich." John crossed over the Ludendorff Bridge at Remagen, fighting his way over. Joe followed with the 7th Armored Division and Bill's truck convoy crossed the Rhine River over a pontoon bridge built by GIs; 330,000 German troops were captured in the Ruhr Pocket. Army engineers built a prisoner of war camp in nearby France with high-wire fences. Uncle Bill supervised a 50-prisoner work detail.

On occasion, Uncle Bill and his buddies received passes. Driven by jeep to Paris, they stayed at the Hôtel du Paris and visited the night spots. Walking the streets, they entered Pigale, the red-light district, where French women in skimpy dresses stood behind large glass windows beckoning GIs to come in and relax. Uncle Bill never told me whether he sampled the goodies or just window-shopped. Thinking about the picture of Monique, I could only guess that all French ladies were beautiful.

From behind the curtain a man in a fancy suit and tie came out. He raised his hands high above his head and held them there. You could see he was different from the other carny workers; his suit fit him nicely and his shoes had a shine. He wore a shiny ring on his little finger and had cuff-links on his shirt sleeves and a shiny pin on his tie. His hair was slicked back and it even looked like he was wearing make-up.

The audience quieted down. It quickly got as still as a church. Dropping his hands, the man spoke with a big voice and a sly look on his face, like he knew something we didn't. *Gentlemen, and if there are any ladies, welcome to our show this evening. This is Monique's next-to-last show and as you know, we close up tonight and move on to our next engagement. Why am I telling you this, you ask? Well, gentlemen, I'm telling you this because Monique told me to tell you she's going to do a special show for you, the kind you'll never forget!* The crowd roared its approval.

I snuck a peek at Richie. I never saw him this happy. It didn't matter that I brought him here to see a naked woman. This was something I dreamed of and what the hell, Richie deserved his dream, too. My only concern was that some jerk in this crowd might squeal on us to Mama and we'd both take a whipping for being here.

Pulling up his coat sleeves, the carny continued. *Before the lovely and scintillating Monique joins you, I want to offer you a chance to take something home with you to remember tonight. It will excite you almost as much as Monique will.* He reached into his suit pocket and pulled his hand out, clutching something in his palm. *What I have in my hand, you cannot get anywhere.*

He opened his hand and held up a small pair of white dice with a small chain running through them. *These little dice are not ordinary dice. No, sir, they are extraordinary. In fact, you could say they're magical.* Everyone's eyes were focused on the dice. Holding them up to his eyes he said, *If you look closely, these appear to be regular dice, except they're smaller. However, if I were to take these dice and soak them in lukewarm water for five minutes, something incredible would happen; the black dots on the dice would disappear. Then if I held them up to my eye and pointed them to the light, I would see Monique, naked and doing things your mother doesn't want you to see!* The crowd laughed wildly.

These magic dice can be yours, gentlemen, for fifty cents! The carny said speaking faster and with more intensity. *Yes, sir, only two quarters will get you Monique any time you want or need her! There will be assistants on each side selling them, but you've got to move fast 'cause we can't keep Monique waiting too much longer. She's hot and she's ready to go. If you do buy the magic dice, stick them in your pockets so you don't lose these precious squares. And remember, during the performance, keep your hands out of your . . . pocket so you don't play with your . . . your magic dice until you get home.* The crowd roared with laughter. *Thank you, gentlemen. The gorgeous Monique will be out as soon as we've run out of these. Enjoy the show!*

Almost instantly, hands started waving in the audience to signal the men selling the dice. Money came forward and dice were passed back. People started looking at the dice causing onlookers to dig quickly into their pockets to buy a pair, too.

Richie turned to me and said with determination, "Let's get some!"

I looked at him, and while thinking what a pain in the ass he was, I stalled for time to make a decision. You could never get something like this in Binghamton; but then, these dice in Richie's hands could be big trouble. There's no way of knowing what he might try with them.

"What are you lookin' at me for? Get the money out . . . half of it's mine and buy 'em before they run out!"

Richie was trying to boss me around and he was acting more

and more nervous. He was looking back and forth at me and the carny selling the dice. *Oh, what the hell, I thought—how much trouble could a little pair of dice be?* I raised my hand and with the other reached into my pocket for the money. I counted ninety cents in the palm of my hand.

I was glad to see that we could pay the fifty cents for the magic dice and still have enough left over to go to Larry's Lunch for our favorite order, plus have a dime left over to get a soft ice-cream cone and split it.

I watched the magic dice come toward me and reached out and took them in my sweaty hand and squeezed them tightly while I handed the carny man fifty cents. When I opened my hand slowly, Richie leaned over and we stared at the magic dice as though they were a map to a pirate's treasure.

The magic dice felt warm in my hand. I could feel my heart pounding against my T-shirt. Richie's finger touched them carefully. He looked up and we smiled at each other. I closed my hand and put the dice deep inside my pocket. As usual I checked to make sure there were no holes in my pocket big enough for the dice to fall through. Satisfied, I pushed the dice down deeper inside my pocket.

The lights dimmed and a hush fell over the once-noisy crowd. Music started and the curtain opened, and a spotlight hit the curtain. Monique came out. The crowd went crazy. Dressed in a strapless silken full-length dress, Monique was even more beautiful than her pictures as she walked the stage cooling herself with a huge white fan made of feathers. Her legs were long and curvy; her tits firm and pointed. When she turned, her behind looked as smooth and as hard as marble. Her eyes seemed to sparkle and her tongue slid out over her thick lips making them look like a rose in a rain shower. She looked like Rhonda Fleming or maybe it was Arlene Dahl, long and curvy and with a gaze that left you begging for more.

We sat there watching Monique dancing across the stage to

the beat of the music. A lone spotlight followed every move she made. I snuck a peek at the audience and saw grown men with their jaws hanging open and their eyes glazed over. I could tell from the look on Richie's face that this would be a night to remember. His eyes looked like moist red grapes from the heavy smoke filling the air. His eyes never left Monique; he didn't even blink. He was seeing things he had only heard about in the neighborhood. Now, he and I would be seeing the secret parts of a beautiful woman and the way Monique moved them made us wish this night would never end.

Monique strolled about the stage to the music, first teasing then taking off a piece of clothing. With each of her moves, the excitement grew and the audience moaned and cheered wildly as more and more of her body came into view. She came across the stage to our side; each step punctuated by a bump or a grind to the music. A scent of sweet perfume drifted across the stage ahead of her. It smelled just like "Evening in Paris"—the perfume from Jacob Eisenberg's Drug Store. But this was the real stuff all the way from Paris. Maybe it was my imagination, but I could have sworn Monique stared right at me. Our eyes locked on to each other. She looked at me with those warm, inviting eyes as though she saw deep inside me and knew exactly what I wanted. My hand reached down to feel the magic dice pressing against my thigh.

She had two sequined tossils hanging off her nipples. I looked at Richie with his mouth wide open. Monique started to spin the tossils in a circle, faster and faster. She looked like a twin-engine plane revving her propellers for take-off. And boy did she take off. Reaching her hand slowly to her hip, she loosened her slit skirt. It slid down her legs onto the stage to the roar of the crowd.

Monique more than kept her promise. Before she was through, she shared every nook and cranny of her shimmering body. She began her act covered by a feathery fan and when she finished, all she wore was a smile.

Words cannot describe what we saw that evening. The tent

inside was hot and steamy. And when Monique left the stage for the last time, the crowd erupted into a deafening roar of clapping, whistling and shouting thanks to her for giving it all to us.

As soon as we left the tent, Richie and I ran for home. The carnival lights and music soon faded as we raced to get back to the Kelly block. Our breathing quickened in the darkness; the show still playing in our heads. Maybe she'll return . . . next year. Until then, I could feel her inside the magic dice rubbing against my leg as I ran.

We went down State Street to Chenango, then over the DeForest Street Bridge to Front Street. It was longer this way, but the chances were better we wouldn't run into anyone that might slow us down. On the way, we passed rows of dark houses, lifeless as graveyards at midnight. In the distance, the high pitch of a railroad whistle was a welcome relief to the sound of our sneakers scuffing the pavement. Every now and then, we would pass through a patch of light spilling onto the street from inside a house.

I could have run all night; I felt as if I were floating like one of Monique's feathers. She had taken Richie and me to a different world where we were warm and happy and not afraid.

"*Lukewarm* is what he said," Richie reminded me as I held the tap open in the bathroom sink and watched the empty jelly glass fill up.

"This is lukewarm. I know what lukewarm is," I said getting a bit annoyed.

Richie and I carefully and quietly walked the glass into our bedroom and sat on the edge of the bed. I reached into my pocket and felt the dice in my fingers. They were warm and smooth. I lifted them up by the little silver-colored chain. Richie's eyes seemed to grow when I started to lower the dice into the water.

"We'll take turns soaking them," Richie said.

"OK. You go first," I answered.

"No, you go!" Richie countered.

"If I go first, I get to look at them first."

"Bullshit! Why should you look first? I gave as much money as . . . Hey, I put in more money than you did!" Richie said.

"Screw that! I'm the oldest. I don't take orders from you!"

"Yeah, just make sure you hold them the right way!" Richie muttered, knowing he better shut up and not push me too far.

We both watched as the dice went into the glass. I held the chain over the side while the dice settled into the water.

Richie and I sat waiting for the time to pass. Richie signaled me that it was his turn and without fussing, I put the chain over his finger carefully. He bobbed the dice up and down a few times in the water, then he sat without moving a muscle, just staring at the dice floating in the glass jar. The look on Richie's face reminded me of Spencer Tracy as Dr. Jekyll, the mad scientist. I wondered whether getting these dice and taking Richie to see Monique was going to cause me a lot of grief. I knew we were going to fight over who keeps the dice and where the dice are hidden and who gets to spend time with Monique and how much. What happens if they get lost, or worse, what if Mama finds them?

I would have to worry about all that later. For now, I'm waiting for Monique. I wondered what she was doing inside those dice. The carny said, *Things your mother don't want you to see.* Monique had already showed us everything she had. What could be left?

The five minutes felt like five hours, but finally the time had come. I reached over and took the chain from Richie's finger and lifted the dice slowly out of the water. I jiggled them a couple of times to throw off any water left on the dice.

I walked the dice over to the window. Richie tried to pull the green shade up, but it was broken. He then lifted it up from the bottom and the light from the street-lamp outside streamed into the bedroom. Getting on my knees, I lifted the magic dice up to the outside light. I squeezed my fingers on the top and bottom of one of the dice and placed my eye up to it. I shut my other eye tight and stared through the dice. I couldn't help but think if anybody saw us now, we'd look like Dr. Frankenstein and Ygor in the lab trying to bring a monster back to life. Richie barely gave me a few seconds when he tapped me on the shoulder to signal his turn.

"Wait a minute for Chris' sakes," I said, still focusing on the dice.

"What do you see? What's she doing?" Richie whispered anxiously.

I couldn't answer. I kept staring into the dice. Then I turned the cube to each of its sides and looked in.

"C'mon! Let me look!" Richie said impatiently.

"Wait a second," I responded as I took the second cube and put it quickly to my eye. I rotated it to all sides.

"C'mon, this is crap! I wanna look," Richie said raising his voice.

"Sshh! Do you want Mama to hear us? Here, look," I said handing the dice to Richie and trading places with him.

Richie put his eye to the dice and in seconds he spun the cube around to all sides, then repeated the same with the other cube. His shoulders slumped as he brought the dice down from his eye. "I didn't see a friggin' thing. There's nothing there except black dots," Richie said softly.

"Yeah, I know," I answered.

"We probably screwed up. We didn't soak them long enough," Richie said.

"I think we did."

"Bullshit! We don't even have a clock. We just guessed!"

"Maybe."

"Or maybe the water wasn't right. It probably wasn't lukewarm enough!"

"It was lukewarm . . . not too hot, not too cold. I know what the shit lukewarm is! Do you think I'm that stupid or what?"

"I'm going to try it again. I'll start all over."

Richie took the dice back to the bathroom. I could hear the water running. Maybe Richie was right. Maybe he'll do it. But I had stared deep into those dice and didn't see a thing except black dots. I lay down on the bed as Richie came into the bedroom. In an instant he was kneeling on the floor peering through the glass jar at the dice soaking inside.

I lay back on my pillow and watched Richie work into the night to bring the magic dice to life. I had never seen him so determined. I tried to stay awake, but I was so tired I couldn't hold on.

When I woke in the morning, I opened my eyes to see the water-soaked wrinkled fingers on Richie's hand next to me. He was fast asleep. A light breeze lifted the green shade against the window sill. On the floor beneath the window were the dice next to the half-filled glass.

Lifting them up to my eye, the dots remained like a black curtain behind which Monique was hiding. I took a knife and tried to scrape away the black dots. Nothing happened.

I DON'T REMEMBER exactly when or where or how the magic dice got lost, but when they did, no one said a word. I felt bad that the carny guys cheated us out of fifty cents, sucking us all in. I felt especially sorry for Richie, because he was never going *to see the things your mother don't want you to see,* promised by those magic dice. But then again I figured he had already seen more than Mama wanted us to see. And that had to be worth at least fifty cents.

28.

BINGHAMTON PRESS   SEPTEMBER 4, 1945

STORY OF JAP'S PRISON SAVAGERY TOLD

6 FROM AMONG 13 TIER MEN ON *MISSOURI* AS NIPS SIGN

It's Over

A picture on the front page of the paper showed a funny-looking man with a pen in his hand wearing glasses and a suit with a high shirt collar, tie, and vest, signing papers at a desk on the deck of the *U.S.S. Missouri*. U.S. Navy men watched in the background, and you knew the war with the Japs was finally over. Three years and eight months after they bombed Pearl Harbor, Mr. Mamoru Shigemitsu, the Japanese man in the suit, surrendered on orders of Emperor Hirohito and the Japanese Government.

I sent another letter to Uncle Bill somewhere in Germany. I wanted him to know I started a scrapbook and was cutting out stories from the newspapers about the war and about baseball. I told him I cut out a story, about Ernie Pyle, an American newspaper writer who got killed covering the war. He was shot by a Japanese soldier on the Pacific island of Le Shima. A sign was put up by the GIs from the 77th Infantry Division that read: LOST A BUDDY, ERNIE PYLE, 18 APRIL 1945.

I also wrote him about Detroit's Hank Greenberg just getting back to the Tigers after four years in the service. Playing for the American League Pennant on September 30, St. Louis led 2-1 against Detroit when Greenberg homered in the ninth inning to win the game. The Tigers then went on to take the World Series. I mentioned I was going to the bars up on Clinton Street to see if any of them would sponsor our baseball team next year. I told him I didn't have any luck yet. The bar owners kept saying, *Maybe later on when the guys get home and business gets better.* I wrote Uncle Bill that even Tonda at Elmo's, the owner who sponsored his basketball team said he couldn't spare any dough. Tonda told me to come back again when, *You're as good as Billy Vrabel, Punky Koranka, and Bobbie Kadlec—then maybe I'll sponsor you.* I told him that could be a heck-of-a long time and not to hold his breath. I finished the letter by telling Uncle Bill that everyone at home was fine and we were all waiting for him to get back.

The word went out that all Boys' Club members were invited to meet and welcome back a former Club member who was credited with being the first paratrooper to land on D-day. No one wanted to miss this, so we were all crowded around Captain Frank G. Lillyman in the auditorium at the Club waiting for him to speak. He wore his full-dress uniform with the 101st Screaming Eagles Airborne Division patch and all his medals. He was skinny and tall and didn't look like a strong guy. But then he began to speak and you just knew he was a special man. He spoke about leading the first American Pathfinder's onto Normandy. He described how the plane carrying his unit roared through the night sky. He watched men trying to stand steady, ready to jump as the plane bounced and tipped. Some were praying; everyone looked scared. No one knew what was waiting out there once they left the plane.

Captain Lillyman said he stood in the door waiting for the signal and when it came he jumped out into the darkness—his chute jerked open and he looked about and saw the sky full of parachutes carrying men and equipment. He said he looked down and saw total darkness. He described the stillness as he and the others glided down. It seemed like a lifetime waiting to touch the earth. As he neared the ground he said he could see it coming fast. He prepared to land and he hit hard. He then heard the others landing, some hitting trees, some hitting water, some screaming from bones being twisted or broken.

We all sat still listening to someone who was actually there, fighting the war. Everything Captain Lillyman said we listened to with our mouths hanging open. His voice, his telling it, carried us to a place as if we were there and we had lived through it. He ended his talk to us by thanking the Boys' Club "for teaching me teamwork which is the reason I'm here now."

We got to shake hands with him and to look into the face of a real live hero.

Little by little, more of the men started coming home. Hardly a day went by that the Erie and Lackawanna trains from Hoboken didn't bring at least one soldier, sailor, airman, or marine home. Fathers, mothers, wives, and children watched from the depot platform, staring down the track, waiting for the train to come into view. Children ran around the station, playing as if it were just another day. But 555 men from the area would not be coming home. For their families the wait was over. These sons, husbands, brothers, and fathers gave their lives in service to their country; an estimated 1,500 other area men had been wounded, and for some of them the wounds meant getting home would take awhile.

The military used a point system to bring the men home. Soldiers got one point for every month in the service, two points for every month overseas and five points for every battle star awarded for being in combat. The men with the most points came home first. They boarded boats out of the port of Dieppe in Lahore Harbor in France and crossed the Atlantic.

Uncle Bill got discharge orders and was happy to be coming home, but hated the water. The trip from Dieppe to New York on a transport boat carried 1,200 GIs home. For twelve days at sea, Uncle Bill was sick and stayed in "sick bay." Entering New York Harbor at night, some buddies carried him to the deck to see the Statue of Liberty. "It was a great sight and *the lady* looked beautiful," Uncle Bill said.

When Army men landed they processed through Fort Dix in New Jersey and got their discharge papers and their final orders. Just as they had left, they returned, one by one. First Uncle John, then Uncle Joe, then Uncle Bill. Everyone was there to meet the trains pulling in with its bells clanging and whistle tooting. When the big steel wheels screeched to a stop and the steam from the brakes hissed, you waited and watched as men in uniform began to step off the train and onto the platform, carrying their canvas duffle bags with their names stenciled on them in black letters. Loved ones ran to greet their men with hugs and kisses and pats on the back. There were a lot of smiles . . . a lot of tears.

Uncle Bill's brother Joe met him at the train station on Lewis Street and they walked home together, over the Clinton Street Bridge, up Clinton to Oak, and then down to Dickinson and the Kelly block.

GRANDMA WAITED AT home for her boys. The war years had taken her sight, but not her tears. She patiently waited until she heard the sound of her boys' voices. And when they hugged her and she felt their faces, she knew her boys were home.

29.

VETS LOOKING FOR JOBS

SOME GOING TO SCHOOL ON G.I. BILL

In the Alley Behind Elmo's

Early Sunday morning the bells rang in the tower of Saint Cyril Church high above the stale stink of beer joints standing empty and dark along Clinton Street. The church bells called out in crisp tones for one and all to come to God and spend an hour searching for His plan for their lives. Outside the church, on a small strip of grass, white wooden crosses stood in the early morning light. The names on them were church members who already knew God's plans. Louis Machovec, John Kapral, Martin Strotsky were among the fifteen names of those Saint Cyril parishioners who laid down their lives for their country. Next to the crosses, small American flags flapped, brought to life by an invisible force, an occasional gust of wind.

For the living, God's plans remained a deep secret. It was inside the church in the flickering faces of statued saints, through the smoky haze of incense and the trickle of blood on the twisted, suffering Face on the Cross that the faithful searched for clues.

Nuns in black robes and starched white collars prayed in silence while little ladies in babushkas lit candles. Groups of women chanted prayers in Slovak and rubbed worn rosary beads with their wrinkled fingers. Prayers echoed throughout the church, piercing every nook and corner, winding upward to vaulted ceilings where images of winged angels floated on white, puffy clouds eager to carry the prayers to heaven above.

Saint Cyril Church tended to the souls of First Warders. Newborns were baptized, the dying received last rites, and young men and women vowed their lives to each other in marriage on the altar of God. St. Cyril's fed and clothed the poor, and sometimes priests "loaned" money to families with no means to repay. When Saint Cyril's men died in the war, its priests consoled grieving families, their white collars stained with the tears of broken hearts. When the dead were brought home from battlefields far away, the priests blessed the remains and prayed the Prayer for the Dead above the native earth waiting to receive the fallen hero, the beloved son.

Preaching hope and salvation didn't always reach beyond the thick, plastered walls of the church. The war was over, but there were some on the street still struggling to reconcile the horror of war and the idea of peace.

"In the alley behind Elmo's at 1:00," Uncle John said to me.

I didn't know why, but it sounded important. It had to be if he wanted me there. Something was going on. Ever since the guys got home from the war, things happened. Clinton Street buzzed again, even more than before. Everyone seemed happier and because our guys won the war, even kind of cocky though there wasn't any real reason to be.

I pulled the red wagon at full speed to the corner of Dickinson and Mygatt to pick up a block of ice for Grandma. Mr. Patrick, the iceman, would have to move faster than usual. On this day, not even the gigantic goiter attached to his neck would give him an excuse for less than fast service.

Mr. Patrick, a block of ice and if you could, I'm in a big hurry.

"Yeah, yeah, everybody's in a hurry now that the war's over," Mr. Patrick said as he took the ice tongs hanging on a nail on the ice shack and disappeared inside. It was a warm Sunday and a typically quiet and lazy day with most people sitting on their porches drinking lemonade and listening to the World Series between the Detroit Tigers and the Chicago Cubs. It was typical except for what was to happen shortly in the alley behind Elmo's at 1:00.

By the time Mr. Patrick came out of the ice house lugging a clear shiny twenty-five pound block of ice, his goiter had turned purple from the cold. Squeezing the tongs on each side of the ice, he dropped it into my wagon. Handing him a dime, I grabbed the wagon handle and started running down the street.

"Hey, be careful or that ice won't make it home," Mr. Patrick yelled.

"Yeah, OK, I'll be careful," I yelled back without looking at him.

The ice bounced and slid inside the wagon even though I pulled it up the smooth side of the street. I flew up the Kelly block stairs and grabbed the tongs on top of Grandma's icebox just outside her kitchen door. I raced back down the steps and sunk the tongs into the heavy block of ice and yanked it out of the wagon. It was already melting as I tugged it up the stairs with the ice in front of me so that in case it slipped off the tongs, I'd be able to use my legs to stop it from rolling down the steps.

Opening the icebox, I lifted the ice into its space and closed the door tight. I yelled to Grandma that the ice was here. Without waiting for an answer, I ran down the stairs and grabbed the wagon and carried it back up the stairs and rolled it to the back where Grandma lived so that no one would steal it.

Running back down Dickinson Street, I turned in the direction of the alley in the back of Elmo's. After climbing several fences, I jumped over the last one and saw a crowd milling about in the alley. I looked around to see if any of my buddies were there, but I couldn't see any. I was sorry I didn't have the time to round them up. Most of the crowd were men home from the war and a lot of older kids. I spotted Uncle John and went and stood next to him. For such a big crowd, it seemed very quiet. I guessed if it got too noisy, the cops would show up and break things up before they got started.

Heads turned when a kid ran down the alley from Clinton Street yelling, *Here they come!* The crowd got louder as everyone turned to look up the alley. "Rabbit" Ziac came down first; "Nordie" Kapral followed. These were two of the toughest, hard-drinking men in the First Ward. Rabbit had been in the war, Nordie had a crippled leg and was turned down. The night before they had been drinking in Elmo's Bar and Rabbit and Nordie had words between them. They agreed to settle their differences in the alley at 1:00 today by fighting with their bare fists.

They took off their shirts down to their bare chests. Rabbit tightened the belt around his waist, his stomach firm and his chest and arms full of muscles. Nordie retied his shoes tighter. One of his legs was shorter than the other; he walked with a limp. When he stood up, his arms bulged with muscles. Like bulls snorting in a ring, Rabbit and Nordie took turns cleaning out their noses by holding a finger on a nostril and blowing out.

The crowd formed a ring around the two. I pushed through to get a ringside view. They kicked up dust from the dry dirt in the yard as they circled each other. I knew Rabbit. Uncle John had taken Richie and me fishing with some of his buddies after they returned from the war. Rabbit was one of the guys in the car who, like all the others, had booze on his breath as we rode for hours in the dead of night. By the time we got to our fishing spot, Richie and I were a bit woozy. I liked Rabbit and was pulling for him.

The crowd began to stir when the fighters raised their fists and started to move slowly, their eyes fixed on each other. It seemed to take a while for the first punch to land. Suddenly, a left thrown by Rabbit cracked against Nordie's ribs. Kapral jumped back, kicking up a cloud of dust as he almost lost his balance. The crowd roared. They circled each other again, their eyes focused but calm and unafraid. A right slammed against Rabbit's chest and it slid off as Rabbit rotated away from Nordie's punch. The crowd groaned at each punch thrown.

Now the punches came in flurries—a left to the ribs by Rabbit, then another followed by a right that sank into Nordie's stomach. Swallowing for air, Nordie landed a right to Rabbit's ribs, then followed with two lefts to the chest, splashing Rabbit's sweat onto the crowd. Rabbit stepped back and circled Nordie. The crowd closed in tighter, waiting for the big punch to land to the head, but both fighters seemed content to pound the body. Voices in the crowd began yelling for their favorite fighter. I glanced at Uncle John, a lit Chesterfield hanging from his lips, shadow-boxing with the fighters inside the circle.

"C'mon, Rabbit. Hit him for Chris' sakes!" I yelled.

The crowd was getting louder as the fighters traded punches in the alley. Red marks and scrapes dotted Rabbit's and Nordie's bodies. Their mouths hung open as their chests struggled for air.

"Nordie . . . hit him good," someone shouted to him as he sank a left into Rabbit's stomach. Nordie ducked a right to his head and Rabbit followed his miss with a vicious left to Nordie's rib-cage that buckled Nordie's legs. Nordie straightened and his right fist dug deep into Rabbit's gut followed by a left to the head that opened a cut under Rabbit's eye. The crowd reacted when blood began to roll down Rabbit's cheek. Wiping away the blood with his bare hand, Rabbit faked a left and landed a vicious straight right to Nordie's nose. Nordie staggered back with blood flowing from his nose. Sensing an end, the crowd grew more excited.

The two fighters circled each other, kicking up dust and straining for air.

"It's almost over," Uncle John yelled to me.

"How can you tell?" I shouted back.

"They've both drawn blood and they're getting too tired to go on much longer."

Slowly, as if they had just heard what Uncle John said, Rabbit and Nordie's arms dropped. Staring at each other, they stepped toward each other, reached out and shook hands as they gasped for air. Picking up their shirts, they put their arms over each other's shoulders and started walking back up the alley toward Clinton Street as the crowd cheered.

"Now what?" I asked Uncle John.

"Now they go up to Elmo's and clean up the blood and have a beer and call it even."

"And that's it?"

"That's it," Uncle John said as he left to join the crowd following the fighters.

I waited for everyone to clear out. All that were left were a few kids running around pretending they were Rabbit and Nordie fighting. I wandered over to where the fighters had stood. I saw the blood spattered in the scuffed-up dirt. Even though no one got knocked out, I was glad Uncle John told me about it and I was glad I was there to see it. I thought Rabbit won.

THE MEN WERE home from the war. Clinton Street was busy once again and the bars and the shops were full. But from the slugfest in the alley and with more and more blood showing up on the sidewalks outside the beer joints along Clinton Street, a lot of the men were still itching for a good fight.

30.

BINGHAMTON PRESS   DECEMBER 24, 1945

YULETIDE JOY DIMMED FOR SOLDIER'S FAMILY AS DEATH TIDINGS ARRIVE

Sgt. Allan J. Rice Was Killed in Action Over Burma

The Night My Brother Shot Al Jolson

With all the men coming back home for good, things seemed to be returning to normal, little by little. But there were exceptions.

It just happened that among the people in the crowd coming out of the last show at the Ritz this particular night was a neighborhood tough guy—Dickie Perworchik. From the bustle and chatter of the crowd, it must have been a good movie. Dickie happened to see me going by and without as much as a hello, hitched up his pants with his two forearms and jerked his head and said, "You, you dirty rat, you. You shot my brother. Now you're gonna get yours."

"You must have liked the show," I said as I glanced from the Cagney billboard to Dickie.

"I'm packing a rod," Dickie said as he reached under his armpit.

"*A rod*, Dickie?"

"Yeah, yeah, a rod, a gat. I'm packin' heat."

I hadn't seen the Cagney movie, but I could see Dickie was really into his *role*.

"He shot your brother? But Dickie, you don't have a brother."

"Yeah, yeah, he shot my brother, the dirty rat. Nobody shoots my brother and gets away with it. I'm gonna plug him," Dickie said while hitching his pants and jerking his head again.

Fascinating things happened when people went to the Ritz. A guy like Dickie could go in as Dickie Perworchik and an hour-and-a-half later out comes James Cagney.

The only way to keep up with who was who was to see every movie that played at the Ritz. Usually, imitating a screen character lasted until the next movie came in, which was every two days. But for Dickie, he was Cagney for over two weeks and I started to get worried. Then, *Little Caesar* arrived and Dickie became Edward G. Robinson. *Yeah, yeah, that's right, kid. I'm the boss. I give the orders. I call the shots. You got that, kid?* I thought he still sounded like Cagney, he just didn't hitch his pants and jerk his head. Instead, he pretended to have a cigar in his hand when he pointed at me, *the kid*.

At the movies, you could be anyone you wanted to be. You could sit in the dark of the Ritz and become the star who was up there on the big screen. Movies made you smart, tough, daring, funny, rich, successful—a hero. You believed that was you up there saving the lady in distress or catching the killer in a trap or beating John L. Sullivan for the Heavyweight Championship of the World. That wasn't Cary Grant or Pat O'Brien or Errol Flynn, that was you up there doing the kind of things you'd never find on the streets of the First Ward. At the Ritz you could have any kind of life you wanted, if only for a day or two.

In no time, guys from the Ward danced like Fred Astaire with

Ginger Rogers and sword-fought on a Spanish war ship like Errol Flynn, discovered gold in the Sierra Madre like Humphrey Bogart, caught cattle-rustlers with Hopalong Cassidy, fought a bull like Tyrone Power, rode through the dust bowl in Oklahoma during the depression like Henry Fonda, swung through the jungle on a vine like Johnny Weismuller, growled like Bob Hope when he saw Dorothy Lamour. But, best of all, Ward kids fought the Japs and the Nazis and whether they lived or died, they fought like John Wayne and Lloyd Nolan to the end.

My buddies never turned down a great line, no matter who said it. After a Bette Davis movie, Vic, a regular in our gang, lit a cigarette and took a puff and said with disgust, *What a dump. What a dump.* Whenever I heard this line, I often wondered what she'd say if she saw the Kelly block.

The women stars were big and beautiful and tough: Joan Crawford, Barbara Stanwyck, Lana Turner, Katharine Hepburn, Betty Grable, Rita Hayworth, and Bette Davis. They would drive the men playing opposite them crazy.

Adventure waited for you at the Ritz, on the screen and off. The movies made you feel that anything and everything was possible. They filled you with daring and set no limits. I learned to laugh in the throat like Sidney Greenstreet in *The Maltese Falcon* . . . whine like Peter Lorre in *The Beast with Five Fingers* . . . look at the full moon and twitch my face into *The Wolfman* like Lon Chaney Jr . . . speak with a British accent like Cary Grant in *Gunga Din* . . . clink a glass and say, *Here's lookin' at you, kid*, the way Bogart did with Bergman in *Casablanca* . . . smile like Alfonso Bedoya in *The Treasure of the Sierra Madre*, and turn mean and say with a Mexican accent, "We don't needa noa stinkin' badges" . . . give Lou Gehrig's farewell speech at Yankee Stadium, echo and all, like Gary Cooper in *The Pride of the Yankees* . . . demand to know Who's on First? like Lou Costello did to Bud Abbott . . . laugh crazy like Richard Widmark in *Kiss of Death* . . . hunch over and walk like Groucho Marx in *Duck*

Soup . . . growl like a cowardly lion as Bert Lahr does in *The Wizard of Oz* . . . walk stiff-legged like Boris Karloff in *Frankenstein* . . . suck blood like Bela Lugosi in *Dracula* . . . rule the streets like Leo Gorcey and Huntz Hall in *The Dead End Kids* . . . and *nyuk, nyuk* like Curly in The Three Stooges.

I never liked the love-story movies. Someone was always crying or dying or lying. There was too much kissing and I could never understand what happened when the movie faded to black, as when Jane Russell opened her mouth and licked her lips at us in *The Outlaw*.

But then, Charlie brought in the *The Jolson Story* at the Ritz, starring Larry Parks as Al Jolson, and this one would turn out to be a real problem. The movie was a big smash and people packed the theater and kept coming back to see it over and over again. Everyone left the Ritz singing Jolson songs: "California Here I Come"; "Toot Toot Tootsie Don't Cry"; "I'm Alabami Bound"; and "Mammy, My Little Mammy." Charlie had a hit and he let it run.

Yonkie Warner got hooked on Jolson so bad he thought he really was Jolson. No matter where he was or what was going on, he'd start singing like Jolson. When he sang "Mammy," he got on his knees and real tears rolled down his face as he sang for his momma. He was pretty good; not only did he sound like Jolson, he had Al's hand gestures and body moves down pat. He even started acting Jewish. We thought he'd get over it at some point, but he kept it up and it started to get annoying.

Still, we liked Yonkie and even felt sorry for him. His father delivered coal and with black soot all over him, Yonkie's father really looked like Al Jolson in black face. Yonkie didn't talk about his family. His mother and father came from the hills of West Virginia and were really poor. In a way, you couldn't blame him for wanting to be someone else. So we put up with his Jolson routine and prayed that it would end soon.

When he was Jolson, it changed Yonkie completely. He was cocky and pushy. He especially tried to impress the girls, but no matter how hard he tried, the girls wanted nothing to do with him. To them he was just plain old Yonkie Warner.

No one knew for sure whether it was true, but there was talk Yonkie went to see the Jolson movie every day. Things got worse as the weeks went by. The real Yonkie was fading away and in his place was Al Jolson. I really tried to like Al, but he was a smarty-pants, always thinking he knew what was right. He thought all the girls loved him and that people in the First Ward were only now starting to discover his talent. One day he told me his parents were against his being in show business and that they wanted him to become a rabbi. I told Yonkie that maybe he should go to the synagogue and pray. If that didn't work, maybe he should think about leaving town and joining vaudeville the way Jolson did in the movie. I was really worried about Yonkie and I was also starting to get worried about my brother, Richie.

Richie didn't care much for Yonkie, and he definitely had no interest in Al Jolson. So, it came as no surprise to me that Richie couldn't stand Yonkie's act. What I didn't know was how aggravated Richie was from hearing Yonkie doing Al Jolson all over the First Ward.

"What's the matter with that asshole, Yonkie Warner?" Richie asked me one day after school.

"What's wrong with him?" I responded, annoyed that my kid brother was criticizing one of my friends.

"He's a real jerk, going around like Al Jolson. Every time I see him, he's dancing and clapping his hands together and singing some stupid song."

"That's botherin' you?"

"It's botherin' everybody! When is he going to stop this shit? Nobody thinks it's funny!"

"Yonkie's OK, it's just that he really likes Al Jolson's music and it makes him happy."

"Happy? The guy's got a screw loose. You or one of your gang better tell him to knock it off."

"He'll quit soon. Believe me, just wait and see," I said trying to sound like I knew what I was talking about.

Most folks looked forward to the end of day when late at night the Kelly block quieted down, everybody longing to rest from their troubles and worries. In the stillness, the haunting sound of a Lackawanna train clanking over the tracks across the Chenango River Bridge could be heard as it chugged west parallel to Clinton Street on its way to Elmira. But now, not even the late nights brought peace. With Yonkie doing Jolson there was no rest, no end.

I should have seen it coming or at least stopped it when I had the chance, but something funny happened one night. It was Saturday night, very late, and Richie and I were trying to get to sleep after a long and hard day of running with our pals. Richie finally stopped tossing and I figured he was asleep. My eyes felt heavy and when the sound of the train came through it seemed to carry me away with it. But through the lonely wail of the train whistle I began to hear a sound familiar and frightening. I listened closely and it was Al Jolson's voice telling everyone he was "Alabami bound." How I wished that Lackawanna and Erie train were heading south, with him on it.

Soon, the train faded and the voice became louder, stronger. Coming out of a near sleep, I knew it was Yonkie Warner coming down Dickinson Street in the dead of night, singing Al Jolson. I felt Richie start to move next to me as Yonkie's voice came closer and louder.

Son of a bitch, I heard Richie mumble as he sat up, listened for a moment, and then got up. Richie reached under the bed. I thought it was for the milk bottle to take a pee. But before I knew it Richie brought up his BB-gun and slid the barrel onto the window sill. I wanted to stop him, but for some crazy reason, didn't.

California, here I come! Right back where I started from! Yonkie's voice sang out in the darkness. He acted as if Dickinson Street were his stage and he was strutting it like a Minstrel Man in front of an adoring and invisible crowd. Yonkie had a great imagination, but he didn't have an ounce of common sense. He didn't know it was time to bring the curtain down and bow out of everyone's life.

Yonkie was getting closer and I watched Richie's finger steady on the trigger and his eye sighted down the long barrel of his BB-gun. Suddenly, I felt as if I were sitting in the best seat at the Ritz watching a real thriller. Yonkie reached his big finish with, *Big time baby, don't be late. Open up that Golden Gate! California, Here I . . . ."*

Richie squeezed the trigger. The BB shot whistled through the night air striking Al Jolson, cutting him off before his big finish.

"Ohhhh, shit!! What's going on? What's happening!" Al screamed in confusion as the BB struck him high on the chest.

I suddenly found myself next to Richie at the bedroom window. Once again, Richie cocked the BB-gun, aimed, and pulled the trigger, sending another shot toward the wounded and confused entertainer. I watched as this one hit him in the middle, below the belt, in a really bad spot.

"Oh, you crazy bastard—you dirty sucker—you filthy puss-head!" Jolson cried out. He was hurt.

I watched Richie slowly pull the gun back from the window. We both listened as Al Jolson continued up Dickinson Street screaming his anger in every direction. Just like the train, his voice grew weaker and weaker as he got farther into the distance. We waited till we heard him no longer and, without saying a word, we laid our heads down on the pillows and listened. All was quiet.

FALLING ASLEEP THAT night, we had no idea how bad Yonkie's *wounds* were, but one thing we knew for sure: Al wouldn't be appearing at the Kelly Block Theatre anytime soon.

31.

BINGHAMTON PRESS   APRIL 2, 1946

SCHOOL ENROLLS 300 EX-GI'S, 600 EXPECTED BY END OF WEEK

Primo

Talking about a monster A-bomb, someone said he was a monster—a real live one. Peewee, Tootsie, Mike, Jugbug, Vic, Yonkie, and I planned to see him firsthand. We would meet at LaTorre's Friday night and sneak into the Kalurah Temple across from the Boys' Club, and see for ourselves if Primo Carnera, the former World Heavyweight Champion and now a professional wrestler, really looked like Frankenstein's Monster.

I woke early that Friday morning and, like most mornings, I looked for food. I wished I could still be in the Fresh Air Program at school and get a morning snack, but I was too old for that now. Mama had left for work and Fran was already gone to school to meet friends. Opening the cupboards, the emptiness inside matched the gnawing feeling in my stomach. With no ice in Grandma's icebox, the smell inside added insult to injury. I tore into my last piece of bubble gum and gave half to Richie. I promised him there would be something for him when he came home during the lunch break.

"I'm hungry now," Richie said.

"Yeah, I know. I am, too. But there's nothing here to eat."

"There's never anything to eat. I'm sick of it," Richie added.

"There's nothing we can do. Mama's broke."

"Again? How're we supposed to live?"

"We'll live. Don't worry."

"Look at how skinny you are. How're you gonna fight anybody if you're all skin and bones?"

"You've gotten me in enough fights. I don't do too bad, do I?"

"You don't always make it look easy."

"Yeah, yeah."

"There better be something here for me to eat when I come home."

"I told you I'd take care of it."

"Get me one of those lemon pies, OK? And some candy."

"Yeah, yeah."

"Where're you getting the dough?"

"I'll take care of it."

"Oh, you're going to steal the stuff, aren't you?"

"I said I'd take care of it."

Richie knew I'd do whatever it took. And so when he got home at the lunch break there was a small carton of cold Crowley's milk, a chocolate Tasty-Cake package of cupcakes, a small Tasty-Cake lemon pie, and a Milky Way. I offered him some of the tomato soup and crackers I was having, but Richie liked his lemon pie and cold milk. It was enough to get us through school that afternoon.

Later that evening someone showed up at our door. It was one of the few times someone ever came to visit Mama. I heard the knock at the door and when I opened it a tall young woman with a little girl smiled at me. The woman asked for *Theresa*. Mama came into our small living room and waved her friend in.

"Mary, how are you? It's good to see you," Mama said.

"I'm fine, Theresa. This is my little girl, Margie. She's a lot bigger than the last time you saw her."

"She sure is, but she's still very beautiful," Mama said. "Mary, this is Ronnie, my oldest son."

"I thought so. He's gotten big."

"Yeah. Fran and Richie aren't here right now. Let's go in the kitchen and sit. You're still in Connecticut, huh?"

"I sure am and I really like it there."

"You don't think you'll come back to Binghamton?"

"Probably not."

There was something different about the young woman visitor. The way she walked with her shoulders back and her head up high. There was a clean, clear look in her eyes. Her voice seemed sure. Where did she come from? Why was she here? I stayed behind as Mama, the woman and her daughter entered the kitchen. I lingered out of sight around the corner to listen a while longer.

"You're just here for a visit, Mary?" Mama asked.

"Yeah, Tree, I'm going back in a few days. I was able to get some time off, but I've got to get back to work."

"What are you doing there?"

"Tobacco. I'm working on a tobacco farm."

"How's that for you?"

"It's unbelievable. You work hard, but the money's good, really good."

"That's good."

"You're still at E. J.'s?"

"Yep, still at the factory in Johnson City."

"Hey, Tree, I wanted to tell you, Ronnie could make some good money next summer in Connecticut."

Listening in, my stomach started turning.

"They're looking for workers. They need them bad. They'd pay Ronnie sixty cents an hour and he'd work ten to fourteen hours a day, six to seven days a week. They don't pay overtime."

"How old does he have to be?"

"Fourteen, but I could talk to my boss. He'd let Ronnie work and pay him off the books. They do that a lot. Tobacco is big in Connecticut. They grow the tobacco that's used for the outer wrapper on really good cigars. It's a huge business."

Listening in, I couldn't say anything, but I was scared. Connecticut seemed like a really long way from home. I'd never wandered too far from the First Ward. I was looking to spend the summer on the river with my pals. Mama seemed quiet, like she was thinking about it.

"He's only eleven," Mama said.

"It wouldn't matter. My boss would do it if I ask him."

"Where would he stay? Who would feed him?"

"All the boys live in outbuildings on the farm. They get food and they get to pack lunches when they're in the field working the tobacco plants."

"I don't know . . . he's pretty young."

"They're bringing boys in from all over, Puerto Rico, Pennsylvania, anywhere they can get them. Girls from all over Connecticut and Massachusetts work on the farms, too. They keep the boys and girls separate."

"Who'd watch over him?"

"I'd keep an eye on him. And I'd make sure he wrote to you and I'd show him how to send money home. You could use some extra money couldn't you?"

"Are you kidding?"

"Connecticut is a beautiful place and the farms are big and the tobacco needs working. What do you think?"

I held my breath waiting for Mama's answer. I didn't want to go. It would be like going away to war. I was scared and afraid I'd never come back if I went away.

"I'm gonna have to think about it."

"OK. Let me know before I head back in a couple of days."

"You know what, Mary? I appreciate you're stopping by, but I think I'm gonna keep Ronnie home for now."

I couldn't believe it. Mama didn't give me up. She didn't

send me away. I slipped quietly into my bedroom and waited for the visitor to leave. I knew she really needed the money, but she wouldn't let me go.

"OK, Theresa. But if you change your mind, get hold of my mother and she can let me know. In the meantime, here's a little gift for you and your kids," Mary said reaching into a large paper bag. She gave Mama a shiny pillow with an American flag on it, with fancy cords all over its edges. The writing on it read: GOD BLESS OUR FIGHTING BOYS. Mama thanked the woman and when she left she tossed it on our sofa.

The visitor seemed nice enough, but I never wanted to see her again. I never heard another word about tobacco farming in Connecticut and I was glad, really glad. The First Ward and the Kelly block weren't much, but they were home and I never wanted to leave, no matter what.

When I reached LaTorre's, all the guys were waiting there for me. We wasted no time heading toward the bridge and Kalurah Temple. On the way, the only thing we talked about was Primo. The newspaper said he was six-foot-seven and weighed 275 pounds. He was going up against Killer Kowalski, and the winner would face Gorgeous George for the world title.

Kalurah Temple covered an entire block. It belonged to the Shriners Club and they built it, inside and out, to look like something out of ancient Egypt. The Temple could handle a large crowd, and people came there on weekends to see circuses, prize-fighting, and pro wrestling.

Primo brought out a huge crowd. This made it easier for us to sneak in. There was a side-exit door halfway down the block. All we did was wait for the right moment to jimmy it open and slip inside. Once inside, we closed the doors. Glancing up the long and wide stairway leading to the main floor, we saw the light shining dimly through a blanket of smoke. The noise of the crowd got louder as we moved slowly up the stairs. Once on top, we slid, one-by-one, into the crowd. Then we met up again and moved about the large space until we eventually settled in the upper balcony that wrapped around the main floor above the ring below.

Now we waited for the big event. The lights dimmed and a huge roar meant the monster would be coming out. First, a spotlight hit Killer Kowalski dressed in a shiny gold robe. The crowd cheered as he made his way toward the ring: *Killer, Killer, Killer* they chanted.

The Killer entered the ring and spun around, waving to the fans. Now, the wait began. The crowd wanted Primo and he was not to be seen. Soon, the crowd began to stomp their feet on the floor. It got louder and louder and suddenly, it stopped. A hush fell over the crowd. A spotlight flashed into a far corner. A giant of a man entered into its brilliant light. The crowd let out a gasp. Everyone remained silent as he stepped toward the ring. His face looked like it was chiseled out of rock. His jet-black hair and the stiff-legged way he walked really did make him look like Frankenstein's Monster.

The crowd began booing him. The more they booed, the meaner he looked. Some men around us called him *Dago, Wop, Greaseball.* They looked like veterans who probably had fought in Italy and were still mad. Stepping into the ring, Primo towered over Killer Kowalski. His robe opened and fell to the floor. His massive body rippled with muscles. His eyes alone looked like they could kill. None of us said a word, except for Yonkie, who muttered, *Holy shit.*

In the center of the ring, the announcer introduced each fighter. Killer Kowalski got a big cheer; Primo got a thunderous chorus of boos. Primo reacted by waving his fist at people at ringside and then into the balcony at us. We all stood up and shook our fists back at him knowing we were far from his reach.

Primo and the Killer got their instructions from the referee and went to their corners to wait for the bell. The bell gonged and Primo stepped stiff-legged toward Killer. Primo grabbed Killer and pulled him into a headlock. The crowd groaned. Primo looked like he could have snapped Killer like a twig. Somehow, Killer spun and broke free from Primo. Then with a punch to Primo's stomach, Primo doubled up and the Killer jack-hammered him to the canvas with a blow using both fists to the back of Primo's head. The crowd roared. Killer grabbed his hands in pain as if he had just smashed them into a concrete block. The crowd moaned. Meanwhile, Primo shook his head to clear it as he struggled to his feet.

For the next half-hour, the two fought to destroy each other. Pounding and slamming, gouging and punching, sweat poured over their bodies as their chests heaved for air. The crowd urged Killer on though it appeared he was tiring. My friends and I shouted till our throats were raw, hoping Killer would beat the monster.

Primo suddenly didn't like the third man in the ring, referee Marty Cardone. Marty was trying to keep the fight clean, but Primo wanted Marty to mind his own business. Primo turned and grabbed Marty and lifted him up and threw him out of the ring. The crowd gasped when Marty landed hard. The crowd booed while they carried Marty to the dressing room. Pete Minnow climbed into the ring to finish reffing the match. The crowd booed Primo's every move the rest of the way.

Killer slapped at Primo with his enormous arm and accidentally poked Primo in the eye. The crowd roared. Blind and in a rage, Primo charged Killer and when he got his hands on him, Primo lifted him off the canvas and spun him around at least five times then slammed him to the canvas with a thud. Killer didn't move. The crowd sat in stunned silence. Primo then crashed his huge body on top of Killer and the referee slapped the canvas three times. The crowd booed as Primo rose to his feet and stood over his beaten foe. When Primo kicked Killer laying motionless on the mat, the audience threatened to charge the ring. Primo responded with a horrific bone-chilling growl and the crowd backed off.

Pete Minnow tried to raise Primo's hand as the winner, but he was too short to lift it, so he motioned to Primo to raise his hand.

Primo responded with a raised fist and let out another bloodcurdling cry, then stepped through the ropes and headed to the dressing room.

The grumbling crowd left the arena quickly. Our gang decided that Primo acted like a big-shot and was in need of a lesson. We planned to challenge Primo. To do so, we thought it would be better to be at the other end of the building, a good block away, when Primo came out.

"He thinks he's hot shit," Tootsie said.

"Yeah," everyone agreed.

"Killer could have beaten him," Peewee chimed in.

"Primo was lucky," Mike said.

"You could probably kick his ass, Mike," Jug-bug said.

"Yeah, Mike. You could take him," Vic added.

"He's just a big sucker," Yonkie said, as if we needed to be reminded.

"We'll see how big he is when he gets his ass out here on the street," I said.

We waited for a long time on the dark and empty street. It was quiet except for an occasional car passing by. Suddenly, we saw some figures moving on the corner under the street light. Among the six or seven people, one towered above all the others. From the way he walked we knew it was Primo. Even from a block away, he looked bigger than a street light.

All the guys looked at me as I cupped my hands and yelled as loud as I could, "Primo! Yo, Primo! C'mon, I wanna kick your ass! It's payback time for what you did to Sharkey! Remember him?"

That got their attention up the block and they turned in our direction. Primo stopped in his tracks.

"Yo, Primo, c'mon. You heard it right. Get your ass down here and we'll show you how First Warders fight."

Primo took two steps in our direction and let out a deafening roar. We turned suddenly, and in a flash bolted at full speed toward home. Straining to distance ourselves from the monster, we huffed and puffed like racehorses. Out of breath, we began slowing down when we reached the other side of the Clinton Street Bridge. We walked silently, gasping for air. Every now and then, I looked back to make sure no one was behind us. None of us knew how fast Primo could run or how quickly his extra-long legs could close the distance between us. Without warning I broke into a sprint again just to be sure. In an instant my buddies were on my heels, thinking I had spotted Primo. We caught our breath and wondered silently what might have been if Primo had any speed.

WE LAUGHED THE rest of the way home. Every now and then we glanced over our shoulder—just to make sure no monster was following us.

32.

BINGHAMTON PRESS   OCTOBER 25, 1946

MAYOR AUTHORIZED TO LEASE LAND TO STATE FOR VETERANS' HOME

Retreat

I t would last about an hour, or so, Mama said. I didn't know how she knew that since she never went to one as far as I knew; she never even really said what they did there. But I was going. No one ever explained anything . . . you just did what you were told. And that was that.

Mama scrubbed and ironed my clothes. She said I had to be clean, really clean. She meant business, so I soaked so long in the tub the skin on my hands wrinkled like an old man's. I didn't know a thing about this retreat I was going to at Saint Cyril's Church with Uncle Joe. All I knew it was for the men and boys of the First Ward. Richie was lucky; he was too young to go. Mama finally told me the retreat was like going to a revival, the kind they held on the vacant lot on Murray Street.

Saint Cyril's offered one-hour Catechism classes on Saturdays for the students from Daniel Dickinson public school. It was like going to Catholic school. Fathers Matthew, Alfred, and Stephen and Sisters Angela, Joseph, and Valeria taught the classes. The priests and nuns didn't look that tough; the small nuns and thin priests looked average, but there was something about them—something in their eyes, the look, the way it could make you feel. You were afraid they were like Clark Kent, Superman, who acted like a wimp and Diana Prince, Wonder Woman, who looked soft in her street clothes, but then you saw what they turned into. Word got around about priests and nuns. You heard stories of how they even took down some of the worst guys in the ward. You heard about priests and nuns taking the meanest and most troubled kids out of class and when they came back the toughies' eyes were red from crying. What did they do to them to turn them into Jello? Tootsie and Peewee told me to keep my mouth shut and to listen to every word coming out of their mouths. They told me not to pretend to be listening because they could tell. And they warned me never to look at the big clock on the wall. So for one hour a week, in that Catechism class, I was in a totally different world, a world in which no one fooled around. I couldn't believe how Tootsie and Peewee could go to Saint Cyril's full-time. No wonder they were so tough.

Catechism class taught me about God and about being a good Catholic. I learned about Adam and Eve and the apple in the Garden of Eden. I learned how the devil makes you sin and about all the different sins. According to the teachers, it seemed like almost everything you did was a sin. Then I learned about confession and how to clean yourself of your sins. Sister Valeria taught us the Act of Contrition.

I memorized the Ten Commandments, the Lord's Prayer, and the Hail Mary. Many lessons were about Jesus; how He lived, how He was crucified for us. It wasn't easy, but the Sisters made us repeat the prayers over and over again until you could say them in your sleep.

Almost everything you heard in Catechism class was new stuff you never heard before, but the biggest surprise was when the teacher told us everyone had a soul. Sister Joseph said you couldn't see it or touch it or hear it, but it's inside each one of us. All the kids looked around at each other wondering what this all meant.

When I was seven-years old I made my First Communion at Saint Cyril's. Somehow Mama came up with the dough and bought me a white suit and a brand-new pair of white leather shoes. The shoes were too tight, but I couldn't tell Mama they hurt. I carried a little white prayer-book and black Rosary Beads. A Scapula hung around my neck inside my white shirt. The night before receiving the holy bread, I went to confession and told all my sins to a priest behind a dark screen. Sister Valencia said confession was like taking a bath . . . it washed away all your sins. From that time on, whenever I took a bath I always watched the water swirling down the drain and thought if sin were dirt, I had a lot of confessing to do. It was scary trying to remember all the bad things I had done and then go squeal on myself to a shadowy face behind a screen.

But this retreat thing; this was a new one. What's it all about? I guessed I'd soon know.

A light drizzle fell when Uncle Joe and I stepped out of the Kelly block and headed toward the church. We borrowed Aunt Irene's umbrella, the one with big pink flowers on it. It helped some, but I could feel the mist hitting my pants. We didn't say anything as we walked together down Dickinson Street in the fading light of day, one of the telltale signs that fall was on its way. The skies above the valley surrounding Binghamton darkened as the clouds settled in for what would seem their usual long stay through fall and winter. Only the far-off spring or a glimpse of the sun could send the gloominess on its way.

Every now and then on our walk, Uncle Joe spit tobacco juice from the Druggist Tuck tobacco he liked to chew. I watched the spit fly through the air and splatter on the street near the curb. He was a good shot; he never once hit the sidewalk. But, on occasion the wind would suddenly gust and swirl. Not wanting to get caught off guard, I kept a close eye on the bulge inside Uncle Joe's cheek. When the compact little ball inside his cheek rolled and his lips started to move together like a baby sucking a bottle, I knew he was moving the tobacco juice to the front. Suddenly his head moved back, then jolted forward and parting his lips, black spit spewed into the air. The swirling wind played with the flying gob turning it into different shapes before it crashed onto the pavement. I decided to walk upwind, to make sure I didn't walk into church with any stains on me.

As we got closer, we could see other guys heading toward the church. It was probably a smart thing to have the retreat on a Wednesday night instead of near the weekend when it would be harder to get the men away from the saloons up on Clinton Street.

The church doors slammed behind Uncle Joe and me echoing our arrival. Uncle Joe dumped the wad from his mouth just before we went in. It felt good to leave the windswept misty night air and the flying tobacco juice and enter the church. Inside, sweet-smelling candles burned and flickered as we took our seats in the middle of the almost-empty church. Uncle Joe and I must have gotten there a little early, but we soon heard the doors opening and shutting around the church and the creaking sound of feet scraping along the polished wood floors. Men came, some alone, others with a son or brother or nephew. Most of the men were like Uncle Joe—vets home from the war. A few of them limped—one walked stiff-legged, a couple of them had crutches. One guy came in with one arm. The expressions on their faces looked like they were sleepwalking. I recognized some of these guys from around the Ward, mostly from seeing them hanging out around the bars on Clinton Street. They came in and scattered about, choosing to sit by themselves, away from others. I looked around the church hoping I'd see at least one of my pals, but none were there. Most of the young kids there were the "goodies" in the Ward. Soon, the smell of rain-soaked clothes replaced the sweet smell of candles.

Every movement, no matter how slight, made noise in the hollowness of the church. The stillness inside never found perfect peace from the coughing and banging and shuffling of the people inside. The church began to fill and in the rare quiet moments you could hear a hard rain begin to beat on the church roof. Hanging high above from the ceiling, pockets of light fell upon us. I wondered how anyone got way up there to change light bulbs when they went out.

I glanced over at Uncle Joe. He never drank, so I never had to get him home from Clinton Street. He never got a scratch on him fighting in Europe. I was glad he was home safe and sound. Like most of the other vets when they got home, Uncle Joe signed up for 20/20, for the vets. They got twenty bucks a week for twenty weeks. I heard him telling Mama he was thinking about going to drafting school in Albany on the GI Bill. Give Uncle Joe a pencil and paper and he could draw anything and make it look real and beautiful. He had a special talent, but he wasn't interested in art. Before joining the Army, he spent the last five years setting bowling pins at the Deluxe Alleys on Henry Street. If he left again, even to go to drafting school, I'd miss him all over again.

The church bells striking outside brought a strange quietness over everyone inside. There was a long pause after the last note of the bell struck that echoed loudly and faded slowly. From the back of the altar a dark-hooded figure wearing a black cape suddenly appeared and walked slowly toward us like a dark cloud forming. His heels clapped on the wooden floor. Standing in front of the first pew, he dropped the hood from around his face. He looked about the church into the faces waiting for him to speak. I had never seen him before. He was a priest, but he wasn't from around here. He looked different from any priest I had ever seen before. A dark, neatly trimmed beard framed his bony face. His penetrating eyes sat deep inside his head. Not young, yet not old, his thin body shifted inside his robe. The light overhead made his thinning hair glow.

RIGHT: Uncle John in Army dress uniform after completing training. *(Private)* *BOTTOM, LEFT*: Uncle Joe in Army fatigues during field training exercise. *(Private) BOTTOM, RIGHT*: Uncle Bill (on right) with buddy (company barber) on supply train in Germany. *(Private)*

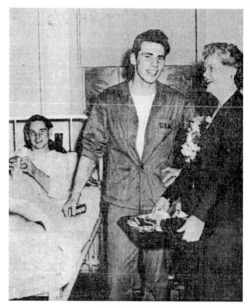

TOP: Uncle John and buddies in Germany taking a break with beer and pipes in hand. *(Private)* *BOTTOM, LEFT*: G.I. with captured Nazi Swastika Flag in Germany. *(Private)* *BOTTOM, RIGHT*: During a hospital visit with wounded serviceman, Arnold Miller of Binghamton tells Mrs. Frances Whittemore about his joining the army at 15. He saw a year's overseas duty, was discharged, and enlisted in the Navy on his seventeenth birthday. At left is Joseph Folweiler of Philadelphia who was wounded D-Day plus 5 in Normandy.

TOP: Credited with being the first paratrooper to land on D-Day at Normandy, Captain Frank G. Lillyman, of the 101st Airborne Division's Screaming Eagles revisits the Boys' Club where he was a former member and thanks Roy Payne and the Victory Volunteers for all their help. That's me on the right, proud to put my arm around a real hero.
BOTTOM: From L to R: William W. Driver, Edwin V. Chandler and Harold Ruth of the Community Chest's Annual Drive help me practice to speak publicly about how the Boys' Club will benefit from the money raised.

The hometown crowd gathers downtown to celebrate the end of the war . . .

. . . and continues late into the early morning hours.

TOP: A wedding at St. Cyril's Church on Clinton Street. *(Private)* *BOTTOM*: Crosses outside of St. Cyril's on Veteran's Day honor those parishioners who gave their lives during World War II. *(Private)*

TOP: A 21 Gun Salute with Taps by the Bugler mark the solemn occasion of honoring the fallen. *BOTTOM*: Flags dress the markers of all deceased veterans at all cemeteries. *(Private)*

TOP: Uncle John's marker at Spring Forest Cemetery in the First Ward. Uncle Joe is interred in the same plot with his brother, but his marker has not been placed yet. *(Private)* *LEFT* Sgt. Manuel Balin's gravesite at Beth David-Riverside Cemetery off Conklin Road. *(Private)*

Elizabeth Barish Vrabel, "Ma,"our grandmother, with great-grandsons Ricky (L) and Mikey Acquisto (R). *(Private)*

"Look at you," Father's voice spoke gently. "Look around at those near you." Heads turned awkwardly. "Most of you men are back from the war, a war that took you away from your homes to fight on fields and towns and villages you never even heard of before. Everyone praised your sacrifice and your service. Now that you're home again, it's a different story. I have seen what war can do to the soul—on the battlefield and at home. There's little to be proud of . . . I know because I hear the confessions and the things I hear tell me you're all going to hell, each and every one of you. And if these young men here follow in your footsteps, they too will surely end up in hell." His voice gradually rose. "You'll all end up burning in the fires of hell." His powerful voice echoed throughout the church as if God were speaking.

Sometimes when he spoke, his words rolled out like thunder; other times they cracked like lightning. Every now and then he whispered a word or phrase like a gentle breeze; then followed with words roaring out of his mouth like a raging wind.

I felt Uncle Joe tensing up beside me. He had just been in combat. I'm sure what he was hearing was news to him and not good news. After surviving the Nazis, he comes home to hear he's going to hell. And what about me? What did I do?

This sounded serious. This was nothing like the revivals on Murray Street with all those happy people singing and shouting their hearts out.

"Your flesh is going to burn," Father's voice roared. No one moved a muscle. No one took a breath.

The palms of my hands began to sweat. I knew I had done some bad things and I'd been told many times by many people to "go to hell," but no one had ever looked at me and told me I was going to the real hell and mean it. A sense of panic ran through me. I had to know what I did to deserve this.

"You have sinned." *Yeah, but who hasn't,* I argued in my defense.

"Lust, fornication, adultery, and coveting—sins of the flesh that will be paid for in hell." *I don't even know what those words mean, so how could I be guilty?*

"The devil has hold of your soul. He knows how easy it is to get you to ignore God and listen to him, the prince of darkness." *I guess I hear the devil talk to me, but his voice sounds a lot like mine.*

"Who do you think you're kidding? God knows who you're listening to." *I don't think I'm really listening to the devil. But sometimes I do things I know I shouldn't.*

"God knows how you're wasting the life he's given you. You men like to go up to the bars on Clinton Street and drink your troubles away." *I knew that one hurt, as I looked around the church.*

Father moved in front of us like a cat. He looked up to heaven and down at hell, his head shifting from side to side as he pointed to men and boys, his long bony fingers sticking out of the sleeves of his dark robe. Sometimes he seemed to be rising into the air. He lifted his crucifix and waved it at us like the doctor waved the cross at Count Dracula to keep the count from getting to the girl's neck.

"You've come back from the war. You saw the killing and the filth of war. God saved you and brought you back. A lot of your friends and fellow soldiers didn't come back. Where do you think they are now? If they could come back now, do you think they'd be wasting their lives boozing and carousing every night? *Probably, if they're First Warders.*

"When you go to hell, there'll be no mercy, no relief, no second chance, and no return from the searing, burning smell of flesh—your flesh." *No one ever told me this before. I heard about hell in Catechism class, but it was just a word about a place for really bad people. I don't think I'm that bad—I mean compared to others I've seen.*

"Yes, you're bad. Even you young boys, you know what

you're up to . . . what's on your minds . . . what you're after. You're evil. You're sinners. There is no hope for you." *Wait till the guys here this. Man, are we in trouble.*

I could feel my throat tightening; my mouth was dry and it was hard to swallow.

"Getting cleaned up and coming to church and getting down on your knees doesn't mean you are loving God. God gave you life to suffer and die." *This is not good news. I don't know what Uncle Joe thinks, but the two things I'm most scared of are suffering and dying.*

"You boys—you run in gangs like packs and look for trouble." *What's wrong with our gang? Tootsie and Peewee, two of my best friends in our gang, are even altar boys—at this church. And we don't look for trouble; trouble just seems to find us.*

Father went on, telling us how we failed and rejected God in favor of the devil. Moving back and forth in front of the altar, he said we had taken up with the devil and fallen for his earthly pleasures.

"You have sinned," Father boomed. *Yes, I stole things But mostly things I needed. Well, some stuff I swiped from Philly's, Kresge's, Sears-Roebuck, the A&P—I really didn't need, but it was stuff I wanted.*

"You have sinned," He repeated, raising his voice. *OK I go into Uncle John's foot locker in his bedroom and look at the pictures of naked French ladies.*

"You have sinned!" he shouted out. *Yeah, I swear a lot when I get mad and I lie a lot if I get caught.*

"You have sinned," he said, his voice straining. *Yes, I go to the magazine rack at LaTorre's looking inside women's magazines for pictures of girl's parts. But the only thing I ever found was an ad way in the back showing a woman wearing a girdle. And besides, you had to look fast so Mr. LaTorre didn't see you looking at women's magazines and know what you were up to.*

We were unclean, he told us. *It was like he knew I still thought about Monique and still wonder what could have been inside the magic dice.* We had turned our backs on God, he reminded us. For certain God would not forget. And when we came face-to-face with God and He passed His final judgment on us, the loss of heaven would be even more painful than the fires of hell.

Father seemed to grow larger and his voice got deeper as he spoke. I wondered why he couldn't be more like Bing Crosby in *The Bells of St. Mary's*, a kind priest with a smile on his face who sang with a soft, sweet voice.

I waited for some good news, but none seemed to come. If there was any, I probably missed it because he got me thinking and worried about all the bad things I had done. I could feel the sweat rolling down the back of my neck. There was no way of getting around it, there was no way of fooling God or Father. According to Father, I was doomed. I was weak. I was not deserving of God's love. In short, I was a sinner and hell was where I was heading. Unless. . . .

"Repent!" Father shouted. "Beg for mercy. Sin no more. One day you will find out where you're going to—heaven or hell." *Yeah, but first you have to die to get the answer.*

We sat for way over an hour and Father never let up. He started throwing in some other words: *repentance . . . forgiveness . . . mercy . . . healing . . . grace . . . redemption . . . salvation . . . love.*

Then, he stopped. He stood silently and looked about the church. This long pause had me worried because I didn't know what was coming next. To my joyous relief, he reached over his shoulder and pulled the hood over his head and turned and vanished behind the altar like a spirit. Everyone remained seated. One by one the men dropped to their knees and bowed their heads. The silence was soon broken by the crackling, coughing, and hacking of the smokers in church. Lungs released their deposits as men spit into their handkerchiefs.

When Uncle Joe went to his knees, I joined him. When he bowed his head, I followed. My mind and body were too weary from the pounding this strange priest had given us. I felt my shoulders slump. I peeked over at Uncle Joe and saw his lips moving slowly, forming words I couldn't hear or understand. He was my hero, he and his two brothers. Uncle Joe and Uncle Bill were gentle men; Uncle John never stood down from a fight. They had fought in the war, risking their lives and limbs and had beaten evil men. I liked putting on Uncle Joe's uniform jacket with the stripes and emblems and medals. I felt proud and grown up. Now, the priest said Uncle Joe was a sinner and he was going to hell and there was nothing I could do about it. I glanced over at Uncle Joe and saw a shiny line under his eye. When he blinked a tiny tear rolled down his cheek and fell onto his sleeve. He reached over and covered it with his hand. I had never seen a tear on a man before.

I closed my eyes. My thoughts began to drift. I started to think about the summer just past and the fun we had down by the river and the games we played. I could hear the guys yelling—I felt the hot sun—I could smell the cocoa butter melting on my burning flesh. I could touch the cool, soothing river water and smell its strange bouquet.

WE RAN LIKE the wind this summer, so fast, not even the devil could catch us.

EPILOGUE

S oon after the war, we left the river behind, taking with us the memories of the joy and fun she gave us. We slowly drifted away—while we were still ahead. The river could turn on you without warning; it was just her nature.

As we got a little older and our wings started to spread, some friends began to go in different directions. You always held on to those closest to you. Now and then you'd run into an old buddy or hear news about someone—the good and the bad.

We moved on from the quiet rushing of water to the loud clatter and clacking of balls in the smoked-filled pool hall owned and operated by Irving Crane in a walk-up building on Henry Street. Crane was a world champion billiard player who held several world records. He was always immaculately dressed and a gentleman who insisted on good manners, tolerating nothing less in his establishment. A man of scrupulous morals and character, he was known as *the Deacon* by his competitors. When he died, years later, Crane's obituary carried an observation by Rudolph Wanderone, also known as Minnesota Fats, the legendary pool hustler. He said, "Irv Crane would have been the only guy to notice the horse under Lady Godiva."

As a child growing up during the war, I saw beautiful faces, full of hope and possibility, bold faces open to life. My friends and I took different paths. No matter which road they took, I can still see their faces, hear their laughs, and know their hearts. We were wartime friends with much in common during an uncommon time.

The passing years dull but do not erase the memory of the early years of our lives. Nor do the years gone by lessen the hold those times have on our hearts. We remember those years and the pain as well as the joy we experienced. Before, during, and after, the war affected everyone in some way.

Those who fought in World War II were truly amazing. Their story is one of unbelievable sacrifice and courage. Most GIs were children of immigrants who endured, along with their parents, a global depression, poverty, and prejudice, only to be called on to leave their families and their children, to fight on foreign soil, not for months or a year or two, but "for the duration." Many left as boys and came back men. There were those who returned and had seen too much war and were not the same. Some never returned. They lie far from home in places like Anzio, Normandy, Corregidor, and Iwo Jima—all Americans, sons of Irish, Italian, Greek, African, Slovak, Polish, Russian, Lebanese and English descendants. They are of many religions. Five-hundred-and-fifty-five men from Binghamton, Johnson City, Endicott, and surrounding Broome County gave their lives. Another estimated fifteen-hundred were wounded.

Following the war, families whose men were killed-in-action received notices from the government that they could choose to have the remains of their loved ones brought home at government expense or let them stay to be buried among their comrades at American Cemeteries overseas. Many families chose to let them lie where they had fallen.

I have visited American cemeteries outside of Florence, Italy, and Maastricht, The Netherlands, where our men are interred. These sites are immaculate and serene. Simple white marble crosses and Stars of David convey name, rank, unit, home state, and date-of-death. At the front gates solemn words of tribute are chiseled in huge hand-polished marble walls overlooking these fallen comrades. Wherever one of our men killed-in-action cannot be identified, these are the words on his marker:

EPILOGUE

HE RESTS IN HONORED GLORY
AN AMERICAN SOLDIER
KNOWN BUT TO GOD

Many cemeteries overseas rarely have American visitors. I commented to a U.S. cemetery superintendent that, "War seems such a waste. These men, as generations pass, will soon be forgotten." He responded that, "Every year, on Memorial Day, the people who live around the cemeteries where the fighting took place show up at the grave-sites by the thousands to lay flowers and pay homage to the Americans who fought and died to make them free. They have been coming, the young and the old, generation after generation, to this day, to honor the sacrifice and courage of our GIs."

When our fighting men returned victoriously after the war, they lifted the spirit of our neighborhoods. They came home heroes in our eyes, and though some had difficulty adjusting, they were respected and admired. Like the depression they had lived through and the World War they survived and won, the veterans came back to face yet another challenge—an uncertain future. They had to pick up the pieces of their lives and fit in, as we all did.

Most of the men who returned are gone now. They rest under green and shady slopes on the hills that rim the valley where they were born and reared. At Calvary-Saint Patrick, Spring Forest, Riverhurst, Slovak Catholic, Temple Israel and Beth David Riverside, and St. Michael's Cemeteries—their graves are decorated faithfully on Memorial Day and Veterans' Day every year. There are still a few old soldiers living. Some still march in the holiday parades down Main Street. Soon they too will be gone.

With the evolution of high-tech weaponry and our military services made up of professional men and women warriors, it is safe to say there will never be another Greatest Generation—soldiers made up of common citizens. The Greatest Generation had their *rendezvous with destiny*. Now it takes its place in history with past patriots who fought on the long and never ending road of liberty, at Bunker Hill, the Alamo, Gettysburg, and Chateau Thierry—World War I.

The war years gave me many heroes. At that time my uncles—John, Joe, and Bill—stood at the top of my list. Before the war, Uncle John worked in the Civilian Conservation Corp (CCC) one of President Roosevelt's job programs to counter the devastating effects of the Great Depression. It gave young people a chance to earn a living and to help their families. After the war, they returned and took advantage of the 20/20 Program. After that ran out, Uncle John worked in construction for awhile until he landed a job with AGFA ANSCO in the First Ward. Uncle Joe went to school on the GI Bill and became a top-notch mechanical draftsman. He traveled around the country to work with a number of large manufacturing companies. Uncle Bill got a job in construction and then went back to work, part-time, for Izzy Lipshutz's grocery store on Clinton Street. While there, he returned to Central High for six months and received his diploma. He then moved on to work for the American grocery store before opening up Jumbo's Market on the corner of Dickinson and Oak Streets. It was his store, just a few doors down from the Kelly block.

Soon after the war, veterans and young men and women with a high-school diploma could get a job at IBM. At IBM and most other major companies you could raise your family, grow old, and retire.

Although I never knew my father, he deserves to be called a hero because he made the ultimate sacrifice—giving his life in service to his country. The first son of Italian immigrants, the native name *Cappellacci* was somehow Americanized early on to *Capalaces* by city school administrators and teachers.

Many years later, I came to realize what a real hero my mother was. With no education and no support she brought up my sister, brother, and me. Women of Mama's day had it tough. First-generation immigrants born of uneducated parents were left alone, in many ways, to make their way through life. Often deprived of parental support and love, they lacked the nurturing and guidance to prepare them for adulthood. From the Great Depression to World War II, many women struggled in an alien society, oftentimes devoid of civilized manners and social coherence. Ignorance was pervasive and women were forced to have work before they could have a life. Even on the job, there was little respect for women. Social grace and compassion were rare. People were quick to label and condemn. Against this background was the make-believe life portrayed at the neighborhood movie houses that fired the hopes and dreams of women with the possibility that life might one day be better. For many, this reality faded to black, the way the movies ended.

Mama worried a lot. She was fiercely protective of us. We learned early on it was better not to give her any bad news or to get hurt. It could trigger a fiery reaction in her. Most of our problems we kept to ourselves.

Mama was a dreamer, a spirited woman who loved movies and loved to laugh and dance. She sacrificed her entire life for her children and grandchildren. One time she took Richie and me to see the Three Stooges live at the Capitol Theatre and we sat way up front watching Moe, Larry, and Shemp carry on. The crowd laughed throughout the show. Nobody laughed louder than Mama. Though far from perfect she had a tough life and never gave up. She took great joy and pride in all our accomplishments.

My grandmother always remained my biggest hero. An immigrant girl, she loved her new life in America and always remained joyful and happy even in the direst of times. Though she amassed nothing in material things she left a treasure to us all in knowing her. The centerpiece of her legacy was kindness and it flowed with grace and love. She was a gentle soul.

My sister Fran and brother Richie are my heroes as well.

Together we took on a lot of challenges and shared the good times and the bad. And we survived.

Years later the young guys and gals I knew growing up during the war took on special status. Most came from families with little. They didn't complain. Many took the hands dealt them without anger or regret. They lifted themselves and kept the faith through rapidly changing and challenging times. Most revered their parents. Their friends were precious and friendships often lasted a lifetime. Above all we shared one common bond. We were once little guys and gals trying hard to become men and women, even though we weren't. We were growing up, but had no idea what that meant. All across my hometown, these people remain true heroes to me to this day.

I didn't realize it at the time, but I came to understand why the Boys' Club played such an important part in our lives. It kept us from being alone—it made us act and think about today and wonder about tomorrow—it gave us a place where we all belonged—where we were welcome.

Some of the guys I grew up with are gone. John (Yonkie) Warner, Mike Ganisin, and John (Jug-bug) Jones. They are missed and remembered.

Whenever I get back to Binghamton, I always pay a visit to Clinton Street. I walk the street where in my youth many of my dreams found inspiration. This once-vibrant and life-filled corridor is now but a relic of itself. Here I see the decaying remains of my youth. I pass by mostly empty buildings and vacant lots where vital businesses and well-kept housing once stood. The once-crowded street full of noisy and proud people is quiet and empty except for a few old men dropping by the few faded beer joints still left along the strip.

The once proud clouds of white smoke rising skyward from stacks throughout the valley rise no more. E. J., IBM, GE, Agfa-Ansco, Links, Fairbanks, Ozalid's, Kroehler Manufacturing are gone. All of the once-thriving factories in the surrounding communities are closed and rotting, victims of "progress" and "business strategies." They are but another notch in the great rust belt that stretches across much of upstate New York today.

Some men and women stayed in Binghamton through the good and bad times. They remained committed to the hometown they loved. They have stayed in the trenches giving support in every way to help the community rekindle a brighter future. It seems the human spirit is such that when hope is linked to action, most anything is possible.

A new Boys and Girls' Club was just built on Clinton Street where I once lived in the alley in back of Elmo's. A new government building went up where Olum's Furniture once stood at Clinton and Mygatt. An international U.S. corporation has built a new business park and manufacturing plant in the First Ward, employing sixty locals. These are the first major new construction projects in the Ward since World War II.

A long-time trucking company on Clinton Street has expanded its business model and is now providing high-tech logistic support to industries—securing records, data and files in a high-tech environment. Next to a vacant lot where the Ritz Theatre once stood, a new eatery is busy serving hearty breakfasts and lunches to a growing community-wide customer base. Small trees were planted along the sidewalks that bloom in the spring.

A NEW SPIRIT is stirring along the strip, the Ward and the city calling out to a new generation. Find *your* heroes, they are all around you. Create *your* stories, they are already in you—waiting to be written.